Hybrid Voices and Collaborative Change

Routledge Critical Studies in Discourse

EDITED BY MICHELLE M. LAZAR, *National University of Singapore*

1 **Framing Discourse on the Environment**
A Critical Discourse Approach
Richard J. Alexander

2 **Language and the Market Society**
Critical Reflections on Discourse and Dominance
Gerlinde Mautner

3 **Metaphor, Nation and the Holocaust**
The Concept of the Body Politic
Andreas Musolff

4 **Hybrid Voices and Collaborative Change**
Contextualising Positive Discourse Analysis
Tom Bartlett

Hybrid Voices and Collaborative Change
Contextualising Positive Discourse Analysis

Tom Bartlett

LONDON AND NEW YORK

First published 2012
by Routledge
711 Third Avenue, New York, NY 10017

Simultaneously published in the UK
by Routledge
2 Park Square, Milton Park, Abingdon, Oxfordshire OX14 4RN

First issued in paperback 2014

Routledge is an imprint of the Taylor & Francis Group,
an informa business

© 2012 Taylor & Francis

The right of Tom Bartlett to be identified as author of this work has been
asserted by him in accordance with sections 77 and 78 of the Copyright,
Designs and Patents Act 1988.

All rights reserved. No part of this book may be reprinted or reproduced or
utilised in any form or by any electronic, mechanical, or other means, now
known or hereafter invented, including photocopying and recording, or in
any information storage or retrieval system, without permission in writing
from the publishers.

Trademark Notice: Product or corporate names may be trademarks or
registered trademarks, and are used only for identification and explanation
without intent to infringe.

Library of Congress Cataloging-in-Publication Data
Bartlett, Tom.
  Hybrid voices and collaborative change : contextualising positive
discourse analysis / Tom Bartlett.
      p. cm. — (Routledge critical studies in discourse; v. 4)
  Includes bibliographical references and index.
  1. Discourse analysis. 2. Linguistic change. 3. Pragmatics.
  I. Title.
  P302.B3623 2012
  401'.41—dc23
  2012000778

ISBN 978-0-415-89338-1 (hbk)
ISBN 978-1-138-88923-1 (pbk)
ISBN 978-0-203-10937-3 (ebk)

Typeset in Sabon
by IBT Global.

For Mary: You are the context to my text.

Contents

	List of Figures	ix
	List of Tables	xi
	Transcription Conventions	xiii
	Acknowledgments	xv
1	Bucking the System: The Revoicing of Hegemonic Discourse	1
2	Background	39
3	Participatory Voice in Development Discourse	78
4	Local Prestige, Local Power	122
5	Taking Control	157
6	Interdiscursivity, Capital and Empathy	181
7	Positive Discourse Analysis: Spaces of Collaboration and Resistance	209
	Appendix 1	233
	Appendix 2	235
	Appendix 3	237
	Notes	239
	References	243
	Index	251

Figures

2.1	Set of process and participant types analysed in legal documents.	66
3.1	Positioning Triangle (adapted from Harré and van Langenhove 1999).	119
3.2	Positioning Triangle of Sara's intended real-time positioning?	120
3.3	Positioning Triangle of local interpretation of Sara's positioning?	120
4.1	A 'Positioning Star of David'.	131
4.2	Network of modal use in interviews with Andrew Martins, Uncle Henry and Gordon Wilson.	143
4.3	Network of projections in interviews with Andrew Martins, Uncle Henry and Gordon Wilson.	151
4.4	Interaction of different modes of power based on analysis of modality and projection.	155
6.1	RU structure of Text 6.2, lines 113–130.	196
6.2	Sara's construal of SUAs.	198
6.3	Uncle Henry's construal of SUAs.	199

Tables

2.1	Approaches to Empowerment (after Cameron et al. 1992a)	65
2.2	Processes and Participant Roles in Article 20(3) of the Amerindian Act	66
2.3	Participant Roles in the Amerindian Act	67
2.4	GOG and Amerindians as Performer in the Amerindian Act	67
2.5	Overseers and Beneficiaries of Actions, Amerindian Act	67
2.6	Participant Roles for Evaluate, Amerindian Act	68
2.7	Performers in Money and Business, Amerindian Act	68
2.8	Participant Roles in the NRDDB Constitution as Compared with the Amerindian Act	69
2.9	Performer Roles Compared between Amerindian Act and NRDDB Constitution	69
2.10	Overseers and Beneficiaries of Actions, NRDDB Constitution	70
2.11	Participant Roles for Evaluate Compared between Amerindian Act and NRDDB Constitution	71
2.12	Performers in Money and Business, NRDDB Constitution	71
2.13	Relating Participant Roles to a Typology of Empowerment	71
2.14	Empowerment as Constructed in the Amerindian Act and the NRDDB Constitution	72
2.15	Empowerment as Constructed in the Amerindian Act, the NRDDB Constitution and the Iwokrama Act	72
4.1	Division of Modals by Superordinates	144
4.2	Modals of Obligation by Speaker	145
4.3	Modals of Possibility by Speaker	146
4.4	More Delicate Present Possibility	146
4.5	Modal Force by Speaker	148
4.6	Distinctive Tendencies in Modal Use by Speaker	148
4.7	Allocation of Involvement, Uncle Henry and Gordon	149

xii *Tables*

4.8	Allocation of Organisation and Work by Speaker	150
4.9	Affect and Cognition by Speaker	151
4.10	Subdivision of Cognition by Speaker	152
4.11	Force of Knowledge and Opinions by Speaker	152
5.1	Summary of Salient Lexicogrammatical Features as Analysed in Texts 3.1 and 5.1 to 5.5	179
6.1	Rhetorical Features of Sara's Contributions in Text 6.1	204
6.2	Rhetorical Features of Uncle Henry's Contribution in Text 6.2	205

Transcription Conventions

W: Now [what X was saying **Eu**: [You gotta	overlapping speech
=	no perceptible pause between words
(xxx)	unclear speech (roughly one x per syllable)
(shortfall here)	best guess
(?how it is)	more tentative guess
[. . .]	data omitted
((noise of flipchart))	transcriber's comment
Eu: This what we don't understand. <<rustling of papers>>	action contemporaneous with stretch of speech
far	greater stress than expected
. . . /(p)	short pause in speech (roughly, up to 2s)
(11s)	timed pause in speech
↑	higher than expected pitch
↓	lower than expected pitch
VANESSA	louder than normal

xiv   *Transcription Conventions*

°here and leave this one°	quieter than normal
°°either way°°	far quieter than normal
<that is why the action>	faster than normal
>the current fix<	slower than normal
lo:gging	lengthening of vowel
hello	said laughing

Acknowledgments

I would like to thank all those people in Guyana who are at the heart of this book. The names that follow are the pseudonyms I have used in these pages—but you know who you are. From the North Rupununi, heartfelt thanks for the hospitality, friendship and inspiration to Walter, Nicholas, Uncle Henry, Sam and all the others; from Iwokrama, specific thanks to Alicia, Gordon and Sara.

I would also like to thank Hugh Trappes-Lomax and Miriam Meyerhoff, who supervised the original fieldwork on which this book is based, and to Euan Reid for giving me the belief to carry on when earlier versions (rightly) fell by the wayside. My thanks to Nadia Seemungal at Routledge, and Michelle Lazar, the series editor, for helping the book see the light of day.

My colleagues at Cardiff University have been a constant source of encouragement, in particular Gerard O'Grady and Lise Fontaine, and old hands Gordon Tucker and Robin Fawcett. Thanks also to Alison Wray and Adam Jaworski for feedback on various parts of the book.

And mostly, of course, Mary, Sadie and Jamie. It was thanks to Mary that I was in Guyana in the first place, while the experiences we shared have shaped the family we are. Sadie and Jamie used to tell me off for getting "too linguistical" and Sadie for a while used "dictionary" as the generic term for a book, so the usual reference to the family's patience in putting up with my efforts are in order.

All faults, inconsistencies and inaccuracies are, as they say, entirely my own.

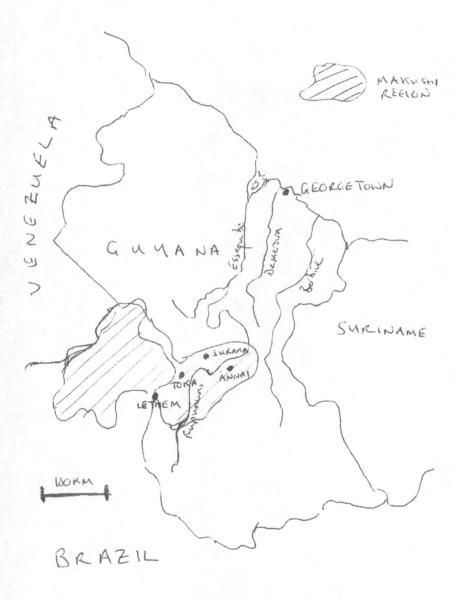

Map of Guyana showing Makushi population. Based on Colchester, M., La Rose, J., and James, K. (2002). Mining and Amerindians in Guyana: Ottawa: North-South Institute.

1 Bucking the System
The Revoicing of Hegemonic Discourse

A lot of people, they feel that the Makushi or the Amerindian culture is so inferior that they don't want to have anything with it. They don't want to associate themselves with it. Even with our youths down here. If you see that when they would call them buck boy, "Wh'appen there, buck boy?", you know they feel offended, like, and they don't feel proud of it, they don't even want to associate themselves with that name.

Walter (Toka, 9/11/00)

Walter[1] is a Makushi Amerindian, the son of a shama man, or shaman, from the North Rupununi savannahs of Guyana, in South America. He is very proud of his heritage, though as a youth he chose the allure of a modern lifestyle, epitomised for him by trappings such as training shoes, over the chance to follow in his father's footsteps and become a shama man himself. While this is a decision Walter now bitterly regrets, the idea that indigenous culture is somehow inferior, something to be ashamed of, to be escaped from, is not at all uncommon, both amongst the indigenous population themselves and the other ethnic groups within Guyana, as captured in Walter's words in the preceding quote. Such a lack of ethnic pride is an understandable consequence of 500 years of subjugation: first, at the hands of the various colonial powers that fought over, bartered for and in turns ruled this strategic section of the "New World" and, since Guyana gained its independence in 1966, at the hands of a post-colonial government that on the one hand portrays the Amerindian population as the guardians of the country's pre-colonial heritage, yet at the same time treats them as second-rate subjects, denied the full rights of citizenship afforded to the other ethnic groups in the country (see Chapter 2 for a fuller discussion of these points and an analysis of the Guyana 1976 Amerindian Act,[2] in which the relationship between the state and Amerindian communities is formally codified). Adding to these historical imbalances between governing authorities and indigenous groups is the presence of international development agencies that for many years treated local populations as the passive recipients of first-world beneficence with no significant contribution to make within the decision-making processes that defined and regulated the development practices which affected their lives.

These various aspects of colonialism and post-colonialism are, of course, related, with the colonial period not only marginalising the indigenous

2 Hybrid Voices and Collaborative Change

community socially and economically, thus establishing the need for development assistance in the post-colonial period, but also accustoming the indigenous community to a strictly top-down system of decision-making in which the local communities occupied the bottom rung. It was therefore a natural, or at least naturalised, process for the international development groups that stepped into the economic vacuums created by the departure of the colonial powers in such contexts to maintain organisational systems that reflected the new centre–periphery relationship as one of donor to beneficiary, of teacher to pupil, or even of role model to aspiring wannabe (see Chapter 3 for a fuller discussion of the discourses of development as these have evolved since the Second World War).

Development practices have changed considerably in the last quarter of a century, however, as many, both inside and outside the development sector, have come to question several of the underlying assumptions behind international development efforts in light of the underwhelming results that had been achieved (Chambers 1997; Cornwall and Gaventa 2001; Cornwall 2002; Escobar 1995). Prominent amongst the re-evaluations of past practice are critiques of the "one-size-fits-all" model of international development (Chambers 1997) in which: (i) development is seen as essentially a unilinear process with non-developed countries following the path mapped out by already developed countries (or "wrongly developed countries", as some critics have labelled them); and (ii) systems of knowledge and expertise are exported wholesale from the centre and imposed across diverse contexts without sufficient consideration of specific local conditions. Stemming from the critiques of the one-size-fits-all model has been a movement to involve local communities to a greater extent within the decision-making process and to combine modern "Western" technological practices with locally appropriate traditional ecological knowledge. For a large part of the period covered in this book, Walter was the chairman of an organisation that was created for just that purpose: the North Rupununi District Development Board (NRDDB), an umbrella organisation bringing together the 13 indigenous communities of the North Rupununi with representatives of the national Government of Guyana and professional development workers. Of these latter, it was an international development organisation, the Iwokrama International Rainforest Conservation and Development Programme (hereafter Iwokrama[3]), who worked with the local communities to establish the NRDDB and who provided logistical support in bringing the 13 dispersed local communities together for the bimonthly meetings that are the main focus of this book.

For some critics, however, such displays of participatory discourse are no more than empty gestures, sops to the latest buzzwords in official policy, while others see them as ignoring, or at the very least downplaying, the relationship between social inequality and unequal access both to and within dominant discourses and so masking the continuing domination of centrist development groups in defining the extent and the means of

Bucking the System 3

local development practice. From a discourse perspective, then, the central problem of development is this: Local knowledge is necessary in order to augment and tailor development knowledge and practice to the specifics of each local context; therefore, local participation within planning and organisation is necessary; however, a history of marginalisation has meant that local communities do not have access to the linguistic strategies necessary to make themselves heard within development discourse, while a *misrecognition* (Bourdieu 1991) of the administrative practices of colonial and post-colonial rule as being based on cultural superiority rather than economic and military power has led to an undervaluing of the very knowledge and organisational capacities that are needed in order to render international development efforts more appropriate to local needs. As a result, it is only to be expected that government and international development workers will dominate discourses involving indigenous groups, with local input remaining at a token level while outside conceptions of "reality" (Chambers 1997), including the needs and capabilities of the local communities themselves, continue to underlie the decision-making process.

Such a scenario is the bedrock of research within the framework of Critical Discourse Analysis (CDA), which is defined by one of its leading exponents (van Dijk 2001:352) as:

> a type of discourse analytical research that primarily studies the way social power abuse, dominance, and inequality are enacted, reproduced, and resisted by text and talk in the political context. With such dissident research, critical discourse analysts take explicit position, and thus want to understand, expose, and ultimately resist social inequality.

It was within such a mindset and with such goals that I undertook my fieldwork in Guyana, and this book describes a variety of discourse events in and around the NRDDB during a three-and-a-half year period, from 1999 to 2002. Living in Georgetown, the Guyanese capital, some 250 miles from the communities of the North Rupununi, I had met with professional development workers from Iwokrama who took me to an NRDDB meeting, where I had the chance to persuade the local communities that my work had something to offer them and to allow me to conduct my fieldwork amongst them. What I confidently offered them was, firstly, a promise to reveal how the institutional format of NRDDB meetings and the imbalance in resources and authority between the communities and the Iwokrama workers was reflected in unequal discourse relations between them; and, secondly, to make suggestions on how to "create a more even playing field" through a redistribution of powerful discourse resources. What I found, however, during my three and a half years travelling between Georgetown and the savannahs, was that the local communities, with the support of Iwokrama, were quietly taking

4   *Hybrid Voices and Collaborative Change*

control of the institutional format of the NRDDB meetings and related events—without any need for my expert advice.

This process of *collaboration* between different social groups and the *appropriation* (Chouliaraki and Fairclough 1999:94; Bartlett 2001) of dominant modes of discourse by the local population as a traditionally marginalised sector of society will be the focus of this book. In this way the case study could be said to belong within the recent trend towards Positive Discourse Analysis (PDA), which seeks to understand "how change happens, for the better, across a range of sites" (Martin 2004:9). There are, however, important differences between the work that has generally been published under this name to date and the approach I adopt here, and in the following section I present an overview of the relationship between PDA and CDA and the key differences between existing PDA and the theoretical and methodological approach to be developed in detail over the course of this book. In particular I emphasise the need for contextual description in critical discourse work and discuss the sociolinguistic concept of *voice* as a key theoretical notion for relating discourse to context.

CRITIQUES OF CDA AND THE EMERGENCE OF PDA

Given CDA's ambitious goals "to understand, expose, and ultimately resist social inequality", it has, unsurprisingly, been the focus of a great deal of critical debate over the last quarter of a century or so. This is not the place to discuss in detail the many issues that have been identified with both the theoretical framework and the methodological approach of CDA (see Richardson 1987; Stubbs 1997; Toolan 1997; O'Halloran 2003; Widdowson 2004); instead I shall focus on a number of specific issues with CDA as they relate to the emergence of PDA as a subdiscipline and from there discuss problems with PDA itself, including some that it has inherited from CDA.

One frequently recurring criticism of CDA work is that it is guilty of "cherry-picking", of selecting isolated instances of discourse that confirm the existing ideological biases of the researcher. In a lengthy critique on this and other aspects of CDA, Widdowson (2004) takes CDA to task on a number of related counts: for limiting its textual analysis to clause-level relations without consideration of the function and effect of these features within the text as a whole (2004:1–16, 89–111); for an overenthusiastic interpretation of grammatical form as being psychologically real and the resulting failure to account for how the pragmatic meaning of grammatical forms can be derived from the context (2004:17–35, 92–96; see also O'Halloran 2003:56–81); for drawing selectively and unsystematically on the range of methodological resources CDA claims to employ (2004:89–111); and for applying even these limited resources partially to selected clauses rather than across whole texts (2004:89–111). Widdowson (2004:103) concludes from these points that the predisposition of researchers in CDA to uncover

Bucking the System 5

the workings of social inequalities within texts (what he calls the underlying *pretext* of such research):

> motivates the selection of features for personal attention. The difficulty is, however, that this interpretative partiality inevitably leaves a vast amount of text unanalysed and unaccounted for. In consequence, what is uncovered are the workings and effects of texts on readers who are pretextually positioned to derive discourses from them which suit their purpose. In short, what we find in CDA are critical discourse *interpretations*. These may carry conviction with members of the same discourse community or others who share the same pretextual assumptions. But they cannot be validated by analysis.

Related to the potential problems of pretextually skewed readings and the limited range of features selected for analysis we have the wider problem of what Blommaert (2005:34–35) calls the *linguistic bias* in CDA. Blommaert identifies three aspects of such bias in CDA work: firstly, its reliance on Systemic Function Linguistics (SFL) for the grammatical descriptions that underpin its methodological framework at the expense of other linguistic theories; secondly, its analysis of available texts without considering the absence of alternatives; and, thirdly, its failure to account adequately for either the social factors behind the production of these texts or the social consequences of their production. I shall return to the concerns raised by Widdowson and Blommaert at the end of this chapter as they are problems that have been inherited by PDA as it has sought to change the thrust of critical work in a more positive direction but has remained squarely focused on the text itself as the provider of meaning. First, I shall turn to the motivations behind that general change in direction.

The avowed goal of CDA to study "the way social power abuse, dominance, and inequality are enacted, reproduced, and resisted by text and talk in the political context" (van Dijk 2001:352, above) has meant that for many researchers, myself included, there has been a tendency in much published CDA work to focus on the negative. This is true even in cases of discourse change, which are seen as strategies for the continued dominance of powerful ideologies in new guises, as with Fairclough's (1995:130–166) analysis of the conversationalisation of political discourse. This approach has often resulted in a 'blame game' rather than contributing to any real solutions, and even "resistance", in van Dijk's wording, can be understood as a negative reaction to hegemonic discourse rather than the potential for discourse to offer genuine emancipatory *alternatives*. Many CDA practitioners have even gone as far as to say that they do not expect to contribute to change, and that their role does not go beyond that of bringing to light what they see as injustices within existing discourse practices. As the theoretical and analytical framework of CDA has developed, however, other leading figures within the field have provided a counter to this pervasive

6 *Hybrid Voices and Collaborative Change*

post-modernist claim that the development of theory and academic analysis cannot contribute to practical change:

> Social forms that are produced by people are being seen as if they were part of nature. There is a compelling need for a critical theorisation and analysis of late modernity which can not only illuminate the new world that is emerging but also show what unrealised alternative directions exist—how aspects of this new world which can enhance human life can be accentuated, how aspects which are detrimental to it can be changed or mitigated. Thus the basic motivation for critical social science is to contribute to an awareness of what is, how it has come to be, and what it might become, on the basis of which people might be able to make and remake their lives. (Chouliaraki and Fairclough 1999:4)

This positive approach to CDA involves shifting away from the analysis of implicit reactionary ideology in texts towards what Kress (2000:160–161, in Martin 2004:7) calls:

> a new goal in textual (and perhaps other) practice: not of critique but of Design . . . While critique looked at the present through the means of the past, Design shapes the future through deliberate deployment of representational resources in the designer's interest . . . The task of the critic is to perform analysis on an agenda of someone else's design. As a result a considerable inertia is built into this process . . . Design sets aside past agendas, and treats them and their products as resources in setting an agenda of future aims, and in assembling means and resources for implementing that.

Martin has been one of the chief proponents of such a change of emphasis, away from the critique of existing dominating discourses and towards the design of emancipatory alternatives; but he also stresses that such design must be underpinned by a knowledge of how discourse works in the social here and now, for good as well as harm. In the article in which he introduces the term *Positive Discourse Analysis* Martin writes (2004:9):

> The lack of positive discourse analysis (PDA?) cripples our understanding of how change happens, for the better, across a range of sites— how feminists re-make gender relations in our world, how indigenous people overcome their colonial heritage, how migrants renovate their new environs and so on. And this hampers design and perhaps even discourages it since analysts would rather tell us how the struggle was undone than how freedom was won.

Martin (2004:7–9) proposes instead a "yin and yang" approach in which "deconstructive *and* constructive activity are *both* required" (2004:7;

Bucking the System 7

emphasis in original). In other words, in every context there will be examples of "the way social power abuse, dominance, and inequality are enacted, reproduced, and resisted by text and talk" (van Dijk 2001:352, above), and discourse analysis can be used to bring these to light; however, such instances form part of a broader picture which also includes instances of collaboration, egalitarianism and bottom-up change, and if we "want to understand, expose, and ultimately resist social inequality" (van Dijk 2001:352, above) then our critical focus must encompass and interrelate both aspects. Despite this change in approach, however, the recent trend towards the positive in discourse analysis has several potential limitations, largely inherited from the CDA framework from which it derives, and these must be taken on board if it is serious in its goal of "setting an agenda for future aims".

Firstly, while Martin is surely correct in highlighting the importance of analysing texts associated with positively evaluated social change just as much as those seen as perpetuating an inequitable status quo, there is a danger that in rejecting the fatalistic stance within some critical approaches PDA will underplay the importance of the determining effects of existing social structures on discourse and be limited to accentuating and celebrating what the analyst considers positive without due consideration of the social factors that created the conditions of possibility for such texts at the local level and how structural features within the wider sociopolitical context might make it possible for such positive change to take hold and spread. Such a strategy would on its own amount to little more than an inversion of the critical pretextual assumptions identified in CDA by Widdowson without moving on to the more difficult design tasks of showing "what unrealised alternative directions exist" (Chouliaraki and Fairclough 1999:4, above) and "setting an agenda of future aims, and in assembling means and resources for implementing that" (Kress 2000:160–161, above). In this respect PDA might be said to have more of a textual bias than CDA, for while CDA contextualises texts inasmuch as it sets out to describe the structural conditions within society which have led to the dominance of one sector over another and related this material domination to the hegemonic status of specific discourse types, PDA has generally limited its contextualisation to the same problematic state of affairs while focusing on those discourses which reject rather than contribute to this situation. PDA analysis is thus largely *reactive*, focusing on texts simply because they "resist" the hegemonic social structure and its associated discourses rather than analysing how the counter-discourses celebrated can gain a foothold within those institutional contexts in which they will be expected to operate. What is lacking in PDA work, therefore, is a detailed analysis of context that not only accounts for how hegemonic discourses continue to circulate and whose interests they serve, but also an analysis of the *tensions* which exist under the veneer of any hegemonic order so as to suggest how the *emergent* reconfigurations of power relations that are realised in

8 Hybrid Voices and Collaborative Change

isolation at the local level in the texts analysed can exploit these tensions to undermine or reorient the existing *structural conditions* of domination within wider society (for a discussion of the relationship between structural objects and emergent practice, see Sealey and Carter [2004]).

A second problem arising from this textual bias is the failure of PDA to consider how the sociocultural background of both producers and receivers affects the *meanings* of given texts. This limitation applies both to the analysis of existing texts and, potentially more importantly, to the design of alternatives. While PDA recognises that within a given social context an understanding of the discourse history in terms of rights and access to discourse and the denial of these is an essential prelude to the task of realigning discourse relations, there has to date been little attempt to undertake a sociocultural analysis of the context that relates the ways of speaking of individual speakers to the discourse customs of their social groups and the speakers' individual positions within these communities.[4] The *meaning* of a text is a function of the social and cultural context in which it is produced and circulated and through which it derives its power; however, while PDA situates complete texts within the broad sociopolitical context of their production and the polemic to which they contribute, the analysis of the interplay of complex linguistic features remains resolutely textual, with the rhetorical features of the language employed analysed in relatively self-contained or universal terms rather than relating them to the specifics of the interactional context and the knowledge and values of the communities in which they circulate.

And, thirdly, if critique-based design is to prove effective it must surely be based on a consideration of the potential for uptake and evaluation of specific discourses, negative and positive, past and future, within the communities whose lives they shape, rather than on the wishful approval of the analyst. Within PDA, however, there seems to be a reliance on the trained linguist to provide the evaluation of the different texts and the linguistic resources employed rather than a concentrated approach to assessing the evaluation and uptake of these texts within the target communities themselves (cf. Widdowson's [2004:170 and elsewhere] critique of CDA). As Toolan (1997:88) puts it with regard to CDA, but with equal validity for PDA: "It is not self-evident that a CDA analysis of a John Major[5] speech, or of a racist discourse, will necessarily more directly lead to a change in the world than, say, a traditional literary critic's commentary on *The Merchant of Venice.*" In this respect, then, PDA would appear to follow CDA in offering critical discourse *interpretations* which cannot be validated by analysis (Widdowson 2004:103). The approach developed in this book is that an evaluation of how texts are taken up should be: (i) based on responses from the intended audience, either within the continuing discourse itself (as is the approach with Conversation Analysis) or in discussion with the researcher;[6] and (ii) interpreted within a broader ethnographic analysis of the practices and relationships within and between communities and individuals and the

Bucking the System 9

relationship of these to the features of discourse of different speakers before specific audiences and within particular contexts. A corollary of this position is that those involved in the process of designing counter-discourses, in "assembling means and resources for implementing" them, must consider whether these new strategies are *assimilable* within the discourse practices of the marginalised groups they wish to assist and whether they will carry any *legitimacy* as alternative discourses within the wider social framework in which they will need to operate. These issues will be discussed further as part of the analysis of situated discourses in Chapters 3 to 6.

These three limitations in PDA can all be connected to the same textual bias that was identified for CDA and an unwillingness (often explicitly stated) to consider non-linguistic features of the context in shaping meaning, in provoking uptake, and in having provided the structural conditions for the texts to be realised at all. To extend the project of PDA, then, it is surely necessary to integrate textual and contextual analyses of communicative practices and to account for the link between language features and social structure.[7] In the following sections I shall talk in more detail about *context* and introduce the sociolinguistic concept of *voice* as a means of linking features of talk to the cultural context of their production and uptake. In the course of these discussions I set out an elaborated agenda for PDA that seeks to overcome the failings I have outlined in my first two criticisms, above, the third having already been addressed.

DISCOURSE: TEXT IN CONTEXT

Contextual factors constrain, orient and provide interpretative frameworks for the production and uptake of *all* texts in various ways and at various levels. While any text, written or spoken, can be analysed for the linguistic features it contains and the formal progression and coherence it displays across its structure, such an analysis would tacitly assume that the text was created in a social vacuum and that it means the same thing to all people. But texts, of course, are not created in social vacuums, as the speakers behind them, their various audiences and even the words themselves, all have social histories. Placing text within its historical and social context is what makes it discourse. Texts as linguistic objects, are, in themselves, potentially infinite in their creative possibilities; discourse, however, as a social practice, as the situated use of language, is highly sensitive to its environment; and creativity, while it is all around, is more circumscribed. This is true even in those areas of language, such as literature, where creativity is perhaps a writer's most important attribute. Think of an innovative writer such as Joyce, Pound or Márquez and consider first whether any of them would have been able to produce the innovative work they did outside the evolutionary framework of less radical texts that immediately preceded them or contemporary shifts in other area of the broader environment and,

10   *Hybrid Voices and Collaborative Change*

secondly, whether these works, had they managed to produce them, would have been understood and taken up by the literary establishment of that time against the general views prevailing on the purpose and accepted forms of "literature". The point I am making here is Foucault's (1972) concept that individual uses of language are constrained by the dominant discourses that are circulating in a given society at a given time and which are used as the benchmarks of common sense and acceptability against which such individual discourse practices are understood, evaluated and legitimated. And if such is true of literature, the essence of which is creativity, then these constraints will apply in spades to those discourses that are aimed at regulating social life and maintaining the vested economic and political interests of the hegemonic sectors of society. Where those advocating positive approaches to discourse analysis can take heart, however, is in the nature of hegemonic power not as absolute, undifferentiated and unchanging control by one sector of society over others, but as "a struggle for power . . . which . . . depends on consent or acquiescence" (Fairclough 2003:218). In these terms hegemonic control is not static, but the continual readaptation of the dominant bloc to changing trends in society and "the naturalisation of particular representations" over others through the manipulation of discourse at all levels (Fairclough 2003:18). Thus, for Fairclough (n.b. 1992), one of the goals of CDA is to show how changes in dominant discourses are *rearticulations* of discursive and material practice designed to maintain the hegemonic control of the existing dominant bloc within society. From a PDA perspective, however, the goal would be to focus on the ways in which underlying social changes in society and the local discourses associated with them bring to light the contradictions and tensions within the hegemonic order and so provide the *wiggle room* for naturalising alternative representations that challenge this order. This is a point that will be developed below and illustrated throughout the book.

While this brief discussion of dominant discourses and the existence of wiggle room relates to my first criticism of PDA practice, above, in terms of its failure to account for the general contextual conditions that constrain the possibility for the emergence of alternative discourses, from the perspective of my second criticism it is also necessary to consider how such alternatives are realised and contested at the local level, where the same structural imbalances in society will be reflected in microcosm. The approach I will take is that in every context which brings members of diverse social groups into contact there will be a struggle to negotiate the meaning of the context in order to control it. In cases, such as that discussed in this book, which bring together local communities and representatives of the dominant order (in this case both the Government of Guyana and Iwokrama as an international development organisation steeped in the dominant discourse of development), this amounts to a struggle between hegemonic and local discourse systems (what Bakhtin [1981] calls *centripetal* and *centrifugal* forces respectively, see below). In order to analyse the contributions of the different participants within such discourses it is therefore necessary to understand how the meanings they make relate to the organisation of each group and the role of each participant within this organisation. The idea that superficially similar speech acts might mean different things in different communities and different contexts is what Blommaert (2005:70) calls the *relativity of function*. While such differences will be inherent across all contexts, Blommaert (2005:72) emphasises the increased importance of this concept within the context of globalisation:

> the functions which particular ways of speaking perform, and the functions of the particular linguistic resources, become less and less a matter of surface inspection in terms of commonsense linguistic categories . . . and some of the biggest errors (and injustices) may be committed by simply projecting locally valid functions onto the ways of speaking of people who are involved in transnational flows.

I suggested above that there was a tendency in PDA to analyse features of texts according to abstract and supposedly universal categories, an example of textual bias that ignores relativity of function and so leads to potential error and continued injustice. I shall return to this idea below, but it is first necessary to introduce a different approach to relativity: Bourdieu's (1977, 1991) concept of *symbolic capital*.

According to Bourdieu, the words of speakers with an accumulation of cultural capital, such as high levels of education or high rank within official institutions, will be imbued with a degree of symbolic capital as long as the speaker employs the formal features of discourse that are conventionally and arbitrarily related to their status. In other word, symbolic capital is the transfer of the cultural capital of the speaker to their discourse, endowing their words with greater prestige and authority than is merited by their content alone and so rendering the speaker disproportionately powerful. I will argue in Chapter 4, however, that Bourdieu's formulation of the concept of symbolic capital is prone to the same universalising tendencies criticised with respect to PDA inasmuch as Bourdieu, on the one hand, emphasises the workings of symbolic power in terms of speakers' relative status within the formal apparatuses of control such as the state and the church and overlooks the importance of speakers' relative status within community life and local institutions and, on the other hand, inasmuch as he assumes a unitary and arbitrary match between cultural capital and the language that foregrounds it. As a result, analyses based on the concept of symbolic capital share the same tendency towards fatalistic determinism criticised in CDA, within which it is frequently applied. The alternative approach I shall take in this book is to assume that symbolic capital is locally contingent, that is to say that speakers will derive such capital in the eyes (and ears) of their audience in relation to their cultural capital within different aspects of local society as well as within translocal institutions, and that there are many and varied means of realising this capital

12 Hybrid Voices and Collaborative Change

in language, the majority of which are not arbitrary. The framework for my approach integrates the concept of symbolic capital within an analytical perspective derived from Positioning Theory (Harré and van Langenhove 1999), a branch of social psychology. The key analytical tool within Positioning Theory is the *positioning triangle*, a schematic representation of the idea that every act (including speech acts) is a social agent's means of positioning themselves with respect to an ongoing storyline (or context). As such the triangle is compatible with Bourdieu's concept of symbolic capital, in that the value of each act within the storyline can be said to be proportionate to the speaker's capital within that context as symbolised by the language they use. In order to make the positioning more sensitive to local contexts, therefore, in line with my comments above, I have introduced conditions between each node so that: (i) the relationship between each act and the storyline is dependent on *the specific audience* to which it is addressed (or by whom it is overheard), each with their own cultural traditions and values, and this entails that (ii) the successful uptake of a position as realised by this act is dependent on the cultural capital of the speaker *before that audience* and (iii) that the uptake of this position through a particular speech act is dependent on the use of language that relates the speaker's words to their adopted position not through universal and arbitrary association but *in locally specific ways*.

I shall expand on this interpretative schema further in Chapters 3 and 4; the key point for the current discussion is that, to account for *relativity of function*, a model of discourse is needed that attempts to analyse the contributions of different speakers, both individual utterances and longer contributions, in terms of the social organisation of the community and the position of the individual speaker within it. This entails matching the experiential content of a speaker's words to the material practices and beliefs shared by their speech community; matching the interpersonal content of their words to their position in the various hierarchies of control that regulate this practice; and matching the rhetorical strategies each speaker employs to the repertoire of community practices for disseminating information and imposing regulations. It is therefore dependent on a prior description and analysis of these features of community life, an aspect that I have claimed is lacking in much PDA research. As suggested earlier, the concept of *voice* is one means of overcoming these limitations, and in the section that follows I will discuss the development of this concept and suggest how it can be utilised in analysing the effectiveness of alternative discourses in their local context and beyond.

VOICE

The term *voice* has gained widespread currency within sociolinguistics, with several different conceptions and definitions being provided by different authors; all these uses, however, ultimately derive from the work of

Bakhtin (n.b. 1981) and other Soviet writers of the 1920s and 1930s. For Bakhtin, to use language is not to turn thoughts to words according to the rules of a predefined and shared language system, as in Saussurean structural linguistics, but rather to recycle the words of previous speakers in new contexts, recalibrating the meaning of the words themselves to suit current needs. Such an act of recycling is not entirely free, however, but restricted by the conventions of the context, with different social contexts having their own history of meanings and so imposing their own framework of acceptability and understanding on any new utterances. In this way Bakhtin saw what had traditionally been considered as unitary languages with a single set of rules as being stratified into particular sublanguages or *speech genres*, each with their own contexts and conventions, and against whose *centrifugal* properties the establishment seeks to impose the *centripetal* force of the unitary language. This concept, which Bakhtin labels *heteroglossia*, is defined by his editors (Bakhtin 1981:428; my emphasis) as:

> the base condition governing the operation of meaning in any utterance. It is that which insures *the primacy of context over text*. At any given time, in any given place, there will be a set of conditions—social, historical, meteorological, physiological—that will insure that a word uttered in that place and at that time will have a meaning different than it would have under any other conditions; all utterances are heteroglot in that they are functions of a matrix of forces practically impossible to recoup, and therefore impossible to resolve.

Under such conditions the use of words becomes a struggle over meaning as speakers strive to match their intentions with the multiple previous uses to which language has been put by others:

> The word in language is half someone else's. It becomes 'one's own' only when the speaker populates it with his [*sic*] own intention, his own accent, when he appropriates the word, adapting it to his own semantic and expressive intention. Prior to this moment of appropriation, the word does not exist in a neutral and impersonal language (it is not, after all, out of a dictionary that the speaker gets his words!), but rather it exists in other people's mouths, in other people's contexts, serving other people's intentions: it is from there that one must take the word, and make it one's own. And not all words for just anyone submit easily to this appropriation, to this seizure and transformation into private property: many words stubbornly resist, others remain alien, sound foreign in the mouth of the one who appropriated them and who now speaks them; they cannot be assimilated into [the new speaker's] context and fall out of it; it as if they put themselves in quotation marks against the will of the speaker. Language is not a neutral medium that passes freely and easily into the private property of the speaker's intentions;

14 *Hybrid Voices and Collaborative Change*

it is populated—overpopulated—with the intentions of others. Expropriating it, forcing it to submit to one's own intentions and accents, is a difficult and complicated process. (Bakhtin 1981:293–294)

These twin ideas, that words and voices are linked to specific genres and contexts and that each act of speaking is an act of appropriation, an act of repopulating other's words with new meanings, were key elements in Bakhtin's work on literary criticism and underpinned the idea that a single author could represent a diversity of voices (the peasant's, the aristocrat's, the intellectual's), each with its own version of reality, in a work of art that is rendered coherent not through a single version of the truth but through the truth as diffracted through multiple voices, a process Bakhtin labels *polyphony*.

Bakhtin's ideas have contributed much to post-modern ideas on literary criticism with its distrust of unitary conceptions of truth and have also been taken up by authors as a means of representing the double consciousness of oppressed and alien groups as they operate within the dominant mainstream. However, the applications of *voice* as a theoretical concept are not limited to the field of literary criticism. If so much is evident even within Bakhtin's own writings when he refers to the tensions between the centripetal force of the unitary language and the centrifugal tendencies of individual speech genres (1981:270), then his fellow Marxist theorist (and possible alter ego) Voloshinov makes the political significance of the struggle over words and voices concept clearer. For Voloshinov (1973:21), if "the forms of signs are conditioned above all by the social organisation of the participants involved and also by the immediate conditions of their interaction" then the word is "an arena of class struggle" (1973:23) in which the dominant forces in society attempt to close down the accepted meanings of words and so inhibit the counter-hegemonic potential that Bakhtin's conceptions of heteroglossia and polyphony imply.

The attractiveness of the notion of *voice* within sociolinguistics, particularly in its critical guises, should be clear, and it is a concept that has been taken up and extended (repopulated, if you like) by several important theorists in the field, all of whom share an understanding of *voice* as a very different capacity from Chomsky's idea of *competence* as knowledge of the grammatical forms of a particular language such as 'English'. Rather, language is seen as a locally and situationally contingent set of functional repertoires and a speaker's capacity refers to their ability to employ these repertoires appropriately in context. The 'language' of linguistic textbooks is not the same as the 'language' of small talk and small talk is different in middle-class suburban England from the small talk in a bar in Guyana, though both may make use of the resources of the 'English language'. And while everybody has a range of repertoires at their disposal—I, for instance, do not talk in the same way when ordering a pint in Edinburgh (or a rum in Guyana) as when I am giving a lecture—access to these different repertoires of language is unevenly distributed across social groups and individuals

Bucking the System 15

within these groups. This is not simply a case of random distribution of different forms for doing roughly the same thing, but a result of the fact that different sectors of society occupy different places within the social hierarchy and have different experiences of the material world, different internal social relations and different traditions of relating events to each other—all of which are encoded in language. Differences in language use are, therefore, not just superficial differences of form, but reflect what Halliday (1978) would call the different *behavioural potentials* open to speakers from social different groups and in different environments. Capacity in different repertoires means the ability to act through language in different contexts, and this involves not just a knowledge of the structures used in this context, but an understanding of the social and situational features they realise and of when it is appropriate to draw on these (Bernstein 2000). I would therefore define *voice* not so much as "the capacity to be understood" (as in Blommaert 2005:255; see below) as "the means of behaving appropriately through language". In this way we can talk of different voices, of "community voice" as opposed to "scientific voice", for example, to refer to the customary ways of making oneself understood in different contexts. A corollary of this is that the use of a particular voice in a new context does not necessarily lead to understanding at all. And within what we might loosely call *intercultural contexts*, there is a tension between different voices that represent different ways of behaving, different social *codes* (Bernstein 1971). What often happens in such situations is that the code of the dominant group prevails, with the result that members of this group are doubly advantaged: firstly, in that it is their experience of reality, their interpersonal relations and their ways of relating events that are privileged, with all the power imbalances that this entails; and, secondly, in that non-dominant groups are unsure of how to behave in the unfamiliar context created, with the result that they are often viewed as incapable. It was just such a situation, the underachievement of British working-class children in school contexts organised according to middle-class norms, that led Bernstein to elaborate his theory of "class, codes and control" (Bernstein 1971, 1973, 1975, 1990). At roughly the same time in the U.S., Hymes was exploring the potential social exclusion of those who do not have a command of the socially esteemed varieties of language that are prevalent in civil contexts in general. For Hymes the immediate tasks for socially concerned linguists at the time were to counter the simplistic view of language variety as merely an unsystematic grouping of deficient versions of the standard language and to replace this with an understanding of language variety as a systematic means of expressing individuality and difference:

> Even if the country remains, so far as the media detect, linguistically simply some sort of mush, those who believe in a society better than we now have should develop a well-grounded critique. What ideal or vision can we entertain in terms of language? Two ingredients of a vision

16   *Hybrid Voices and Collaborative Change*

are longstanding. One is a kind of negative freedom, freedom from denial of opportunity due to something linguistic, whether in speaking or reading or writing. One is a kind of positive freedom, freedom for satisfaction in the use of language, for language to be a source of imaginative life and satisfying form. In my own mind I would unite the two kinds of freedom in the notion of *voice*: freedom to have one's voice heard, freedom to develop a voice worth hearing. (Hymes 1996:64)

The aim of this book is to trace exactly these processes (the relation of which to CDA and PDA respectively should be clear) in the local development discourse of the North Rupununi Savannahs. Below I will set out a model of how the marginalised communities might overcome the "denial of opportunity" that permeates their history over the last 500 years to develop "a voice worth hearing", a voice that carries local social structures into contexts generally dominated by the voices of outsiders; and in later chapters I will illustrate through analysis of situated texts the extent to which the communities of the North Rupununi developed "the freedom to have [their] voice heard", to have it legitimated as a valid voice within this new context. This is an important struggle, particularly in the contexts of globalisation and international development on which this book focuses, as it is a struggle not just for 'understanding', but for the recognition of the underlying bases of community life in the face of external intervention in local affairs on an unprecedented scale.

Blommaert is similarly preoccupied with the sociolinguistic repercussions of globalisation and incorporates this concern as one of his five general principles for critical approaches to discourse analysis:

> We have to conceive of communication events as ultimately influenced by *the structure of the world system*. In an era of globalisation the threshold of contextualisation in discourse analysis or sociolinguistics can no longer be a single society (or even less a single event) but needs to include the relationship between different societies and the effect of these relationships on repertoires of language users and their potential to construct voice. (2005:15)

Blommaert therefore sees the concept of *voice* as central within such a perspective, and goes as far as to suggest that "a critical analysis of discourse in contemporary society is an analysis of voice" because:

> Voice stands for the way in which people manage to make themselves understood or fail to do so. In doing so, they have to draw upon and deploy discursive means which they have at their disposal, and they have to use them in contexts that are specified as the conditions of use. Consequently, if these conditions are not met, people 'don't make

Bucking the System   17

sense'—they fail to make themselves understood—and the actual reasons for this are manifold. My point of departure is: in contemporary societies, issues of voice become ever more pressing, they become more and more of a problem to more and more people. Voice is the issue that defines linguistic inequality (hence many other forms of inequality) in contemporary societies. An analysis of voice is an analysis of power effects—(not) being understood in terms of the set of sociocultural rules and norms specified—as well as conditions of power—what it takes to make oneself understood. (2005:4–5)

Central to Blommaert's argument is the notion of *indexicality*, "meaning that emerges out of text-context" relations (2005:252) and operates in a "non-arbitrary, socially and culturally sensitive way . . . in societies" (2005:253). Blommaert expands on this idea to talk of *orders of indexicality* (2005:73–78), a term that is designed to capture the idea that the indexical connections between context and meaning are ordered in two ways: firstly, in that they are "closely related to other social and cultural features of social groups" (2005:73); and, secondly, in that such indexical systems are differently ranked within "stratified complexes" in terms of the social connotations and the degrees of prestige and power they are afforded by different social groups (2005:74). Blommaert (2008:427–428) expands on the relationship between voice, indexicality and orders of indexicality:

Voice is a social product, and it is therefore not unified but subject to processes of selection and exclusion that have their feet firmly in the social structure. Consequently, voice is best seen materialistically as the practical conversion of socially 'loaded' resources into socially 'loaded' semiotic action, every aspect of which shows traces of the patterns of distribution of the resources. Some resources will be exclusive, others will be democratic; some will mark superiority, others inferiority; some will function well across different social contexts while other's [*sic*] functions are locked into specific niches in society. Some people will have a lot, others will have a few; some have valuable resources while others have low value resources.

In other words, not only will specific voices be *understood* (a term I will develop below) in some contexts but not in others, but also these different voices will carry different types and degrees of prestige, or *legitimacy*, in different contexts. These are both central ideas in the case study that follows where I will attempt to show that Blommaert's concept of *orders of indexicality* carries counter-hegemonic as well as hegemonic potential and so provides a crucial element in the framework for *collaboration* to be developed, particularly as it relates to what I call the *perturbation potential* (Bartlett, forthcoming) inherent in different communication contexts. In

18 Hybrid Voices and Collaborative Change

the following section I outline in condensed form the principles of this concept and its importance for PDA, ideas which will be developed at length over the case study.

PERTURBATION POTENTIAL

Drawing on the previous discussion we can talk of *voice* as a way of speaking that converts local resources into semiotic action and which is generally understood by a specific community whose previous discourse provides the linguistic backdrop against which individual speakers perform. "To make the word one's own" can then be taken to mean drawing on past uses of language and resituating these in a new linguistic milieu that is shared by other group members, *repopulating* the language with new meaning and creating for oneself a position, an identity, in relation to the ongoing discourse. The effectiveness of any such discourse intervention, as argued above, will depend not only on the form of the intervention itself and its relation to community practice, but also on the position of the speaker within that community in terms of their rights and obligations, their recognised knowledge and their history of past interventions. We can therefore distinguish between, on the one hand, *community voice* as the array of shared (if ever-changing) conventions that realise in discourse the intricacies of social life within a given group and within the framework of which individuals express themselves and, on the other hand, the *individual voice* of a single speaker who takes up a position in relation to the ongoing discourse that both announces and acts upon (Thibault 1995) the status that speaker has attained within the specific community, largely as a result of previous discourse interventions. In other words, while speakers may be said to speak from within the same community voice, no two members of a community will share the same individual voice as, on the one hand, they occupy different places within the community, with different rights, obligations and knowledge that can be translated into words, and, on the other, each controls a different *repertoire*, built up of past linguistic experience in a variety of different milieux, aspects of which they can reformulate according to the needs of each new context . In these terms an individual's voice can be seen as "a mesh of intersecting voices" (Kristeva, quoted in Talbot, Atkinson and Atkinson 2003:25), as being "'populated' with a heterogeneous array of voices through which a language user's identity is built up" (ibid.).

For a speaker's voice to be effective in a specific context it first has to be understood, and by this I mean not only in terms of *comprehension*, but also in terms of *empathy*: It must relate to the community voice, must connect with the practices and beliefs that have shaped that voice. Beyond this it must be recognised as a *legitimate voice*, that is, one through which the individual is entitled to identify themselves within that social milieu. While effectiveness is never guaranteed, the more completely these conditions are met, the more effective a speaker is likely to be in achieving their intention. As Blommaert (2005:205) puts it, identity is not an individual attribute but a dialogic practice; it is something that has to be *granted*. In these terms, to be effective equates with being *powerful*, being able to achieve one's purpose. Giddens (1993:104, in Fairclough 2003:41) defines power, which depends upon "resources or facilities" which are differently available to social actors, as the "transformative capacity of human action", the capacity "to intervene in a series of events so as to alter their course . . . the capability to secure outcomes where the realisation of these outcomes depends upon the agency of others". This definition fits well with Blommaert's conclusion, above, that "[a]n analysis of voice is an analysis of power effects—(not) being understood in terms of the set of sociocultural rules and norms specified—as well as conditions of power—what it takes to make oneself understood". What all this means, in short, is that for a speaker to be effective, or powerful, they have to draw from amongst the repertoire of voices available to them to create an individual voice that is appropriate to the specific milieu in which they are operating. While this is a difficult enough matter under normal conditions, in *intercultural contexts* such as my case study, that is to say *polycentric* (Blommaert 2005:254) contexts in which markedly[8] different voices and orders of indexicality are simultaneously in operation, it is more complex still. At its most basic level, it involves translating one culture into the voice of another. At a higher level it involves creating a *hybrid voice* that is at once empathetic, comprehensible and legitimate within both cultures simultaneously. However, if we accept that a speaker's identity has been formed by "a mesh of intersecting voices", that it is both dialogically constructed (Wetherell 2007:672) and a "dialogical practice" (Blommaert 2005:205), then for some speakers, especially those familiar with both sets of expectation in force within a given intercultural context, translation will be a possibility and, for particularly skilled speakers, even the creation of a hybrid voice, "in which features of one genre are embedded within a token of another" (Baumann and Briggs 1990:64), will be possible. In other cases the creation of a hybrid voice will not be an individual effort but the *collaborative* achievement of a variety of speakers each making their own contributions and *revoicing* the contributions of others as appropriate. In the case study that follows, particularly in Chapters 5 and 6, I hope to show examples of both these practices in action as instances of what Bakhtin (1984) calls *polyphony*: truth, or in this case power, as distributed across an array of voices and across a range of orders of indexicality in which different speakers' voices and the identities they construe for themselves are differently legitimate and hence powerful. Most importantly, from the point of view of my earlier criticisms of PDA, the hybrid voices that result from these practices will not only be alternatives to hegemonic voices; they will also potentially be at once *assimilable* within the marginalised culture and *legitimate* contributions within the dominant

20 Hybrid Voices and Collaborative Change

discourse. Each context therefore carries a degree of *perturbation potential* (Bartlett, forthcoming), the scope for altering accepted, often hegemonic, discourse practices, in direct relation to the different voices of the participants present, their place in the communities that they represent, and their capacity to act on these conditions as determined both by the structural constraints of the social context and the speakers' individual skills. The task of PDA for me, therefore, rather than celebrating alternative discourses without relating them to the social bases of their formulation and their potential for uptake, is to bring to light the perturbation potential in each context and to stimulate this potential in practice. This involves, amongst other considerations, moving beyond a focus on the abstract meaning of texts in isolation to provide an ethnographic account of the discourse context that relates the language features of these texts to the social organisation of the groups involved in the encounter, a move which is made possible via the concept of voice, as elaborated above. As a first small step in this direction the case study that follows aims to provide an account of this potential in operation and to analyse the contextual factors that contributed to its successes and failures.

METHODS OF ANALYSIS

From the above discussions it should be clear that *discourse* and *text* are by no means the same thing (and see Widdowson [2004] for an extended discussion of this point). From one perspective we can say that discourse is the situated use of language and that it therefore includes but goes beyond texts as spoken or written words to encompass the range of structural and situational factors that make texts meaningful and that determine whether they will be effective, or even possible, within certain contexts. From the reverse perspective we can say that written or recorded texts are the trace of discourses, the permanent record of the multiple verbal actions that brought a panoply of situational factors to bear on a moment of social interaction and that helped to reshape the context itself. From these ideas follows the oft-stated refrain that "meaning cannot be read off the text alone". Equally as true, however, is the converse idea that text, as the detailed trace of discourse, is our principal way into analysing the meanings of communicative events and that, consequently, text needs to be analysed not only in detail, but in ways that make the connection to discourse specific. There are two particular levels to such analysis in this book.

Firstly, and more generally, I will analyse stretches of text (and occasionally individual utterances) in terms of the linguistic features they display and relate these to the practices and organisational structures of the different social groups involved in NRDDB discourse—that is, in terms of the *voice* they realises as discourse. In analysing texts for voice I will use a different approach from that of Hymes and others. A major basis of

Hymes's (1996) work on voice is the notion of *ethnopoetics*, the exploration of distinctive and consistent underlying structures in the narrative styles of particular subgroups. Much of his work is focused on storytelling and other forms of artistic production, but his approach has been applied to other genres such as asylum applications and education (Blommaert 2008). The analytical framework I develop in this book shares the same concern in describing narrative as locally specific practice as Hymes's ethnopoetics and highlights many of the same features, but it draws on a different range of linguistic variables using, in particular, the descriptive categories developed within SFL as a means of analysing language as a social phenomenon (Halliday 1978; Halliday and Hasan 1985). SFL has a long history of work on voice, particularly within Bernstein's framework, and this will be developed more fully in later chapters (and below I shall justify this approach in relation to Blommaert's criticisms of the role of SFL in CDA). The major component of SFL description that I will draw on here is the concept of language as realising three separate functions simultaneously: (i) the construal of experience, (ii) the enactment of social relations and (iii) the signalling of relations between parts of texts to each other and to the here and now of the context. These functions establish what are referred to as the *field*, *tenor* and *mode* of the discourse respectively (Halliday and Hasan 1985) and, in combination, they activate the *register* of a text or sections within it. From the perspective of voice, register is the linguistic means by which competing social systems are realised in discourse. While *voice* refers to the customary ways of talking within a community or to an individual's realisation of identity through discourse, *register* refers to the properties of the text itself at any point. Identifying voice in practice in these terms is therefore a question of relating the registerial features of a text to the social organisation of the community or to the social identity of the speaker in terms of the shared experience represented (field), the interpersonal relations enacted (tenor) and the rhetorical conventions for disseminating information and regulating practice (mode). Between them, voice and register are thus important analytical tools in determining whose social system is prevalent in a discourse at any time and, in the long run, to investigate what situational variables are instrumental in allowing for different voices to be heard and what the effects are of using different voices on the situation itself (see also Bartlett 2006). As discussed earlier, such an analysis requires a prior description of the relevant community practices, which will be provided in Chapters 2 and 3.

At a second level of analysis, that is, beyond identifying the voice that is realised by any particular stretch of text, it will also be necessary to explore the linguistic means by which the interplay of voices in NRDDB discourse is imposed and challenged, when it creates mutual understanding and when it leads to misunderstandings and breakdowns in the discourse. While the descriptive framework of SFL might be adequate in providing a general description of the voices in play at any specific time

22 *Hybrid Voices and Collaborative Change*

(at least according to the perspective on voice I have elaborated above), in analysing in more detail the mechanisms by which these voices are negotiated I shall follow Blommaert (2005:235) and draw on a variety of "disciplinary toolkits as repertoires from which elements can be chosen and combined, depending on the specific problem that needs to be solved". I shall put off a discussion of these different methods until the chapter outline, below, in order to make the relevance of each method to the problem tackled clear and to avoid repetition. After the chapter outline I shall provide a general overview of the relevance of the specific methods adopted in relation to the broader discourse concepts outlined in this chapter and, in particular, to the criticisms of Widdowson and others with regard to textual analysis within CDA and, by inheritance, PDA practice. Before that I shall provide an example of textual analysis that combines my approach to voice within the SFL framework with other analytical methods in order to illustrate the general methodological framework adopted throughout the book.

NEGOTIATING *VOICE*

The text that follows represents an instance of the struggle between competing voices, albeit a largely friendly one (and this is an important point that will be developed below), and in my analysis and discussion I will elaborate a little further on my framework for analysing voice introduced above. At this stage it is only possible to consider *individual voices*, though with occasional references to the *community voices* that each in its own way manifests; it will be a central goal throughout the book to analyse and illustrate in greater depth the relationship between individual and community voices, but this can only be done after the description of the local context in the following chapters. I have placed this text in the introductory chapter, however, as it is a debate on the process of development itself and so, as well as introducing key participants in NRDDB discourse and illustrating the interplay of different voices as they negotiate and recalibrate the ongoing discourse context, it provides a thematic background for the book as a whole. The text comes from an Iwokrama-sponsored workshop organised to formulate a Community Management Plan in which Iwokrama representatives led discussions on local issues and the systematisation of resource management based on both traditional and imported knowledge. Although the workshop is a format more familiar within the dominant culture, an issue that is raised within the text itself (lines 8–13&113–122), in this case it draws on the cultural resources of both sets of interactants. The community participants whose voices are heard here are both prominent members of Toka village, where the workshop is taking place. Walter (**W** in the transcript) is a native Makushi speaker who has learned English through the school system and local interaction. As stated above, he is the

Bucking the System 23

son of a shama man, and he is also an activist in the radical Amerindian group the Amerindian People's Association (APA). He became chairman of the NRDDB some time after the workshop from which this text is taken. Nicholas (**N**), though a native of Toka, was educated on the coast[9] and speaks English as his first language. He has been Touchau (elected chief) of Toka and Touchau of Touchaus for the North Rupununi as a whole. He is also a pastor within the village, in the same church as Walter and, while he had no official status within the NRDDB at the time of writing, he was a frequent and vocal contributor from the floor. The text also introduces the voices of two prominent members of Iwokrama. Gordon (**G**) is senior wildlife biologist, born in Guyana of Welsh extraction and educated in Britain. Gordon was responsible for setting up various community participation structures and was a major contributor to NRDDB meetings. Sara (**S**) is a social scientist particularly involved in community development, and the workshop from which the text is taken was her project. At this time she had recently joined Iwokrama. The text is part of a feedback session on earlier discussions and covers issues of central importance to this book such as cultural autonomy and the extent and nature of community participation in development practice. Some references are made to flipcharts written up during those discussions. For transcription conventions see page **xiii–xiv**. This is a rather long excerpt, as are many throughout the book, as I think it is appropriate to reproduce such examples to provide a genuine feel for the voices involved, so readers can 'hear' the analysis in the text itself.

Text 1.1 is important not only in terms of the topics it raises, but also in that, as an activity, it is an example in process of the negotiation of voice and the decision-making power that different voices control. As discussed above, *voice* is defined here as the extent to which the three discourse variables of field, tenor and mode (the discourse context) relate to the lived norms of particular groups (the social context). It is worth emphasising at this point the bidirectional relationship between the discourse context and the language features *at risk* (i.e. likely to occur within the text). While the discourse context *activates* appropriate linguistic features, the use of particular features also *construes* (Halliday and Hasan 1985) the discourse context. In other words, the field, tenor and mode of the discourse at one and the same time delimit what can 'legitimately' be said by following speakers but are themselves a product of what has already been said. In this way the discourse context can be seen as dynamic, neither totally restricting nor totally open, but allowing for a gradual recalibration of temporary positions that can, over time, impact upon longer-term positions. In sum, language can be strategically employed to change the context, including power relations and understandings of lived experience, so that in Text 1.1 we see the various participants jockeying for control over the field, tenor and mode of the discourse while staying within the bounds of legitimacy that have already been established. This notion of temporary recalibration and the longer-term effects it achieves will be a particularly important theme throughout the book.

24 Hybrid Voices and Collaborative Change

Text 1.1 Toka, 18/4/00, Management Planning Workshop

```
1   G:  Added to that, then, there's the whole question of (who owns) agriculture,
2       we talked about (xx) and (xx) . . . Another one was the land, the whole question
3       of the relationship between Toka and the Government and what land was
4       available for use . . . and that's tied in with (xxx), tied in with long-term
5       security . . . ?
6   N:  That's. .that should be tied in to ownership of other resources like water,
7       (xxx) . . .
8   G:  Ownership and use of management (product). Management (rights xx).
9       (p)
10      The target (h)as communication we've got in . . . which I think comes into
11      the first thing, that's called mechanisms how. .>how your views can be
12      reflected both< with the government, with UNDP[10], with Iwokrama, with
13      everybody.
14      (p) ((some mumbling))
15      Another big one . . . we've seen . . . that seems to affect a lot of things is creek,
16      your ideas of creek management . . . (detay) reforestation.
17  N:  I think it's a whole restoration process.
18  G:  Restoration (xxxx)?
19  N:  Not only that. But the (xxxx). Because of cultural restoration. Maybe
20      you couldn't finance that, you know? Because what we find there's
21      disadvantage when we've been government, erm, driven programmes, they've
22      been. .financially supported properly. .and our erm programmes are not,
23      traditional ways are not supported so. They have an advantage right away
24      there (xx) find that. . they actually killing . . . government is (xx) not knowing
25      (they) erm killing culture.
26  S:  °Not knowing?°
27  ?:  °(xx)°
28      (p)
29  G:  I'm not sure if this doesn't (xxxx) my interpretation.
30  N:  (What your interpretation is?)
31      ((Interference, pauses and muttering.))
32      I think one of the things we have to do (actually) is we have to be. .(adventure,
33      you know) with a (pi xx). When we develop plans that erm. .the government
34      na[11] see it as being, you know, complementary . . . complementary with the
35      present development strategies of the government, so. .we're not supported, but
36      it should be supported, (na?)
37  G:  But this comes back again to this whole question of whether or not anybody's
38      listening to what you're saying. Which doesn't appear to be the
39      case. At all levels. Sometimes because before in our communities they don't know
40      how to listen. Sometimes they're just not terribly interested in listening.
41      (p)
42  S:  °(xxxx)°if this comes back to the whole question of land rights and what
43      that means. Uhm. .what sort of autonomy do you have over your land,
44      °(xxx)°, these for now (13 legal) square miles, what sort of autonomy does that
45      give you. .and what you can do with that land and not do with that land an'
46      whose business is it. Erm, how do you manage that land. .whose /biz/- ah, all
47      these things need planning=
48  N:  =but let's talk [about self-gov. .governance]
49  S:                 [a number of things] erm=
50  G:  =(gotta find out yer)=
51  S:  =we're not talking about political governance, sovereignty, we're talking
                                                              (continued)
```

Bucking the System   25

52		*about [(xxx governance)]*
53	*N:*	*[but that's what we're] talking about, being able to (them thing),*
54		*control and to manage the different (xxerity).*
55	*G:*	*We talked about=*
56	*N:*	*=community*
57	*G:*	*permanence in the village, from a style that's <u>forced</u> by the government from*
58		*outside, not (wanting to get into) the village, but forced. .a forced process from*
59		*outside. .they'd rather it to be an internally-driven process. .and the whole*
60		*Amerindian the Amerindian Act[12] was based on this that the Government*
61		*wants (to be). .leader, rather that the Amerindian Act says that . . . and, er, that*
62		*the whole. .this whole thing of the village law, the village developing its own*
63		*laws, the Council developing its own laws, the Council being trained for*
64		*dealing with people from inside and outside of the village rather than asking*
65		*the government to deal with the external influences, but also the internal*
66		*influences. Somehow developing mechanisms whereby people are*
67		*compensated for spending all that time <u>doing</u> it, but to do <u>this</u> . . . not, again,*
68		*being dependent on the government to give $3,000[13] a month or whatever it is,*
69		*but. .but for systems to be set up so that the. .community's self-governing it's*
70		*self. .self-sufficient in that context. Community spending. .would like. .to sort of*
71		*spend more time planning with their own (xx)*
72	*N:*	*You don't think the term self-government . . . tha- that's the thing that's been*
73		*creating a big (problem)if you talk about local government [°(xx)°]*
74	*S:*	*[Sounds]*
75		*like sovereignty, and <u>that</u>'s the problem right there=*
76	*G:*	*=It's more [(xxx)]*
77	*S:*	*[(besides)] governance comes in. .or even using those*
78		*words . . . becomes then it's the kind of thing you [see*
79	*N:*	*[yeah, but you see that*
80		*the government would look at it from the international perspective, then it*
81		*would see that self-governance what it means according to the /kak/- the*
82		*(IO) Convention. (ones it's signed on) indigenous peoples. An' [that's*
83		*what we're talking about.]*
84	*S:*	*[(x x*
85		*x x x x x x x x] x x) those conventions, <u>talk</u>-shop. (p)*
86		*Maybe 300 people that write them. [(x)*
87	*N:*	*[Sure I know, but it's still there. And*
88		*those are the implements that [we're supposed to use.]*
89	*S:*	*[And there's no means] by which to enforce*
90		*them.*
91	*N:*	*°(x).°*
92	*G:*	*One of the major issues is that the Government should work*
93		*><u>with</u>. .people. .or <u>for</u> people. .and not. .plan< before planning experiments*
94		*and imposing them. .on people. And it again comes back to*
95		*<u>listening</u> . . . being able to listen.*
96	*N:*	*To put it [more. . . . .] let me give you a development thing which you*
97	*S:*	*[I wonder if]*
98	*N:*	*can . . . community-based, right? [(xxxxx)?]*
99	*S:*	*[Right.] Okay, mmm. Yeah! Mmm, yeah.*
100		*Uhm. . . . . There are a number of. .of observations °(and things)° that, I*
101		*don't know . . . (xxx) uhm I think (that some of them are xxxxx). The ways in*
102		*which the Government has removed <u>power</u>. . from communities, they're not*
103		*just . . . fighting to get co-ownership of communities, but it's. .it's in these*
104		*development projects, it's in these land-management schemes . . . small little*

(continued)

26   Hybrid Voices and Collaborative Change

Text 1.1 (continued)

```
105      things. .it's in how it controls schools, how it, you know, how it does these
106      things. .erm, so, it seems like a lot of the strategy is to (stays more in), take
107      them back. .and at those levels, through development of (xxx). This
108      relationship with the government, though, seems to be. .(devolved???),
109      especially when it comes to village authority structures. Some people on
110      the one hand feel that's it's important to keep having external input,
111      through the police and and things like that because there are issues within
112      the village that are not handled °through the (xx).°
113  W:  We[14] other plan is that we want to (produce) a proposal.
114  G:  Proposal for wha:t?
115  W:  Some form of (xxxx)
116  N:  Was it better ↑communication, or ↓information?
117      °((unclear talk/muttering))°
118  W:  °I think it's somewhere about there.° To get through with some
119      management plan °down there°.
120      (long pause) ((more ?searching))
121  G:  When we were talking about communications system?
122  N:  (xxx we) proposal and we talked about setting up a plan. .or someting.[15]
```

In terms of the field of discourse, the representations of processes, participants and circumstances in Text 1.1 are activated by the topic of discussion: intercultural perspectives on development. The text therefore introduces several key issues such as the meaning of development and the extent of cultural autonomy and the role of the local communities in the discussions surrounding these issues. The text also shows very clearly how the field under discussion is not fixed: Rather, the meaning and importance of key concepts are contested and negotiated as each speaker attempts to impose their own agenda on the discussion and to legitimate their own definition of the state of affairs. At the beginning of Text 1.1, for example, Gordon introduces the topic of "the land" (1–5) and relates this to long-term security (4–5), management (8) and issues of communication (10–13). Nicholas, however, changes the direction of the discussion when he announces (17) "I think it's a whole restoration process" and steers the topic towards the more contentious issues of funding for government-led development and the resulting acculturation (19–25) of the local population, a theme which Gordon relates back to communications (38–42) and Sara then develops in the direction of autonomy and legal rights (44–49). From here on, each of these speakers picks up on aspects of the others' themes and adapts them towards their own. As we have seen, Gordon picks up on the notion of autonomy and turns it back to communications issues, while Nicholas attempts to introduce the key term "community-based" (58&100) into the definition of autonomy, in line with his ideas on cultural restoration. Sara picks up on the term "community" (100) to direct the discussion back to issues of power and control (101–114) by emphasising how the government has wrested authority from the communities. As discussion continues beyond Text 1.1, the emphasis seems to have fixed on communications and community control, but Nicholas is still able to reintroduce his key theme of intercultural issues:

132 *S:*   *(it has to be= =for example) the children are seeing and learning from*
133   *people who are [(x x x x x x x x x)]*
134 *N:*   *[No, but which culture exists. .]which one is dominating?*
135   *Western culture or Makushi culture?*
136 *S:*   *Well, [it's not= =it wasn't a discussion of the cult-=*

Walter is also able to raise practical issues relating to community participation:

147 **W:** *I think that. .I mean after they did this. .this is a starting point and you*
148   *really (depends) on how much time you put in, it could, er, do good for*
149   *the. .the future (one). .and I think that we have to be aware of, er, the time*
150   *do it, (we're looking at) that we can (xx) for individuals at this time of the*
151   *year, but I think we should, erm, have a long (xxx) this.*

And Sara introduces methodological considerations:

177 *S:* *workshops are perhaps not the best way to actually work with the*
178   *communities, uhm, and this is a starting point, your management plan,*
179   *which is. .it's really just a starting point, an impression of what's the best*
180   *way to move forward on. .the methodology perspective, this is a big one*
181   *and that requires a lot of input from. . ↓you in terms of what you think*
182   *works or doesn't work, what's a good time and a bad time . . . things like*
183   *that . . . erm, we really should discuss, when we start discussing the way*
184   *forward.*

The contrasting emphases on method and practice, and their relationship to voice, are a recurrent theme in this book and are considered in some detail in Chapters 3, 5 and 6. The problems with the workshop format itself are highlighted in Chapter 3, including the communicative disadvantage facing the communities when dealing with the authorities, Iwokrama included, an issue that is explicitly raised at a later point in this discussion:

159 *N:* *Well, the next thing that worries me is the definition of. .of=of development.*
160   *Hmm? It's that up here we've got our own definition, we understand this*
161   *as we development, but then that might not be the same thing, we have the*
162   *(x) of indigenous communities.*
163 *G:* *(xx) come back to whether or not the development agencies, including*
164   *Iwokrama, are listening to what the (players) have to say. (xxx) And what*
165   *are the mechanisms for being able to listen. (p) By having you in here are*
166   *we really listening to the community? (p) That's another question, because*

28   Hybrid Voices and Collaborative Change

167   *this is the problem with the Board, I mean listening to what the Board*
168   *says, is that really listening to what the people want, the whole system needs*
169   *(to remodel) to do that.*

Within the field of discourse, the level of terminology is also an important variable, with Text 1.1 lying somewhere on the midpoint of the continuum between everyday and specialist, with terms such as *restoration process* and *cultural autonomy* woven into a generally more informal level of speech.

Moving on to mode, which relates to the role of the text itself as a linguistic construct, a significant feature of Text 1.1 is the degree to which different speakers relate the discourse to the here and now, that is, the degree to which the talk is *contextualised* or *decontextualised*. Using Cloran's (2000:175) schema for identifying different degrees of contextualisation over a stretch of text (what she calls Rhetorical Units, to be discussed in detail in Chapter 6; see also Appendix 1), Text 1.1 can be seen to move between Plans and Conjectures (e.g. 6–16) in which the events described are hypothetical with regard to the present context; Commentaries (e.g. 38–39, 44–45), which relate directly to the present context; and Recounts (e.g. 102–109), which are removed in time from the present context. Later on (not shown in Text 1.1), we have Generalisations regarding methods of information transfer, which are neither time nor place specific, and Reflections on community life, the development process and the role of outsiders, which are related to co-present participants but are non-specific in time. Sustained differences in use of these rhetorical devices from different speakers will be shown to be an important feature of voice in Chapter 6.

Also seen as a variable in mode is the means of transmission of the language: whether it is written, spoken, written to be spoken, and so on. These distinctions in means of transmission have regular effects on the form of discourse. They are also culturally salient practices, as will be discussed in Chapter 5. Text 1.1 is predominantly spoken discourse, though important points are written up on a flipchart. As spontaneous spoken language, the discourse is characterised by the high degree of turn-taking and the complexity of the clausal structures used to get meaning across in unplanned real time (e.g. Gordon's turn from 59 to 74).

Negotiating the content and significance of information requires more than just contesting definitions within the field of discourse, and speakers employ a range of interpersonal linguistic features that affect the tenor of the discourse and, consequently, its direction and pacing. Tenor variables include such strategic variables as who asks questions of whom and how strongly the speakers assert their views; what level of respect they afford their interlocutors, and on what basis; and the solidarities they display. In Text 1.1, the way speakers relate with each other is a function of the complementary social positions that the different speakers represent, both within their own cultural backgrounds and within NRDDB–Iwokrama interaction; the familiarity they have with each other; and the solidarity

Bucking the System   29

that comes from a common goal but that is weakened by the participants' different approaches towards this goal. This all results, in broad strokes, in a tenor of frank expressions of disagreement tempered with deference and an informal tone within a semi-formal framework of turn-taking that nonetheless allows for interruptions and overlaps. This ambivalence in the tenor, as speakers each endowed with cultural capital from different sources come into contact in an equitable setting, can be seen in that there are few direct questions or elicitations for other speakers to contribute (line 30 is a rare example): Nearly all the utterances are declarative statements, while the use of rhetorical questions from Nicholas, for example, serves to reintroduce his key themes as much as to cede the floor (75–76, 100). Similarly, participants consistently use hedges, particularly "I think" (e.g. 10, 17, 32), to introduce points of view and so soften the blow of diverting the focus towards their own areas of concern. However, hedging disappears at several key points in the contestation of the field and there is a clear breakdown in turn-taking procedures at these points. Lines 49 to 59 and lines 75 to 101, for example, are characterised by interruptions and overlaps that are largely missing from the rest of the text as each speaker seeks to impose their own definition on the key concepts of autonomy, governance and sovereignty. The interdependence of field, tenor and mode, to be discussed in Chapter 6, is shown in that at these critical points the mode of the discourse also changes as language turns towards more introspective Commentaries on the discourse process itself, with Nicholas (50&55), Sara (53–54) and Gordon (57) one after the other explicitly directing or stating what is being talked about at the present moment:

50. *N:* =*but **let's talk** [about self-gov. .governance]*
51. *S:*   *[a number of things] erm=*
52. *G:* =*(gotta find out yer)=*
53. *S:* =***we're not talking about** political governance, sovereignty, **we're talking***
54.   *about [(xxx governance)]*
55. *N:*   *[but that's what **we're] talking about**, being able to (them thing), control*
56.   *and to manage the different (xxerity).*
57. *G: **We talked about**=*
58. *N:* =*community*

The participants employ a range of rhetorical means in their attempts to control the semantic development of the discourse here: Nicholas's inclusive command (50) to direct the talk; Sara's contrasting Rheme structure[16] (53–54) to contest Nicholas's command; Nicholas's defining clause (55) to get the discourse back on his track; and Gordon's past declarative (57) to serve as a justification for present action.

What becomes clear throughout the text is that although there is broad consensus on both the general topic of discussion and the interactional roles of the different participants, there are subtle differences at play and

30 Hybrid Voices and Collaborative Change

at various points each speaker reconfigures the variables of field, tenor and mode. This demonstrates the point made above that the discourse context activates relevant linguistic behaviour, yet is open to recalibration through the different construals of the speakers. For example, while the discourse remains within the general field of local development, the different speakers clearly have different takes on what is most relevant to the topic. Similarly, despite the superficially democratic nature of proceedings, the Iwokrama representatives speak more often and generally for longer and tend to lead the discussion, sanctioning or excluding particular paths.[17] In some ways, then, variations in the field, tenor and mode of discourse in this text can be said to introduce *tensions* into the workshop format, and these tensions, over who has the right to speak how and when and who defines the range and specifics of the field of discourse, are reflections in microcosm of the very issues that the participants are discussing within the wider Discourse of Development and, in particular, tensions around whose voice is to be legitimated within these discourses.

CONCLUSION

Throughout this book *voice* stands for ways of speaking that are based on and that transmit a community's way of being—or rather, their ways of being, as no culture is monolithic and it is the variety of experience within a community, their shared diversity, that makes possible the transformations in ways of speaking that I am going to describe. These transformations, as I hope to show, amount to more than a simple *abrogation* (Bhatt 2010:523) by the local communities of the institutionalised discourse of dominant groups in favour of traditional discourse systems; it refers, rather, to the development of new *ways of speaking* that are appropriate to the mix of social groups, with their distinct bodies of knowledge and systems of authority, within the new intercultural context. This process was not a one-sided affair, and the willingness of professional development workers to adapt their ways of thinking and acting was one of the *conditions of possibility* without which the NRDDB could not have developed as a space of shared knowledge and shared authority. In contexts such as the North Rupununi, where the Amerindian population have suffered a double colonisation, first by the Europeans and secondly by the post-independence government, the creation of innovative discourse relations with the dominant sectors of society is, according to Bhatt (2010:526–527), a key feature in the gradual development of a post-colonial identity which:

> can be understood as the emergence of agency and self-awareness: a new semiotic process and ideology of plurality and hybridity, through which people imagine their identities as being dialogically construed through resistance and appropriation . . . [a process which] emerges

Bucking the System 31

in localised linguistic practices as a new differentiation, which welds colonialism with autonomy, past with present, and global with local. Hybridity involves the fusion of two relatively distinct cultural forms, styles and identities, creating a discursive space—a *third space* (Bhabha 1994)—where competing representations of colonised-coloniser, indigenous-foreign and local-global are constantly negotiated.

In reference to the achievements of the Amerindian communities I have, a little playfully, called this opening chapter "Bucking the System". The term *buck*, as can be seen from the quotation from Walter that opened this chapter, is a pejorative term for Amerindians in Guyana, originally used by colonial settlers but now used by the non-indigenous population. In using the term I hope to capture how the Amerindian communities of the North Rupununi are reasserting their pride in their heritage after years of casual and institutionalised discrimination and how, in so doing, they were able, in some small way, to change the system itself. What I present in this book is therefore not the analysis of top-down control over discourse that perpetuates societal inequalities which I had foreseen, but a case study of bottom-up change in institutional discourse which I hope will serve as an inspiration and a model for similar processes elsewhere. My account is partial in that it captures only some of the events within the NRDDB and their background and partial in that it is told from my perspective, within a framework of my design to suit my aims. Nonetheless, I believe it is a true version of events, if one of many, that captures some of the richness of that time from a valid perspective. My perspective is on local development within the North Rupununi and the role of community and individual voice within related discourses, and my way of recounting and analysing events will be framed to suit this perspective. While the analytical methods I employ are not the only way of approaching the concept of voice, which is not in itself the only way of approaching the issue at hand, my account can hopefully be seen as providing one angle on the "truth" that contributes one voice to the *polyphony* created by other accounts of similar situations.

THE STRUCTURE OF THE BOOK

In this introductory Chapter 1 I highlighted what many critics perceive as problems within CDA, some of which led to the development of an alternative approach known as PDA, and some of which were inherited by this new approach. In particular I discussed the limitations of the *textual bias* in CDA and PDA and suggested the sociolinguistic concept of *voice* as a means to overcome this problem. *Voice* was defined as a way of speaking that realises in discourse aspects of speakers' social backgrounds, specifically in the way that speakers' talk captures elements of their material culture, plays out interpersonal relations and organises information in a

32 *Hybrid Voices and Collaborative Change*

coherent fashion. As such I suggested that the concept of voice could usefully be employed to analyse how skilled speakers, either individually or in collaboration, create new discourses styles that are *comprehensible*, *empathetic* and *legitimate* across intercultural divides. I then introduced the SFL concept of register as a means of analysing discourse for voice as it is realised through the *field*, *tenor* and *mode* of texts at a given point and provided a textual analysis to illustrate this.

In Chapter 2 I provide a general overview of the participants in NRDDB meetings: the local, predominantly Makushi population; the Government of Guyana; and Iwokrama which, in collaboration with the local communities, established the NRDDB. I follow this with a more detailed account of life on the Rupununi Savannahs drawn from interview data, fieldwork notes and secondary sources. This begins with a description of the social conditions and internal organisation of the Makushi people, with a focus on their material culture, their interpersonal power relations and their traditional means of disseminating information and regulating activities—those variables that relate, respectively, to the SFL concepts of field, tenor and mode, and hence to my conceptualisation of voice. This is followed by a discussion of how the internal organisation of the local communities has been disrupted by the centrist tendencies of the national government and the pressures of globalisation, including international development. Between them, I argue, these forces have provided a challenge to traditional community practices and undermined local methods of control without providing an adequate and sustainable alternative, with the result that the Makushi communities find themselves caught up in a developmental limbo. I supplement this discussion with an analysis of the 1976 Revision of the Guyana Amerindian Act and the NRDDB's own Constitution of 2001 as a way of comparing the government's perspective on the relationship between Amerindian communities and the Guyanese state with that of the local people themselves, particularly in terms of development practice. For this analysis I provide a quantitative comparison of the allocation of the semantic roles[18] of *overseer*, *performer*, *beneficiary* and *undergoer* to Amerindians themselves, on the one hand, and to outsiders, on the other, within processes of local development as set out across the two documents. Overall this chapter serves to describe the historical *conditions of possibility* that led to the creation of the NRDDB as a site where the local communities, the national government and Iwokrama come together to discuss local development; more specifically, it serves to provide the contextual framework that enables the analysis of text as discourse in later chapters, particularly as a point of reference in determining the extent to which different speakers can be said to adopt the voice of the local community, the institutional voice of Iwokrama, the voice of international development or some other voice.

In Chapter 3 I will focus on the discourse history between the various participants within the NRDDB—the local population, the Government of Guyana and international development organisations—in order to suggest

Bucking the System 33

how this history is a constraining factor on current discourse. I start the chapter with an overview of the "Discourse of Development" as it has been formulated and put into operation by dominant sectors of society, namely, the world superpowers and international aid organisations, and the tensions that exist between the donor–beneficiary view of development underlying traditional development discourse (and which, I have argued above, is in large part to blame for the continuing failure of the development project) and more recent approaches that advocate an opening up of spaces for community voices to share their local knowledge and to participate in organisational structures. Turning to the specifics of the North Rupununi, I will then trace the history of discourse between the international development organisation Iwokrama and local communities to suggest that the tensions evident within development discourse at the international level can be linked to ambivalent discourse practice at the local level as Iwokrama workers struggle to overcome traditional lop-sided discourse practices and community members struggle equally to accustom themselves to their new role as discourse partners. I will then analyse a text from early on in my fieldwork which shows how control over a management training exercise shifts gradually, and perhaps unintentionally, from Walter, as a community elder, to Sara, as an Iwokrama representative, and discuss how Sara's latent *symbolic capital* was an implicit factor in this shift. This analysis entails a two step-process comprising a description of the most salient linguistic features of consecutive sections of the text in as objective terms as such selection allows followed by an interpretation of the section as discourse in action drawing on the conventions of Conversation Analysis, Interactional Sociolinguistics and the descriptive tools of SFL. The analysis of the text as a whole suggests that the various discourse moves of the participants *foreground* their different positions in the local community and as professional development workers and lead to what I suggest is a communicative breakdown that alters the nature of the discourse from that point on. Building on the discussion of this text I outline a heuristic model for analysing discourse in terms of the position speakers take up and the relevance of their social standing in enabling them to do so, or indeed preventing them from doing so.

In Chapter 4 I analyse the concept of *positioning* in more detail, drawing on Bourdieu's (1977, 1991) concept of *symbolic capital* as the prestige speakers carry with them as the result of such social factors as their education, their class and ethnicity, and their status within different institutions. After suggesting that symbolic capital is a more varied resource than in Bourdieu's framework, in terms of both the underpinnings of speakers' prestige and the language that accompanies this, I analyse three interviews with participants in NRDDB meetings, a local farmer and councillor, a community elder instrumental in setting up the NRDDB, and the Iwokrama senior wildlife biologist, to suggest a variety of forms of symbolic capital, and hence of *orders of indexicality*, which are in play within the NRDDB.

34   *Hybrid Voices and Collaborative Change*

This analysis involves a quantitative analysis of the different modal forms and mental projections employed by the speakers in describing local development in order to ascertain and describe the degree and type of capital the different speakers can be said to appropriate to themselves within the field of local development. This is supplemented by a qualitative analysis of sections of each interview to illustrate how these different discourse features work in conjunction to construe each speaker's position. To conclude the chapter I sketch a model of *collaborative discourse* that brings these different capitals together.

Chapters 2 to 4 thus provide a backdrop to the analyses of a series of discursive events from the NRDDB during the period of my fieldwork in Guyana. In Chapter 5 I will analyse five chronologically ordered texts that demonstrate various ways in which local communities can be seen to be taking control, or at least sharing control, of these events, and show how the discursive means by which they achieve this can be related to the concept of *voice* and the different positionings of speakers within the discourse. As the purpose of this chapter is to demonstrate how local control over NRDDB discourse had developed over time, these analyses are contrasted with the analysis of the chronologically earlier text in Chapter 3 and the same analytical techniques are employed.

In Chapter 6 I will analyse two texts in which first Sara and then Uncle Henry, a prominent local elder, attempt to explain the concept of *Sustainable Utilisation Areas* to members of the NRDDB. I will show how, through the alternation of variables in *field, tenor* and *mode*, Uncle Henry's contribution draws on a combination of local and external voices to which he has unique access and through which he manages to successfully explain the concept of sustainable utilisation after Sara had failed to do so. I will suggest, however, that the success of Uncle Henry's contribution relied on Sara's earlier attempt, and describe various ways in which the combination of the capital of different speakers can be brought together in a *collaborative* model of discourse practice.

In Chapter 7 I will provide an overview of the previous chapters, situating them within the wider context of international development and suggesting some caveats regarding the extent to which, and the manner in which, the changes in local discourse identified might impact upon the wider context. I shall revisit my discussion of *PDA* in this chapter, bringing together the various elements of the analytical model that has been developed in the book as an alternative methodology and drawing conclusions as to the potential of the analytical methods employed and the theoretical model developed for application in other discourse contexts. I shall end this final chapter with a discussion of the limitations of my work and suggestions for future directions.

In this overview of the book I have touched on the analytical methods I will use, and it is therefore appropriate at this point to return to the criticisms of CDA methodology that were discussed at the beginning of

Bucking the System   35

this chapter and explain the ways in which I think the range of methods employed can overcome, or at least mitigate, these. I will first consider the various elements that contribute to Widdowson's charge of *cherry-picking* in CDA and then turn to Blommaert's concerns over *linguistic bias*.

Widdowson makes the two related claims that in focusing attention on clause-level analysis CDA is often guilty of misrepresenting the contribution of individual clauses to the text as a whole and that the analysis is not representative in that only sections of each text are selected for discussion. In contrast, my analysis is generally of long stretches of text *in toto* rather than on isolated features, though it will be necessary at times to focus on restricted sections where these are seen to have significant effects on the text as a whole, and in analysing these stretches I focus on relations between the different sections within them, particularly with regard to how these sections contribute to bring together different community voices (n.b. Chapter 6). I also analyse and interrelate a variety of texts from differently situated speakers over a three-year time period rather than focusing on individual texts in isolation. While the choice of texts for analysis is restricted to those areas judged to be of interest, I hope that through the approach I have taken I have avoided tailoring my analysis to my pretextual assumptions (which are many).

Widdowson also discusses the tendency within CDA, as derived from SFL, to treat grammatical categories as if they were psychologically real (as does O'Halloran 2003) without due consideration of their "pragmatic" effect and their contribution to the text as a whole. In Chapter 2 I have compared government and NRDDB representations of different groups' participation within local development by means of a quantitative analysis of the roles allocated to them in the NRDDB Constitution and the Guyana Amerindian Act of 1976. However, in allocating the roles of *overseer, performer, beneficiary* and *undergoer* I have used semantic criteria, thus avoiding the contentious area of the specifically grammatical encoding of meaning. That is not to say that I do not see an analysis of the grammatical means by which these semantic roles are encoded as unhelpful, and indeed I believe it would add to the analysis, but at a second level of analysis which I have not carried out in this case. In those analyses where I have focused on specifically grammatical categories I have done so in two different ways: individually, as they occur within texts (Chapters 3 and 5) and quantitatively across different texts (Chapter 4). In the first instance I have followed the two-step approach of providing first an objective account of their presence before moving on to an interpretation of their function at the point at which they occur. While this second step clearly involves a degree of subjectivity, I have attempted to reduce such subjectivity and to make my interpretations as replicable as possible by first providing the objective categorisation of the features analysed and by basing my interpretation on methodologies from Conversation Analysis and Interactional Sociolinguistics. And in linking these interpretations to the extensive discussion of social and discourse relations between the participants I have attempted to

36 *Hybrid Voices and Collaborative Change*

suggest the interpretations that the participants themselves are likely to draw from the texts rather than those of the (pretextually motivated) expert analyst looking for hidden meanings. Where possible I have attempted to back up my interpretations with either evidence from the continuing text or from interview data. In contrast to the qualitative analysis of text, the quantitative comparison of different speakers' use of modals and mental projections (Chapter 4) cannot provide the contextual features that alter the significance of individual uses (though I have attempted to categorise each use according to its function in context), and I have therefore followed the quantitative data with a qualitative analysis of the speakers' use of these features to demonstrate how they combine to discursive effect. Moreover, the quantitative data are not put forward as necessarily significant in and of themselves, but rather as suggestive of the different degrees and types of authority each speaker appropriates to themselves within the field of local development, an analysis that is linked to the sociocultural background provided and which is used, firstly, to set up a heuristic model of collaborative practice that is then tested against further examples of discourse and, secondly, to add some weight to future interpretations of speakers' contributions, informed as these must be by the discourse tendencies of the individual speakers, which will be salient factors in the local audience's uptake of their words.

Turning to Widdowson's criticisms of CDA for using only selected methods, all I can say is that this is a necessary limitation given the constraints of space (and reader interest), but that I have aimed to use different methods consistently within each analysis as appropriate to the questions being asked of the text at that point.

In sum, in analysing the interrelation of a variety of lengthy texts, using a mix of analytical methods, in relating these texts to an extensive account of the sociocultural background and to evaluations of the text from interview data, and in using quantitative as well as qualitative data to make my analyses more robust, I hope to have avoided to some significant extent the related tendencies towards cherry-picking and pretextually skewed interpretations that Widdowson has identified.

I hope that this multifaceted approach has also gone some way to overcoming the *linguistic bias* in CDA identified by Blommaert. The first aspect of Blommaert's critique is CDA's reliance on SFL in providing its linguist theory, and it could be argued that I have fallen foul of this criticism in adopting SFL's categories of field, tenor and mode as a central analytical device. However, the reason for this relates to Blommaert's (2005:235) view of the role of linguistics within discourse analysis:

> If we see discourse as contextualised language, and take this dimension of contextualisation seriously, we shall be forced to develop a linguistics that ceases to be linguistic from a certain point onwards, and becomes a social science of language-in-society.

This is a view of linguistics that is shared by SFL, and the categories of field, tenor and mode were developed to provide the interface between text and context, as the point at which linguistics ends and social science takes over:

> While in the theory the relation of context of situation [as captured by field, tenor and mode] to context of culture seems clear, the description of the options in the context of culture has never been articulated in any detail. Perhaps one is tacitly saying with Hjelmslev that, at this point, the sociologist and/or anthropologist will take over. Certainly, linguists as linguists are not able to analyse—or are at least limited in the extent to which they can analyse—the crucial properties of culture . . . Perhaps it is worth adding that, in a functional stratal theory of the type that I take SF to be, where the theoretical model attempts to model the permeability of human conditions of social existence and the system of verbal semioisis, there will inevitably arrive a stage where the highest stratum would not be wholly describable in terms of language. (Hasan 1995:267–268)

In other words, SFL is primarily concerned with developing a model that accounts for language as a social construct and which, while it focuses on the specifically linguistic features of the relationship between language and context, carries this description to the point where it can connect with models or accounts of this relationship from the wider social sciences. It is for this reason that I have taken the relationship between voice and the registerial features of language as the basis of my analysis. However, in analysing the mechanisms by which voice is realised and contested in real-time discourse I have not limited myself to the descriptive categories of SFL but have, as Blommaert suggests in the same paragraph from which the above quote comes, used "disciplinary toolkits as repertoires from which elements can be chosen and combined, depending on the specific problem that needs to be solved".

The second aspect of CDA work that Blommaert identifies as displaying linguistic bias is that it analyses existing texts in some detail without consideration of why these texts exist and why alternative texts do not. While I cannot claim to have overcome this limitation in the present work, I hope that in providing an account of the discourse history within and between the participants involved in NRDDB meetings as these constrain the *conditions of possibility* within which the discourses analysed emerged I have at least in some part addressed this problem.

Finally, Blommaert takes CDA to task for not accounting for the social factors behind texts, for failing to account adequately for either the social factors behind the production of these texts or the social consequences of their production—where they come from and where they go to. Blommaert includes this criticism within the point discussed earlier, and I have

38   Hybrid Voices and Collaborative Change

responded to it partially there, but I have included it as a separate issue here as an additional problem is brought to bear when Blommaert says of CDA (2005:35) that:

> analysis starts from the moment there is linguistically encoded discourse, bypassing the ways in which society operates on language users and influences what they can accomplish in language long before they open their mouths, so to speak . . . while . . . a lot happens to language users long after they have shut their mouths.

In similar vein, Scollon and Scollon (2007:620) state that:

> research frameworks which focus on moments of action rather than on abstractable structures such as cultures and languages, must remain inherently open to following out to where the analysis leads the participants. It is not only practically difficult to know what one will need to study next and where, or with whom, it is theoretically limiting to make such decisions in advance of becoming engaged in the actual research. Such *a priori* control of the research agenda is necessarily rejected as a return to an earlier stage of ethnographic development, in which the power to make such decisions would always lie in the hands of the external researcher and his or her academic and professional institutions.

In providing an extensive description of the social context of the North Rupununi and the social relations within and between the different groups (Chapters 2 and 3) and in developing a model of the positions speakers can take up in discourse in relation to these positions (Chapters 3 and 4) I hope to provide some account of "the ways in which society operates on language users . . . long before they open their mouths"; however, beyond analysing increasing local control over NRDDB discourse as a result of previous successful interventions, my analysis stops short of accounting for what happens "after they have shut their mouths", a point I will return to in discussing the limitations of my work and future directions in the concluding chapter.

In conclusion, while my approach addresses some of the principal critiques of CDA and PDA practice, I cannot hope to have fully overcome them and issues will, of course, remain. What I hope to achieve is to set out an enhanced agenda for PDA practice that takes these issues on board in order to move beyond analysing counter-discourses with the same textually oriented methods that CDA has used to critique hegemonic discourses and onto an analysis of how these discourses function in their specific context and how an understanding of their workings might contribute to the design of alternative discourses that are viable within that context.

2 Background

Well . . . I . . . I don't see, you see like I said, it's like in a transition, right? But then, if you take a transition in one way, in the Western way, then you finished being a Makushi, right? You don't want that, right? But what I am saying, there are certain things that we have, that we've had to do without over the years, and I'm sure that our culture is not exactly like our foreparents' was, and so you find, and it happens around the world, that certain aspects of culture goes as other things are adopted that we took from a different culture. But it might be because somebody has found some better way of doing something, right? Over the years that would become the new trend, as the old one dies. Still the person remains who they are.

Nicholas (Toka, 10/11/00)

Within the NRDDB there is an acceptance not only that the traditional way of life is changing, but also, in a seeming paradox, that change is necessary if the communities of the North Rupununi are "to remain who they are" in the face of the social and economic upheaval brought about by rapid advances in transport and communication systems and the increased integration into national and global structures that these entail. A particularly salient example of this process locally is the construction of a road stretching from the inland city of Manaus, in Brazil, to the port facilities in the Guyanese capital, Georgetown, a road that will pass through the heart of the Rupununi communities. Such a development on the one hand threatens a disruption of the local economy and long-standing social structures, along with environmental degradation and increases in crime, alcoholism, prostitution and disease; yet, on the other hand, it holds out the promise of enhanced infrastructure in areas such as communications, medical services and transportation, and so increased access to national and international markets for local goods. Failure to take advantage of these latter developments would ultimately render community structures unsustainable within the changing national and global context, as recognised by Sam Bramley, a prominent community member and sometime chairman of the NRDDB, when he says, "We must use the road, or the road will use us" (see Bartlett 2001). These words demonstrate at once a willingness to integrate into wider society and a determination to be in control of what Nicholas in the epigram refers to as the "new trends" that increased integration will bring with it. To assert such control the local communities cannot work in isolation, but need to make their voices heard and their activities recognised by those who manage the processes of transition at national and international level. As Sam says, in reference to such agencies: "Work with us, not tell us what to do".

40 Hybrid Voices and Collaborative Change

Integrating local perspectives and efforts into wider strategies of development is not a straightforward proposition, however, and is dependent on both objective and subjective conditions for it success. Objective conditions that can either facilitate or constrain effective participation include durable structures such as existing political and social systems, government legislation and economic relations, while subjective conditions include the attitudes and abilities of local and external participants within the development process. A willingness from outside agencies to involve local communities in the discourses that determine the direction and the means of development is a key factor here, as is a recognition from local communities of their own role in these processes, coupled with the skills to adapt their local practices to new contexts. In this chapter and the next I will therefore provide a brief account of the objective sociocultural condition of the North Rupununi within Guyana as a whole and of the history of discourse relations between the local communities and external agencies. In Chapter 4 I will turn to the subjective conditions as these are revealed through the implicit understandings of the different participants as to their respective roles in the development process. Between them, these chapters set out, to a limited extent, the *conditions of possibility* for the appearance of an effective community voice within the discourse of development and contextualise a more detailed account in Chapters 5 and 6 of how, through the skills of both local and external participants, such a voice has evolved within the North Rupununi. In Chapter 7 I will discuss the possibilities and limitations of this voice being heard in the wider national and international context.

As stated in the previous chapter, this will be a partial account, shaped by my focus on voice. In line with this perspective, I will pay particular attention to three broad aspects of community life on the North Rupununi: material conditions, interpersonal relations and methods of communication. In this way it will be possible to analyse the extent to which the instances of discourse analysed in later chapters represent either local or external voice as the reproduction of shared experience, social structures and rhetorical strategies trough the field, tenor and mode of discourse respectively. I do not pretend that this will amount to a full account of the context; unfortunately, I am not a trained ethnographer, and I have only the data I have collected and a handful of secondary sources to work with. Were I to start my fieldwork again, I would do it differently. I have, however, attempted to represent events as fully and as faithfully as I can and to incorporate the perspectives of those involved wherever possible. Three particular limitations are worth highlighting at this point, however. Firstly, most of my local correspondents were high-profile figures within their local communities, and in this regard my account might be seen as an elite perspective. While this limitation is tempered by the fact that it is at least a locally informed account, it remains a shortcoming. Secondly, I have no first-hand data on either community-internal discourse practices or of discourse between local communities and outsiders before the period

Background 41

of my fieldwork, and so cannot present a direct comparison with the data analysed here. I have, however, incorporated accounts of both of these from insiders and observers, while the chronological perspective I take in later chapters in itself invites comparisons over time and suggests an evolution towards a more community-based voice during the period of my fieldwork. Thirdly, describing an encounter between different cultures introduces the temptation to essentialise and reify each culture individually, as well as the meeting itself, especially in such a brief background account as that offered here. To do so would be to ignore the fact that cultures are neither discretely bound nor static. A better model is that of complex dynamic systems that are heterogeneous at any point in time and that over time are continuously being redefined yet develop according to their own internal, if nebulous, logic. Such a position is explicitly recognised by Nicholas in the opening quotation to this chapter: "Over the years that would become the new trend, as the old one dies. Still the person remains who they are." Over-essentialising can lead to superficial conclusions; yet some attempt to identify commonalities to observed behaviour is necessary and, in much the same way as a grammatical description of a language relies on 'a line of best fit' drawn through a system that is consistent neither in time nor space, ethnographers can draw on—and acknowledge—what Spivak (1990, cited in Rattansi 1999:97) calls *strategic essentialism*. As Rattansi (1999:103) concedes, it is not possible "to do without relatively general frameworks of interpretation", although he stresses that writers "have to be well aware of their [accounts'] historical specificity and their cultural boundedness [as being from the interpreter's viewpoint] and the need to accommodate constant revision." In order to counterbalance the limitations of essentialism I have attempted to include a variety of perspectives within these background chapters, though they remain bound by my own viewpoint and goals.

I begin my overview of life on the North Rupununi and the process of development with a brief introduction to the central participants. After that I give a relatively extended account of the material conditions, interpersonal relations and means of communication within the region, and I finish the chapter with a brief analysis of the Government of Guyana's 1976 Amerindian Act, a document that frames, within certain limitations, the scope for Amerindian autonomy and self-development within the national context.

THE MAKUSHI PEOPLE OF THE NORTH RUPUNUNI

According to Guyana's advisory *National Development Strategy* (NDS 2000:277), there are roughly 46,010 Amerindians in Guyana, comprising nine distinct ethnic groups and representing 6.4% of the total population of nearly three-quarters of a million. This apparently represents a decline in the total Amerindian population of 5.8% between 1993 and 1999. Amerindians represent the fourth largest ethnic group in Guyana,

42 *Hybrid Voices and Collaborative Change*

after East Indians (brought in as indentured labour), Africans (brought in as slaves) and mixed race, respectively. These distinctions of race are extremely important culturally, economically and politically in Guyana. The largest Amerindian group, the Lokona/Arawak, live close to non-Amerindian groups on and near the coast, where roughly 90% of Guyanese live. The next largest Amerindian group are the Makushi, situated in the Rupununi savannahs on Guyana's western border with Brazil. Brazilian towns and facilities are closer than the Guyanese population base on the coast and to a large extent the border exists more in theory than practice. Crossings are frequent and easy and no passport is necessary to visit the closest towns and villages where the Brazilian authorities offer healthcare to Guyanese citizens. Radio, and in a few cases satellite television, come to the savannahs from Brazilian rather than Guyanese stations. The map of Guyana on page **xvii** marks the areas where the different Amerindian peoples live.

The Makushi number between 7,000 and 9,000 within Guyana (NDS 2000:277; Makushi Research Unit [MRU] 1996:5) and a further 15,000 in Roraima State, Brazil (MRU 1996:5). The Rupununi Savannahs are also home to roughly 6,000 Wapishana (Forte and Melville 1989:7) and so account for roughly a quarter of all Amerindians in the country (NDS 2000:277). Guyanese Makushi are generally located in the North Savannahs and the Wapishana in the south. These population figures signify a huge recovery from apparent near wipe-out: Between 1835 and 1932 estimates concur on a total figure of roughly 3,000 Makushi evenly split between Guyana and Brazil (MRU 1996:10). I can find no official statistics on the Amerindian languages, which suggests something of the government's attitude towards the country's Amerindian population; however, Iwokrama is currently compiling a wide range of social data in collaboration with local communities. From my own experience in the North Rupununi, I would (very roughly) characterise the area linguistically as follows:

- A sizeable minority of adult Makushi speak negligible English or none at all. This group increasingly comprises the older generations.
- A large section, probably the majority of the population, are native speakers of Makushi, but have learned English in school and through informal and business contacts with outsiders. Levels of competence in English differ significantly, particularly in terms of age and gender, though many from this group would pass as local native speakers.
- A sizeable minority are native English speakers with a mainly passive understanding of Makushi, though they generally have a positive attitude towards the language.
- Many children and young adults from Makushi-speaking families are less competent in Makushi than in previous generations as a result of English-language schooling and the increased use of English within many domains of community life.

Background 43

- There are also plenty of Portuguese speakers in the area, as testified by Frances Johnny, a Makushi of Karasabai Village (Forte and Melville 1989:80): "I would say that Portuguese is the second language in my area. Makushi is first and English third."

As already suggested, the communities of the North Rupununi are currently in a state of social, cultural and economic flux as they come into contact with wider society and international structures to an extent not witnessed since the European intrusion into the region in the late eighteenth century (Colchester 1997:45–46). Once an isolated region, planes now fly daily into the North Rupununi, carrying with them the previous day's papers, and improvements to the road from Georgetown mean that motor vehicles from the capital can reach the villages of Surama, Annai and Toka, the homes of my principal informants, in 12 hours or less.[1] Local medical posts are dotted throughout the region, and there is a hospital in the main town of Lethem, though severe cases must be flown to Georgetown. Lorries carrying manufactured goods, tinned foods, beer and lemonade ply their trade between these villages on a daily basis. As well as creating trading relations between the Makushi and Coastlanders, the transportation of prepared foodstuffs and manufactured goods has long-term effects on local culture not only through the introduction of a monetary economy, but also on the local diet and levels of nutrition, methods of farming and traditional skills. This situation is bound to become more intense in coming years as the road is substantially upgraded to link the Brazilian city of Manaus with the shipping facilities of Georgetown. Clothing is largely non-traditional, and indigenous costume, as well as dances and ceremonies, are reserved for visiting dignitaries such as Prince Charles or for foreign film crews who, having travelled thousands of miles, are often disappointed with the everyday realities of Makushi life.

While community-based authority is still influential, the government-sanctioned authority of councillors, teachers, doctors and police, as well as those employed by development agencies, presents a challenge to traditional social hierarchies and means that the influence of the state is felt in all walks of life, while greater accessibility to the region means that this support can be rapidly backed up if necessary. Since I left Guyana several villages in the Rupununi have obtained Internet access, but at the time of my fieldwork telecommunications outside Lethem were severely limited, often no more than a radio link operated once a day and in times of emergency. National radio could only be heard with difficulty,[2] and there was no terrestrial television, though a few satellite televisions had been set up. Several of these were installed during the 2002 World Cup as the Rupununi is fanatical about its local team—Brazil. Electricity, however, is rare in the region. Lethem is powered by a small and erratic hydroelectric power plant, but outside the town only a few individual shops and houses have

44 *Hybrid Voices and Collaborative Change*

petrol-fuelled generators. UNICEF has recently provided many communities with solar power and lighting for school and community buildings, and some families use car batteries, recharged from the solar power system, to run lights and small appliances such as cassette players.

With this ever-increasing exposure and contact come many challenges, both positive and negative, to aspects of the local cultural system ranging from the Makushi language to communal land holding. This is a period of critical importance for the people of the North Rupununi as they decide how to face up to these challenges, looking to the social and economic potential offered by wider communications and greater access to external resources while remaining cautious of an overenthusiastic embracing of new ideas, often foisted upon them, with their potential for wrong and irreversible development, the loss of cultural and natural heritage, and the widespread cultural anomie experienced in many rapidly transforming communities worldwide. The *Report on Region 9's Poverty Reduction Strategy Consultations* (Regional Democratic Council [RDC] 9 2001), a document prepared by the locally elected RDC after grassroots consultation in about 50 villages, recognises the need for both traditional and modern input when it states in its preface that:

> Communities were very responsive and participatory, it was noted that people are hungry for development, which they said, should occur hand in hand with cultural revival. (5)

That this cultural revival should include the use of indigenous languages is made clear in the consultation document's section on education, which calls for:

> The use of local resource personnel with the necessary language skills to design and educate programmes in 'Indigenous Languages' for schools and member communities. (31)

The need to develop both traditional and new knowledge is underlined in "problems identified under economic opportunities and employment creation", where concerns over the "lack of appropriate modern technology" and "cultural expertise not being passed on or shared to younger generations" (RDC 9 2001:8) reflect the need to embrace existing culture within the development process. This dual approach is mirrored in the section on communications, where proposed solutions to "problems identified under governance" (RDC 9 2001:14) include the suggestion that:

> Government needs to be educated on the ways of the Amerindians and likewise the Amerindian needs to be educated on the ways of the Government. (16)

Similarly:

Background 45

Consultation on any community projects/programmes must be the hallmark of implementing any projects in the community. Local community experts must have a say in the decision making or else valuable funding will continue to be wasted. (ibid.)

Importantly, these remarks and recommendations from the RDC, the regional Amerindian Touchaus' Council and the communities themselves demonstrate that maintaining their cultural identity and their language as they develop expertise in modern technology is a genuine concern of the communities of the North Rupununi; it is not simply the vicarious nostalgia of a middle-class, first-world development elite (myself included).

IWOKRAMA

Iwokrama came into being in 1996, having arisen from a 1989 offer from the Guyanese government to:

make available a part of Guyana's tropical rain forest (since determined to be 360,000 hectares) for use by the international community, under Commonwealth auspices, for developing and demonstrating methods for the sustainable utilisation of tropical rain forest resources and the conservation of biological diversity. (Iwokrama Act 1996:preamble)

Iwokrama's mission statement (NRDDB and Iwokrama 1999:7) specifies that the aim of the programme is to:

promote the conservation and sustainable and equitable use of tropical rain forests in a manner that will lead to lasting ecological and social benefit to the people of Guyana and the world in general by undertaking research and training and the development and dissemination of relevant technologies.

More specifically, Article 6(g) of the Iwokrama Act states that one of Iwokrama's activities is to:

endeavour to preserve and maintain knowledge, innovations and practices of indigenous communities embodying traditional lifestyles relevant for the conservation and sustainable utilisation of biological diversity and promote their wider application with the involvement of the holders of such knowledge, innovation and practice; and encourage the equitable sharing of the benefits arising from the utilisation of such knowledge innovations and practices.

Iwokrama is not directly answerable to the Amerindian communities but to a board of trustees, appointed jointly by the government and the

46 Hybrid Voices and Collaborative Change

commonwealth secretary-general, of which only one *ex officio* member need be Amerindian (Iwokrama Act 1996:Article 11). In practice this *ex officio* board member has been the Minister of Amerindian Affairs, and as such a direct representative of the government. However, Iwokrama is answerable indirectly to the communities; at the time of my fieldwork the bulk of their funding was from Britain's Department for International Development (DFID) and was specified as being for social development. This means that continued funding for Iwokrama and jobs for the professionals employed there are heavily dependent on the continued goodwill of the Amerindian communities towards the project.[3] Iwokrama is also reliant on Amerindian cooperation in providing traditional ecological knowledge (TEK) to supplement their own imported knowledge base while prominent community members are instrumental in promoting Iwokrama projects locally. There is therefore common cause between Iwokrama and the local population, a point to be discussed in Chapters 4 to 6, and it is crucial to Iwokrama that Amerindians continue to see their work as beneficial to their communities and respectful of their cultural practices. These factors mean that Iwokrama workers are simultaneously constrained to work within what is defined as good development practice by their donor organisations while maintaining the goodwill of the local communities whose view of development is not always in accordance with international 'expertise' on the matter (Iwokrama senior social scientist, personal conversation). Amerindian communities are also increasingly dependent on Iwokrama: as an ever-greater source of local employment through their Forest Ranger and Community Environment Worker (CEW) schemes (see below); for the facilitation and funding of local meetings; and as an advocate for development projects at national and international level.

THE GOVERNMENT OF GUYANA

Guyanese politics is dominated by two political parties: the People's National Congress (PNC),[4] who were in unelected control under Forbes Burnham and Desmond Hoyte between 1964 and 1992, and the People's Progressive Party (PPP), who have been in control since the elections of 1992 to the time of writing. Both parties rely on ethnic loyalty for their support and at election times there is frequent and often serious racial conflict. The PNC mainly represents the Black population and the PPP the larger East Indian population,[5] a status that gives it an almost insuperable advantage at the ballot box, to the potential detriment of electoral accountability. However, the Amerindian population could hold the balance of power if it were to vote en masse and so receives attention from the two main parties in the periods immediately prior to elections. Parties representing specifically Amerindian interests have emerged over the years with differing levels of success. In contrast, both main parties, with their origins in post-war state

Background 47

socialism, have strong centralising traditions, as evident in the country's motto *One Nation, One People, One Destiny*. Within the government, at the time of my fieldwork, there was an Office of Amerindian Affairs, headed by a minister, though at that time denied the full status of ministry, a contradiction that speaks plenty of the ambivalence of the government towards Amerindian issues. The NRDDB has many direct dealings with the Office and the Minister for Amerindian Affairs occasionally attended NRDDB meetings during the period of my fieldwork, as did minor government officials and state employees such as health officers, when the occasion demanded. However, the government itself is not a major participant at these meetings, a presence more in spirit than in body.

THE NRDDB

The NRDDB was set up to facilitate meetings and workshops between those communities bordering the Iwokrama Forest and Iwokrama scientists and social scientists, as well as government officials and representatives of other non-governmental organisations (NGOs) and international organisations, as a response to the perceived failures of communication between these groups. I will discuss the NRDDB in more detail below, but it is worth drawing attention here to the problems with Iwokrama's initial outreach work in the communities and the need for more proactive means of communication, as described by Uncle Henry,[6] jaguar-hunter turned gamekeeper, elder statesman of Surama village and a founding father of the NRDDB:

> *As I said it was like knocking on a stone wall. In Georgetown and in the region, nobody had a clue of what Iwokrama, what a research station is like, what it is to do sustainable utilisation of the forest. It was a big fancy word nobody understood, especially in these rural communities. So these workshops now, started to bring, when we did workshops on mammals, we did workshop on birds, we did workshop on fishes, we did workshop on reptiles, this start to bring out the people understanding[7] of what went on. And then the ranger training started to get rangers from the area to the . . . and this started to open people's eyes.* (Uncle Henry, Surama Rest House, 6/3/01)

As well as members of the community in general, NRDDB meetings are attended by a variety of local office-bearers: Makushi leaders, such as Uncle Henry, often with a history of dealings with external authorities; touchaus, with plenty of experience of Amerindian politics at the local and national level; the MRU, a group of mainly women who are documenting and publishing traditional knowledge with Iwokrama assistance; and CEWs, a group set up to explain Iwokrama's work at the community level and

48   *Hybrid Voices and Collaborative Change*

to bring back to Iwokrama, through the Board, the desires, complaints, problems and satisfactions of the local communities. These last are seen as the outreach side of Iwokrama through the NRDDB and are, theoretically, under the control of the latter, though funded by Iwokrama. CEWs are often youngsters with little negotiating experience and, as shall be seen later, practical control over their activities is a constant if understated source of dispute.

NRDDB meetings cover two days every other month, with the first day dedicated to community business while the second day is attended, and largely officiated over, by representatives of Iwokrama. Workshops and other activities often take place in conjunction with NRDDB meetings as they require the participation of community members from throughout the region and transport is difficult and costly. Iwokrama provides road transport to and from board meetings and covers the cost of those who arrive by boat.

MATERIAL CONDITIONS ON THE NORTH RUPUNUNI

Amerindian labour is almost entirely related to traditional activities concentrated on subsistence farming, with the indigenous population living to all intents and purposes outside the cash economy (NDS 2000:277; Forte 1996a:16). In recent attempts to integrate the Amerindian population into the mainstream economy various Guyanese and international aid programmes in the area have been promoting microindustries through the funding of infrastructure, financial training and the setting up of local credit unions. However, these have generally been implemented without adequate consideration of local conditions and have produced little benefit, and often significant loss. At the time of my fieldwork hundreds of pounds of peanuts, the product of an ongoing NGO-sponsored scheme, were sitting marketless at the wrong end of the Rupununi–Georgetown road. Repeated failures such as these have made Amerindian communities reluctant to experiment with the cash economy and only about 1% are self-employed: in fishing, manufacturing, mining and quarrying (NDS 2000:277; Forte 1996a:16). In the few cases where the market economy has made inroads and people have surplus cash, the wider consequences often lead to problems such as the neglect of farmlands, the loss of traditional knowledge and the introduction of poor dietary habits. All these factors contribute to a certain degree of scepticism towards economic development on the part of elders such as Uncle Henry:

> *Development is a process that teaches you to want something you don't need. And if you look at the youths today, very few wants to go in the farm to do things. Then they rather to work with somebody and then go in the shop and buy biscuits or soft drink, some crap stuff*

Background   49

or something. Because it's easy. It's much easier. You don't find the people boiling the weed medicine any more and dispensing it to the youths in the weekend. That was traditional and my mother—she did that every fortnight, Saturday or Sunday morning. [. . .] Today you don't get those things. People don't go to it. They rather go and ask for an aspirin, whether you get, you stump you toe and it getting infected, you ask for an aspirin or something [. . .] and what they don't understand, that the very medicine they buying in the shop comes from the forest from those plants. (Uncle Henry, Surama Rest House, 22/6/02)

What is more problematical, cash surpluses can prove illusory, especially to a community which, according to Nicholas, is not experienced in financial planning and prone to spending money in hand rather than reinvesting it in community development. The spending of these chimerical surpluses thus results in capital outflows from the community, as described by Uncle Henry (Surama Rest House, 22/6/02):

Yes, you see, but the most of the, erm, even the parents now are drifting away to everything modernised—you find a truck comes in here, bringing in things to sell, they want, everybody wants to purchase, but who's producing things to sell back to those trucks that bring them? Where're . . . and where are they getting the money to buy these things? That is the problem. And when they can't . . . they're not seeing that mistake. So I say you have to produce, to sell to bring money in the community. Because if you keep buying, your money is going out and you leaving with the plastic, empty plastic containers. You see, that's the problem.

While NGO-sponsored projects have at least attempted to involve local communities in setting up new sources of income, the private business sector has merely sought to profit from local resources without giving anything back to the community in the form of either profits or well-paid work:

The interior of the country has become an enclave for overseas business interests, a situation reminiscent of the colonial age, when the country was dominated by foreign-owned sugar and mining companies. Those most affected are the country's 60,000 Amazonian Indians . . . marginalised by the development process. Denied adequate land rights and control over decision-making in their own territories they see their environments despoiled and their millennial cultures undermined. (Colchester 1997:1)

Larger industries such as mining have brought some expendable capital into the region, capital that could be used in local community development, yet existing laws are not geared to such a process of internally driven

50 Hybrid Voices and Collaborative Change

development. Indigenous land rights, for example, do not extend to subsoil rights (Forte 1996a:23), and many are "concerned that valuable minerals are being removed from lands belonging to them without any meaningful consultation and compensation" (NDS 2000:280). Rather than serving community needs, therefore, externally driven development serves only to reinforce the subordinate position of Amerindians in Guyanese society. Despres (1975:99), writing not as an advocate for Amerindian issues but as an economist, claims:

> Over the years, the competitive allocation of Guyana's unexpropriated resources has served to order categorically identified elements of the Guyanese population in an arrangement of unequal status and power. Amerindians are marginal to the whole economy and they exist at the bottom of this stratification structure.

As a result, many Guyanese Amerindians have to seek gainful employment across the border in Roraima State, Brazil, which has experienced relative economic expansion (MRU 1996:51), while in the North Rupununi a local study revealed that 49 males were absent from 467 households and 28 households were headed by women (MRU 1996:51).

The issue of Amerindian land rights has long been contentious and the resolution of this issue was one of the conditions set on Guyana's independence in May 1966, a condition that has only partially been met (Upper Mazaruni Amerindian District Council [UMADC] et al. 2000:15). In 1976 4,500 square miles of land was conferred on Amerindian Communities out of a total of 40,000 requested and 25,000 recommended by the Amerindian Lands Commission (Forte 1996b:82). The land conferred represents 7% of the national territory of Guyana, corresponding to Amerindian population figures but not taking into account the fact that, for example, Makushi traditional subsistence requires "wide swathes of the varied ecosystems of the North Savannahs" (MRU 1996:287). At the time of my fieldwork[8] only 60% of Amerindian communities were provided with title to *any* of their traditional lands. Worse, rights were guaranteed for neither the land titles themselves nor for the related rights of usufruct, which the minister responsible for Amerindian Affairs had the right to adjust or withdraw at the stroke of a pen (NDS 2000:279). In the aftermath of the 'Ranchers' Rebellion' of January 1969,[9] "the revolt that raised the bogey of secession and the loyalty of the Amerindians to Guyana" (Colchester 1997:49–52), not only was the granting of land titles delayed with key frontier areas excluded altogether, but Amerindian ownership of lands was made conditional on continuing loyalty to the state, a condition imposed on no other sector of society and clearly racist in origin. Those of mixed race had to forfeit all rights of Amerindians over state lands, as did Amerindian women who married non-Amerindians (though the converse is not the case; see NDS 2000:279). Those wishing to mine to a depth of more than six inches were required to give up their

Background 51

rights as Amerindians. Between them these regulations seem to *essentialise* Amerindian society as racially pure, non-industrial and reliant on the Guyanese state, themes that will be taken up in the following in an analysis of the Amerindian Act. There are practical as well as ideological reasons for the government's position: Given the increase in mining activities nationally and their growing strategic importance worldwide, increased Amerindian control over the development of community lands would be in direct conflict with central government's own economic interests. As a result, while multinational companies are increasingly given access to exploit traditional Amerindian lands, claims from the Amerindian communities themselves have until recently lain unattended to (Forte 1994:26). Economic conditions mean that local communities themselves are also responsible for despoiling lands as a short-term survival strategy as:

> there is a threshold of poverty below which the poor . . . become disproportionately destructive, either by directly destroying resources which could nurture them for years or indirectly by giving outsiders access to resources under indigenous control. (Forte 1996a:56; see also Colchester 1997:123)

As an alternative to both traditional subsistence activity and the few jobs available in industry, the interior regions of Guyana are looking to the ecotourism boom of the last decade or so in countries such as Costa Rica. However, despite the breathtaking landscape of the interior, social problems on the coast and extensive failings in infrastructure at the national level mean that Guyana is no Costa Rica, and it is unlikely huge numbers of ecotourists will come. Nevertheless, in a non-cash economy such as the North Rupununi relatively low numbers can be significant in themselves and small-scale local infrastructure is developing to benefit both community-based projects and individual workers (Williams 1997:41). But, as with other industries, the technical assistance and financial investment necessary for such ventures will have to come from outside agencies, either national or international. The financial power of these outsiders combined with the poor formal education of indigenous groups means that the norm is for the incorporation of local communities into the ecotourism industry only "at the lower end of the pay scale" as "cooks, waiters, construction workers, boat drivers and groundskeepers" no longer in control of development locally (Forte 1996b:18).

INTERPERSONAL RELATIONS

A recurring theme in local accounts of traditional practice is that Makushi culture was formerly sustained and reproduced through an equilibrium of knowledge and authority that vested power in the hands of the few,

52 Hybrid Voices and Collaborative Change

with the remainder of the population becoming obedient to the strictures imposed upon them through a process of mythologisation of the regulatory framework and its acceptance as normative consensus. Uncle Henry (Surama Rest House, 22/6/02) vividly describes this conjunction of expertise and social status as a reproductive mechanism within an absolutist mode of instruction/regulation:

> *Yes, our foreparents had their . . . their system and it wasn't something written, it was something passed from generation to generation, from father to son, from mother to daughter. And they had certain beliefs, and some still carry the belief, but the problem now is most of that traditional knowledge and belief is lost. You see, for instance, there are certain places where the ancient people never wanted you to go and hunt or fish or if there's a place where they know, they knew the breeding areas, swamplands, they knew the wetlands were the breeding grounds for these certain species, and they would have that as a taboo, you can't go there and hunt, they tell you if you go there, something would happen to you, and if you insist, somebody is a daredevil and wants to go and rove it, they would set up their, what you call the shama man, the piai man, and he would organise with one of these guys who can imitate the kanaima [shape-changer[10]], and he'd dress and give the guy a good fright, and they never go back there, and then he would go and say, "Indeed there is something there", and that kept them away.*

Cooke (1994:29–30), after Habermas (1984), labels as *conventional* such modes of *communicative action* where "[w]hat counts as good reason may be determined in advance, and inflexibly, by the traditions and the normative consensus prevailing in a given society or community" (29). Again following Habermas, Cooke (1994:30), sees these modes as counter-developmental and to be replaced by a post-conventional *communicative rationality*, defined as "critical and open-ended". However, in the case of the Makushi, while the myths that regulated community practice are no longer generally misrecognised as consensus and the authority of the piai man is diminished, new ways are yet to be found to replicate the social purpose of this authority in maintaining livelihoods. As Uncle Henry (Surama Rest House, 22/6/02) puts it:

> *The hardest thing for the community to face is to retain their culture, their . . . their traditional way of life. You cannot . . . they would not be able to retain it 100%, but at least you can retain the important part of it. The change, it drift away to the modern life, the developed way of life, it's like a moth drawn to the fire, you see. And it's difficult. I mean you have to teach them to prepare themselves to cope with that way of life that is going to meet them. It's like you are preparing for a*

Background 53

tornado or a hurricane. So when it hits you, you can withstand it. You put the shutters up.

One reason for the dissipation of the piai men's authority is that knowledge is now more evenly shared within the community. Nicholas (Toka, 10/11/00) describes this change, echoing Uncle Henry's own comments:

> [T]he old man used to say there is a mermaid in that pond, you mustn't go in there, that they were actually preserving the fish . . . But those old people don't know that, but I, my knowledge, now I could look at it, know there was nothing in there because I went there and caught fish, plenty of fishes, and I know the old people actually put that in there, but then you can actually go back and when you go back and you start studying this, the shama man, they should get a lot of (xxx) knowledge in the shama man, (xx) that's untouched, you don't get that so. That's untouch[11] so far. But when you go and look at how they operate, right, the things that they do, the things that they say, and you could see that they actually instil that fear if they don't want a certain pond to be like affected or so, they would tell you well so and so, so and so would happen and this will happen. But when you know, you know somebody like me would know that wouldn't happen.

This disruption of traditional authority systems has resulted in a 'crisis of the commons' scenario within the system of stock management. Previously under the control of local elders:

> local people now indiscriminately fish and hunt during the spawning and breeding seasons of fish and animals as old proscriptions against hunting animals with eggs or young have broken down. The authority of the village councils and Captains is frequently questioned, particularly with regard to defining hunting sites and times. The general view that wild animals belong to everyone means that people feel they can hunt and fish as much as they like. There also seems to be developing a general feeling that people should harvest as much as they can, because otherwise someone else will harvest the animals. (NRDDB and Iwokrama 1999:16–17)

Such breakdowns in community cooperation demonstrate the interdependence of economic activity and control within the social system. This has far-reaching consequences, as illustrated by Nicholas (Toka, 10/11/2000):

> We might say, "Okay, let's go into large-scale agriculture". Yes, some people might be ready, the majority may not be ready. So . . . you know . . . how to meet tha'?. Because you could get one set of people going ahead of some, so the next thing you're doing, rather than having Coastlanders

54 *Hybrid Voices and Collaborative Change*

> *come in and, like, exploit Amerindians, you have Amerindians exploiting Amerindians, and that would be more deadly, because, now, you can move the Coastlander, but you can't move the Amerindian.*

Another reason underlying the change in authority systems is the change of social context brought about by the encroachment of outsiders, the multiplication of issues to be regulated and the increased complexity of these. This has led to the need for the *specialisation* of knowledge (Berger and Luckmann 1966:95) and the spreading out of authority amongst many experts rather than its concentration in the hands of local elders and shama men. Communities now see the need to form specialist committees to exploit fishing resources, for example, and to monitor depletion of stocks in conjunction with government authorities and with the help of international experise and funding (NRDDB, 3/3/01). While such changes might resemble a move towards Habermas's communicative rationality, in many more spheres of community life the disappearance of conventional authority has left behind it a vacuum, a vacuum which many parties, not all of them benevolent, are willing to fill. The result is a complex of competing power relations deriving from such diverse sources as the moral authority of local elders, traditional and imported expertise and the political authority of the government. The relationship between these variables and development discourse will be key concerns in later chapters, where I consider ways in which specific communicative events fail or succeed and suggest areas for collaboration through the exploitation of different configurations of such sources of authority. In these terms the aim is not the universalised communicative rationality of Habermas but more a *discourse across difference*, where different voices operate in an environment of mutual understanding, acceptance and cooperation.

TRANSMISSION OF INFORMATION

In this section I will contrast traditional methods of educating children into the Makushi way of life with the methods employed within the schooling system. In the following chapter I will contrast local communications systems in general with those set up by external agencies.

Given the breakdown of community authority systems and the knowledge base behind them, described above, it could be said that the problems provoked by the modernisation of economic relations stem from modernisation's inability to produce a system of regulation and instruction appropriate to itself. One failing seems to be that whereas the old methods of instruction, aiming at self-sufficiency and sustainability, married theory and practice and related new information to local life, state schooling in the Rupununi relies on a *banking model of pedagogy* (Cummins 1996:153) in which the teacher's role is to impart largely abstract knowledge and skills to *tabula rasa* students

Background   55

in return for their integration into the non-local system. While this model of education has existed in local schools for a long time, the increased reach of state authority within Amerindian communities means that its influence within Makushi practice has grown over recent decades, just as the authority of local elders has waned. And as the aim of this model is to integrate students into the dominant power/knowledge systems, it fails to engage with the alternative indigenous system and the practicalities of daily life in the Rupununi, often leaving students disastrously adrift in both worlds. Walter (Toka, 9/11/00) contrasts the two processes (**W** is Walter; **TB** is me):

W: *The Makushi culture is not something that you learn, you know, on a book or something, it's something that is be passed on, yeah, from your parent, parent['s] parent, that's why, the thing that I would know, the sum of the thing that I know, what my father taught me, is what his father taught him, what his father taught him, going back, all the way back.*
         [Tom asks about teaching children during hunting and fishing.]
W: *Yeah, as we go now, you would see, look how many things you would learn in, for instance in a school now, you would be doing spelling or reading, and you may be able to cover like 20, 40 words. Now, from the time I leave here, when we go riding, he tell me "Daddy, what is that?"*
TB: *Oh, so you're not just teaching him fishing?*
W: *No::, is not just fishing, it's as you see, you learn it. You say "That's a bird, what's its name?" and, you know, you call it. "Look at those mountains", what it mean, and you know, all these things. [. . .] You see why they would learn faster there, it's more active also. Now you're not seated in one place, you're just looking at one direction, looking at one blackboard and one person and so, you know.*

With respect to the school system, the NDS (2000:281) recommends the following approach:

> Education for Amerindians should be wide in scope. It should not only address issues of formal education for children in the school system, but should extend to empower Amerindians of all ages to improve their standards of living. Education and training policies should be of such a nature that they enable Amerindians to deal with other contemporary issues that affect them. Strategies should therefore be designed to ensure that they encompass all aspects of human development.

The current situation, however, remains far from this vision and serves to undermine Amerindian self-image rather than developing it to meet changing needs:

56   Hybrid Voices and Collaborative Change

> Despite the best intentions . . . education has a non-traditional focus that may not be applicable to community development. Students are therefore not inculcated with an appreciation of the value of their own traditions. In addition, many cultural aspects of Amerindian life are being eroded. (NDS 2000:281)

Moreover, according to Forte (1996a:18) only 0.1% of the interior population have received any form of post-secondary education, and trained primary teachers in Amerindian villages very often come from outside the region. Even in official documents such as the NDS (2000) I can find no serious statistics on education levels. Colchester (1997:137–138), however, has the following to say:

> Amerindians have the country's lowest levels of formal education, with the smallest proportion going on to secondary and higher level grades. The lack of secondary schools in the interior means that the few children who do pursue further schooling are often obliged to travel down to the coast. There they suffer discrimination and cultural pressure to conform to coastlander standards.

In an attempt to improve the situation, in 2002 a new secondary school was opened in Annai, North Rupununi, to supplement the school in Lethem, almost 100 miles away. There are also 'Hinterland Scholarships' for children from the interior to attend secondary school in Georgetown and at other coastal schools and between 1963 and 1989 1,063 children were educated at the government's expense under this scheme (Forte 1996b:10). However:

> This programme has not helped the cause of Amerindian development to date. The reasons include the fact that there have been few jobs to return to in the villages. Most scholarship students who do graduate and hope to benefit from their schooling have had to look outside the region of their birth for jobs. So, ironically, the scheme has the result of selecting the brightest Amerindian children for the purpose of effectively banishing them from their home villages. At the same time, the overall performance of the interior scholarship winners has been poor. (Forte 1996b:10)

In fact, 14% of these scholars achieve no formal qualifications at all (René van Dongen, UNICEF, personal communication). This raises many serious questions, among them the relevance of course content to interior issues and daily life. Even in subjects such as agricultural studies which would appear to be relevant, the concentration on the coastal sugar and rice economy renders the subject inapplicable to hinterland farmers who do not produce these crops. Presumably materials with which the students were familiar

Background   57

would not only enhance their academic performance, but also give them the option of returning to the interior with skills matching the development needs of the region. Instead, poor schooling provision, the lack of relevance of the national syllabus and the improbability of state education improving employment prospects have led to a huge dropout rates amongst the Amerindian population, a slack Uncle Henry (Surama Rest House, 22/6/02) would like to see taken up by a return to traditional knowledge adapted to a more formal mode of instruction and contributing to the local economy:

> So that when these children . . . there are a lot of dropouts in the indigenous population there is a lot of dropping out, you got a 90% dropouts in school. As soon as they reach third form, they are out. [. . .] Now, we want to use those dropouts . . . to put them to learn, that is why we're going to have a section there with industrial arts section, teaching carpentry, cabinet making, you know, so you can train children, young men and women, to do things like catering, (xxx) section where you teach the young women to cook, to sew and (x). So even if they are at home they can sew clothing or something and make a dollar. You don't need to go to Brazil to be a domestic over there, and you can do it over here, you know, live in your—we have land, go to the soil, do agriculture.

The need to relate formal education to the practicalities of daily life is crucial not only in terms of providing future generations with relevant practical skills, but also in order to engage the students' interest, drawing upon and developing their own expertise. Such a *contextualisation* of new knowledge is also an important factor in disseminating information within development fora such as the NRDDB, as will be explored in Chapter 6.

In a situation such as the Rupununi, where the majority of schoolchildren enter the education system monolingual in an indigenous language, there is also a need to provide a serious and coherent programme of bilingual education. However, despite pre-election lip service in an attempt to win the all-important Amerindian vote, the government has done little to implement such a serious bilingual policy as such a programme would, as Colchester (1997:138) points out, be incompatible with the government's integrationist policy of *One People, One Nation, One Destiny.* There are, however, some positive recent developments, as in the case of Adrian Gomes, headmaster of the Aishalton Secondary School in the Wapishana area of Deep South Rupununi and chairman of the Wapishana Literacy Association (Wapishana Wadauniinau Ati'o—WWA), who has completed an M.Sc. in TESOL from Leeds University in England and so is as qualified as anyone in the country on bilingual education. However, when I worked along with Adrian and the WWA promoting Wapishana education for nursery schooling and the first years of primary I found the government attitude towards his efforts generally uninterested and ill-informed. Another

58 Hybrid Voices and Collaborative Change

potentially positive development was the appointment of a hinterland education coordinator in 2000. The coordinator at that time, Mr. Edward Jarvis, is a dedicated and compassionate educator who has smoothed the channels of communication on the issues in Amerindian education. But his duties covered a vast area, in terms of both responsibilities and geography, and he had to compete with attitudes towards bilingual education within the government that rarely if ever extend beyond an unquestioning belief in the notion that monolingualism is a natural advantage, with English as the language of choice. And while organisations such as the WWA promote the use of indigenous languages in education and many teachers, particularly at nursery and primary levels, use these languages substantially in practice, there are serious doubts in the minds of many parents and teachers as to the usefulness of using indigenous languages in education (see Hornberger and López [1998] for a detailed account of a similar situation amongst Amerindian communities in the Andes). As a result, any bilingual programme will have to be strongly promoted amongst the population before the issue is fully understood and accepted. At present there is a feeling that indigenous languages are purely for informal use, with English supplanting them in higher-prestige domains. At the newly opened secondary school in Annai the head teacher there tried to prohibit the use of Makushi even in the dormitories. When I asked Walter (Toka, 9/11/00) about the head teachers' attitudes to Makushi he described similar, if less dramatic, attitudes:

W: *Some of them still respect it a lot, as much as they would respect the English language, but in some cases I see that they kinda look at Makushi as their means of communicating with their community, with the Makushi people.*

TB: *But not in the school, is that what you're saying?*

W: *Nah, not in school, they won't do that in school.*

TB: *Makushi for the village, English for the school?*

W: *U-huh. Yeah.*

TB: *And even Amerindian teachers and headmasters are doing that, yeah?*

W: *Yeah, they're doing that.*

As well as the usual problems relating to individual development associated with the current practice of total immersion into the dominant second language (see e.g. Cummins 1996, 2000), a further consequence of this policy is that English becomes associated from an early age with power and discipline, potentially leading to expectations that those who command the language also command authority. Furthermore, English-language teaching follows a traditional grammar-based approach, one of the prominent aims of which is to eradicate any traces of Guyana's English-based Creolese from the speech of the Amerindian population.[12] This emphasis on 'good grammar' means that children are not trained to use English to express

Background 59

themselves. It is hardly surprising, therefore, that in negotiating situations between minority groups petitioning through English as a second language, on the one hand, and native English gatekeepers, on the other, many minority participants fail to contribute anything beyond a bare minimum or, as in the more tolerant institutional setting of the NRDDB, prefer to use Makushi when they need to express themselves. Walter is aware of this problem and as chair tried to persuade people to express themselves in the language they felt most at ease in (NRDDB 2/11/01, Annai Institute):

> *if you can't speak properly in English, if you can't bring out the whole essence of what you're saying, I would prefer you spoke in Makushi.*

However, the pressure to conform with institutional norms and the feeling, expressed above, that English is the language of prestigious domains meant that very little Makushi was used in NRDDB meetings, despite the presence of an excellent interpreter and gifted linguist.

THE LOSS OF TRADITIONAL KNOWLEDGE: AN ENCYCLOPAEDIA IS CLOSED

Interrelating the contextual variables of material culture, interpersonal relations and methods of communication, it could be said that the changes in the indigenous context brought about by their increased integration into the wider society have provoked crises in the fields of indigenous community activity, the set of which activities comprises a community's material culture. These crises in turn are connected to breakdowns in the interpersonal systems that regulate community relations, and the information systems through which the communities sustain and reproduce traditional knowledge and values. This interrelation is apparent in Nicholas's description of the shama man's former power in controlling fish stocks and how enhanced fields of knowledge have altered the tenor of interpersonal relations by undermining the authority of the shama man and the means of communicating instruction and regulation. Completing the circle, the result is that Makushi material conditions are further affected through factors such as the overharvesting of increasingly scarce resources, a greater reliance on cheap imported foods and the loss of traditional knowledge relating to subsistence farming and medicine. In other words, external control of the economy threatens the coherence of the dynamic system of culture as a whole. In such a scenario the most obvious route to coherence is to fill the vacuum left by the collapse of the indigenous system with the national system in its entirety. The motto *One Nation, One People, One Destiny* suggests that this is the end of history as envisaged by the government. For while they frequently adopt the rhetoric of participatory democracy, the popular perception is either that the government has no idea of what

60   Hybrid Voices and Collaborative Change

participation means in practice (Tony Melville, Touchau of Touchaus for Region 8, Guiana Shield Conference, 6/12/00), or that the rhetoric is no more than a facade to cover their true intent, This would seem to be the case when, after urgings for an Environmental Impact Study on the proposed road from Brazil, the government "tried to stifle public debate about the road and discouraged the consultants from holding public meetings to gather local people's opinions" (Colchester 1997:56). According to Forte (1996b:68), and reminiscent of the justifications of the Conquest:

> The most striking factor about the first phase of the road building is that the Amerindians, who form the majority of the population of the area through which it passes (Region 9) were the last to know about the awarding of the contract to [Brazilian mining concern] Paranapanema. The official attitude is as if the trail to Kurupukari [in the Iwokrama Rainforest] will be passing through no man's land, *terra nullius*.

While state assistance has brought about advantages to the local communities in such matters as the provision of infrastructure, subsidised transport and a level of organisation necessary following the disappearance of traditional community action, Escobar (1992, cited in Spiegel, Watson and Wilkinson 1999:175) captures the ambivalence of a triumph of paternalism as envisaged in this case by the Government of Guyana and underlying existing interactions between the state and indigenous communities:

> One cannot look on the bright side of planning, its modern achievements (if one were to accept them), without looking at the same time on its dark side of domination . . . Planning inevitably requires the normalisation and standardisation of reality, which in turn entails injustice and the erasure of difference and diversity.

One symptom of the "normalisation and standardisation of reality" and the "erasure of difference and diversity" is the loss of traditional knowledge. This process was described above by Uncle Henry with particular reference to medicinal knowledge, but it is applicable across many fields of material and symbolic culture. Anthropological research into traditional exploitation of forest resources carried out in the region by Christie Allan demonstrates a great gulf in traditional knowledge between the older generation and young and middle-aged Makushi (Christie Allan, presentation of research findings to Surama Village, 21/6/02). Nicholas (Toka, 10/11/00, Tape 27) places this process in the context of diminishing competence in Makushi and the consequent failure of intergenerational transmission of the elders' knowledge. He claims that what is passed on in English is "only scratching the surface of Makushi culture" and describes the loss of access to the elders' knowledge as "like an encyclopaedia being closed". To make matters worse, it is the elders, with their barely tapped store of traditional knowledge, who participate least

Background   61

in modern institutional fora, as these often rely almost exclusively on English and contain a measure of written documentation, modes of transmission in which these elders are at the very least uncomfortable and from which, in the worst case, they are totally excluded (Uncle Henry, NRDDB Meeting, Annai Institute, 4/11/00). In excluding both the knowledge and power of elders, institutional fora can be said to have closed whole discourse systems. To further exacerbate the problem, the government practice of bringing in outsiders to carry out work in the region has meant that there is no compensatory transfer of imported skills and hence no capital transfer either. To highlight a case in point, Walter (Toka, 9/11/00) considers that it would have been better to establish a brick-producing capacity in the region rather than to bring in the bricks from outside:

> *It should have been a contribution of the government. But then they didn't want us to gain any money, like, or something like that coming from those bricks.*

Nicholas (Management Planning Workshop, Toka, 18/4/00) makes a similar point with regard to the financial support given to externally-devised projects:

> *Cultural restoration, maybe you couldn't finance that, you know? Because what we find there's disadvantage when we've been . . . government, erm, driven programmes, they've been . . . financially supported properly . . . and our erm programmes are not, traditional ways are not supported so. They have an advantage right away there (xx) find that. . they actually killing . . . government is (xx) not knowing (they) erm killing culture.*

Elsewhere Nicholas complains that very little money from aid budgets ultimately goes to Amerindian communities, but is accounted for in the wages of foreign aid workers (my family included!) and a coastal Guyanese workforce. Walter (NRDDB Meeting, Yakarinta, 18/1/02) likewise labels a process whereby millions of dollars are spent on providing wells for indigenous communities without a penny reaching local pockets as "a backward kind of development". His point is that if money does not come into the community they will always have to rely on outside patronage rather than reinvesting the money in their own projects and developing a measure of genuine local autonomy. Any measure of autonomy is anathema to the government (see the discussion of the Amerindian Act below) and I have at times felt that international aid organisations are keener on drawing indigenous communities into international controls than on either passing on skills or encouraging self-sufficiency and sustainability. Uncle Henry (Surama, Rest House, 22/6/02) shares this cynicism with regard to private enterprises operating in the Rupununi:

62   Hybrid Voices and Collaborative Change

> Because the business sector fully understand that once the indigenous population get to know the true meaning of sustainability, well then they would start to manage their resources and their chances of making a lot of money would be cut.

Overall it can be said that there has been a decline in the prestige afforded to indigenous cultural resources while there has been no compensatory capacitation of the indigenous community in prestigious domains previously excluded to them. As a result, in the wake of the impact of modernisation, the local community has not been allowed to re-establish an equilibrium on its own terms; instead, external actors have rushed in to stake their claim in every aspect of community life. This disequilibrium and the net loss of prestige for local cultural resources has resulted in the *misrecognition* (Bourdieu 1991), by Amerindian and non-Amerindian alike, of external structures as inherently superior, an attitude encountered from the first days of schooling, where English rather than Makushi is seen as the suitable medium of education. A similar process of devaluation of their own culture by indigenous groups is made clear in the opening quote of Chapter 1, where Walter says, "A lot of people, they feel that the Makushi cul-, the Makushi or the Amerindian culture is so inferior that they don't want to do any . . . they don't want to have anything with it." Similarly, in discussion with representatives from Iwokrama, Nicholas had referred to "Western culture" as "winning out" over indigenous culture, a point he elaborated on later (Toka, 10/11/00):

TB: *Which culture would you say is dominating at the moment?*

N: *Dominating? The Western culture is kinda . . . is more ahead, but erm, you still gotta understand Amerindian culture is not dead . . . very alive. I want to say, I don't think the people dominate (in) Iwokrama.*

TB: *I think . . . yeah . . . I think, well I think that was in context it made more sense, I think it meant 'winning out', when you're here, in a village like Toka, you see the Makushi culture, you see the Western culture [and you were worried]*

N: *[I wouldn't really think] 'winning out' was the proper word too. What I would say, it's erm, it's more vivid, right, you can see more of it. But then if you go back . . . okay, you do business, you meet the people, you approach the way they think, you can see that the Amerindian culture is still inside of the people, it's ingrained inside of the people, right? So it's, I mean, "What a man is inside", you know the Scripture, "I would see it in secret", right? "As man thinketh in his heart, so is he." So, the way the people think, the way they believe, the way they feel about life is purely Makushi. But then the environment that they live in is Western.*

Background 63

What Nicholas has captured here is Bourdieu's idea that those socialised in a particular context develop a *habitus*, a "system of dispositions" (Bourdieu 1990a:59) that is appropriate to their environment. A social agent's habitus is their preferred and largely subconscious way of behaving: ingrained, naturalised and extremely difficult to override. However, when displaced from their *field of socialisation*, social agents are unsure of how to behave and, conversely, often behave in ways that are misunderstood by those in whose natural field they are operating. If the alien *field of action* is a dominant culture, as in the case of the indigenous peoples of Guyana, the response of the members of this dominant group is often to attempt to acculturate the 'other' and assimilate them into their culture. However, this approach carries with it dangers of stagnation and anomie, as Nicholas (Toka, 10/11/00) points out:

> *You can't change totally, to change the people totally you would have them again in a position where they wouldn't know where they are going.*

In this scenario, the minority group is lost because their cultural dynamic has been broken, unable to accommodate the nature and rate of change. However, if the rate and nature of change are controlled, it is possible for the cultural dynamic of the minority group to absorb and adapt this change in a process of development:

> A community inherits a specific way of life . . . which sets limits to how and how much it can change itself. The change is lasting and deep if it is grafted on to the community's suitably reinterpreted deepest tendencies and does not go against the grain. A community's political identity then is neither unalterable and fixed, nor a voluntarist project to be executed as it pleases, but a matter of slow self-recreation within the limits set by its past. (Parekh 1995, cited in May 2001:73)

The need for a community to remain true to its cultural past as it develops, then, contains more than just sentiment or 'romanticism': It is a means to protect against 'wrong development', where indigenous peoples feel like "refugees in own country, begging for a little bit of this, a little bit of that" (Uncle Henry, Management Planning Workshop, Surama, 29/3/00). Nicholas (Management Planning Workshop, Toka, 18/4/00) is, as usual, more dramatic. Summing up the government's willingness to fund plans from national and international organisations but not from indigenous groups themselves, he concludes:

> *We die as a people; so that is passive genocide.*

These failings can be related then to a mismatch of field and habitus in that, by and large, new practices have been either entirely inappropriate to the North Rupununi or could not be *assimilated* into the indigenous cultural

64 Hybrid Voices and Collaborative Change

dynamic. Such assimilation is only possible through a continuous linkage between knowledge and practice, with the socioeconomic and discourse relations between the various stakeholders developing in an integrated fashion.

In the later chapters of this book I will attempt to show how the evolution of an appropriate voice is a step towards restoring community pride in its own culture through the recognition of local authority systems and traditional knowledge. However, to be effective in the new context, I will suggest that both traditional authority systems and fields of knowledge need to interact with imported knowledge to create a new voice. Such a development depends on structural conditions that legitimate a diversity of voices (a *polyphony*, in Bakhtin's terms) and so open up new space for community members previously excluded by the mismatch of habitus and field to contribute their expertise and opinions. To finish this chapter I will analyse the revised Amerindian Act of 1976 to show how the attitude of the Government of Guyana to its indigenous population was far from conducive to increased Amerindian participation in contributing to its own development, and rather legitimated the unfavourable structural conditions as outlined in this chapter so far. I shall contrast the assumptions of the act with the Constitution of the NRDDB to show the disparity between the roles envisaged for the local communities within the two acts. In the following chapter I will examine the history of discourse between Iwokrama and the communities of the North Rupununi, as a product of discourse development internationally, to suggest that this also left a lot to be desired. In later chapters I will analyse discourse from my period of fieldwork to show how subjective conditions such as the disposition of key Iwokrama workers and the discourse skills of prominent community members have contributed to overcoming the objective conditions in bringing together the authority, knowledge and rhetorical practices of the local community and professional development workers in a radically new voice.

THE CONSTRUAL OF CONTROL AND IDENTITY IN THE AMERINDIAN ACT AND THE NRDDB CONSTITUTION

In this section I will analyse the 1976 Revision of the Amerindian Act[13] and the NRDDB Constitution in terms of how they make provision for community input into local development policies and the extent to which they promote community involvement in carrying these policies out. As suggested in the previous section, a sense of local self-esteem, of pride in Amerindian culture, is an essential precondition for such a collaborative space to be opened up, and I follow the quantitative analysis of participation as set out in the two documents with a brief qualitative analysis of the (often implicit) construal of Amerindians and the Amerindian way of life, especially within the Amerindian Act (for a more detailed version of these analyses, see Bartlett [2005]).

Turning first to participation, Table 2.1, developed from a schema proposed by Cameron et al. (1992), relates community involvement across the two parameters of local decision-making and implementation to four broadly defined approaches to development: *paternalism*, in which outsiders both make decisions about activities that affect local communities and act upon them; *cooptation*, in which outsiders make decisions but local communities enact these; *advocacy*, in which local communities make decisions but are not empowered to enact them; and *local autonomy*, seen as the most progressive approach to development, in which local communities both make decisions and act upon them.

The initial analytical method employed in comparing the texts is to subcategorise the activities allocated to the different participants in each document and to quantify and contrast the degree to which either the government or Amerindians themselves are construed as the central participants within different activities, as set out in Figure 2.1. The end-terms in this systems network do not represent the actual lexical items used within the two documents but the most delicate level of grouping considered both meaningful and workable. Non-end-terms represent less delicate groupings that provide alternative angles for analysis. The analysis that follows outlines the level of control ascribed to either the communities or outsiders within the different categories of activity. Four levels of control can be distinguished: overseers, performers, undergoers or beneficiaries of the activities in question.[14] The overseer role refers to any participants explicitly stated as initiating or authorising a process undertaken either by themselves or by other participants. Performer refers to the participants who (explicitly or implicitly) are construed as undertaking actions, and also to the subjects of attributive statements (thus every process has a performer). Beneficiary refers to those for whom or on behalf of whom the text explicitly states that an action is carried out, and also to recipients of information or of goods and services. Undergoers are those on whom an action is carried out. As well as the ascription of specific roles to different groups, the analysis will focus on overseer–performer, performer–undergoer and performer–beneficiary relationships within the different activities.

Example 2.1 is Article 20(3) of the Amerindian Act, which is unpacked into its constituent processes and participants in Table 2.2:

Table 2.1 Approaches to Empowerment (after Cameron et al. 1992a)

	community choice of action?	*Community action?*
paternalism	X	√
advocacy	√	X
cooptation	X	√
local autonomy	√	√

66 *Hybrid Voices and Collaborative Change*

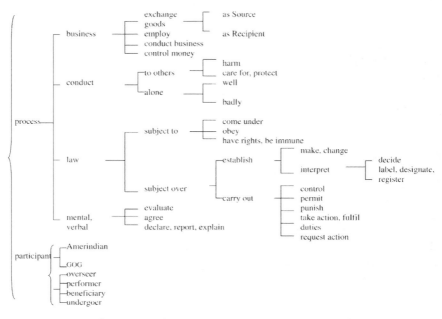

Figure 2.1 Set of process and participant types analysed in legal documents.

2.1 The proceeds of any such tax shall be paid to the district commissioner and shall be utilised by him exclusively for the benefit of the District, Area or Village in respect of which it has been levied and raised, and for such purposes and in such manner as the Chief Officer may approve.

Table 2.2 Processes and Participant Roles in Article 20(3) of the Amerindian Act

Process	Overseer	Performer	Undergoer	Beneficiary
legal:subject to:obey:PAY		(Amerindians— agentless passive)	proceeds of tax	GOG: district commissioner— TO
business: control money: UTILISE	GOG: Chief Officer— APPROVE	GOG: District Commissioner— BY	proceeds of tax	Amerindians: District, Area or Village—FOR THE BENEFIT OF
law:establish: make/change: LEVY AND RAISE		(GOG: District Commissioner— agentless passive)	proceeds of tax	Amerindians: District, Are or Village—IN RESPECT OF WHICH

Table 2.3 Participant Roles in the Amerindian Act

Participant	Total roles played	Overseer roles	As % of roles	Performer roles	As % of roles	Ben. roles	As % of roles	Undergoer roles	As % of roles
GOG	277	86	31%	173	62.5%	10	3.6%	8	2.9%
Amerindians	213	4	1.9%	103	48.4%	51	23.9%	55	25.8%

Table 2.3 compares the roles allocated within the Amerindian Act to the Government of Guyana (GOG) and to Amerindian groups.

From these figures it is clear that through the Amerindian Act the government construes itself as more active in the process of Amerindian welfare development than the Amerindians themselves. For example, in 62.5% of all references to the Government of Guyana (GOG) it is allocated the performer role, as compared to 48.4% for Amerindians. Taken from a different perspective, GOG is construed as performer in 62.7% of all processes in the Act compared with 37.3% for Amerindians, as shown in Table 2.4.

Returning to Table 2.3, GOG is construed as overseeing 31% of all the activities in which it is involved while Amerindians oversee a paltry 1.9% of their own actions. Conversely, Amerindians are construed as beneficiary and undergoer in 23.9% and 25.8% of their activities respectively, compared with 3.6% and 2.9% for the government. These last two roles construe the Amerindians as extremely reliant on outside actors leading development activities, accounting between them for 49.7% of all Amerindian activity compared with a mere 6.5% for the government. This dependency relationship can be further highlighted by interrelating the allocation of different participation roles, as in Table 2.5.

Table 2.4 GOG and Amerindians as Performer in the Amerindian Act

Performer	Total performer roles	As % of performer roles
GOG	173	62.7%
Amerindians	103	37.3%

Table 2.5 Overseers and Beneficiaries of Actions, Amerindian Act

Performer	Total	Other as overseer	As % of actions	Other as beneficiary	As % of actions
GOG	173	1	0.6%	30	17.3%
Amerindians	103	39	37.9%	5	4.9%

68 Hybrid Voices and Collaborative Change

This table shows that whereas only 0.6% of all processes with the government as performer have a different participant as the overseer, 37.9% of all Amerindian performer roles are overseen by others. Similarly, the government is the beneficiary of only 4.9% of Amerindian actions, whereas Amerindians are seen as the beneficiaries of 17.3% of all government actions.

Particularly relevant to the concepts of local autonomy and voice is the allocation of performer roles for processes of evaluation. As Table 2.6 shows, these number 20 to 5 in favour of the government, representing 11.5% and 4.9% of total performer roles for each respectively.

Looking at other specific areas of activity we can see from Table 2.7 that the government is the performer in money dealings 18 times (10.4% of all their actions), a role never allocated to Amerindians, even though the money is for Amerindian concerns and the government is three times explicitly stated as dealing with money on the Amerindians' behalf. A similar picture appears in business matters, for while the respective percentages as performers in business matters might appear to favour Amerindian groups, 11 out of the 16 processes are initiated by the government. None of the government's money dealings are initiated by other groups.

The paternalistic tone of the act that this analysis reveals is widely recognised by activists in Guyana. Walter referred to the "passive" role of Amerindians within it, while the Amerindian Peoples' Association (APA 1998:1) says in its *Plain English Guide to the Amerindian Act*:

> The 1976 Act is based on previous laws concerning Amerindians that date back to the early 20th century. This was when Guyana was still a British colony and Amerindians were not considered capable of representing and speaking for ourselves. The same way of thinking is still

Table 2.6 Participant Roles for Evaluate, Amerindian Act

Performer	Total performer roles	Evaluate	As % of performer roles
GOG	173	20	11.56%
Amerindians	103	5	4.9%

Table 2.7 Performers in Money and Business, Amerindian Act

Performer	Total	Money (other-initiated)	As % of performer roles	Business (other-initiated)	As % of performer roles
GOG	173	18 (0)	10.4%	5 (0)	2.9%
Amerindians	103	0	0%	16 (11)	15.5%

Background 69

present in the 1976 Amerindian Act. It is extremely paternalistic, offensive in many respects, discriminatory and provides almost no protection for our rights.

In contrast to the government's construal of control within Amerindian affairs, the NRDDB Constitution of 2001 sets out the roles and relationships that the Amerindian communities of the North Rupununi see for themselves and outsiders, including NGOs. Table 2.8 shows the distribution of participant roles in the NRDDB Constitution and compares this with the figures for the Amerindian Act.

In the Constitution, the government and NGO groups are construed as performer in 57.1% of all references to it, compared with 57.6% of all references to Amerindian groups as performers. Both sides are thus seen as predominantly active in their own right. Amerindians, however, are given more responsibility in absolute terms, as performers in 89.1% of all actions in the Constitution, as compared with 37.3% in the Amerindian Act, as shown in Table 2.9.

Returning to Table 2.8, we see that in the NRDDB Constitution the role of overseer accounts for 14.3% of total GOG/NGO roles and 15.3% of total Amerindian roles, representing virtual equality in contrast to the huge discrepancy in favour of government overseeing in the Amerindian Act (31% of all GOG references compared with 1.9% of Amerindian references). Beneficiary accounts for 14.3% of GOG/NGO roles and 12.9% of Amerindian roles in the Constitution, again representing virtual parity in

Table 2.8 Participant Roles in the NRDDB Constitution as Compared with the Amerindian Act

Participant	Overseer:		Performer:		Beneficiary:		Undergoer:	
	Const.	*Act*	*Const.*	*Act*	*Const.*	*Act*	*Const.*	*Act*
GOG/NGO	14.3%	31%	57.1%	62.5%	14.3%	3.6%	14.3%	2.9%
Amerindians	15.3%	1.9%	57.6%	48.4%	12.9%	23.9%	14.1%	25.8%

Table 2.9 Performer Roles Compared between Amerindian Act and NRDDB Constitution

Performer	*Total Performer roles*	*As % of performer roles in NRDDB Constitution*	*Comparative % of performer roles in Amerindian Act*
GOG	12	10.9%	62.7%
Amerindians	98	89.1%	37.3%

70   *Hybrid Voices and Collaborative Change*

contrast to the Amerindian Act, where Amerindians are portrayed as beneficiaries far more than the government (23.9% of all Amerindian references as compared with 3.6% of references to GOG). As regards the undergoer role, the Constitution once again represents virtual parity, with 14.3% of GOG roles and 14.1% of Amerindian roles as undergoers, while in the Amerindian Act 25.8% of all Amerindian roles are as undergoer compared with only 2.9% of government roles.

In terms of role allocation, then, the overall construal of each participant is almost identical here, unlike the hugely skewed Amerindian Act. However, there are significant differences when we consider interactions between participants as represented by combinations of participant roles. Table 2.10 shows that only 3.1% of Amerindian actions in the Constitution are overseen by other participants, as compared with 37.9% in the Amerindian Act, while 66.7% of GOG/NGO actions are overseen by the NRDDB in the Constitution, compared with 0.6% of other-overseen GOG actions in the Amerindian Act. And while GOG/NGOs are the beneficiary of 3.1% of all Amerindian actions in the Constitution as compared with 4.9% in the Amerindian Act, Amerindians are only once seen as the beneficiaries of GOG/NGO actions in the Constitution, representing 8.3% of all GOG/NGO actions, compared with 17.3% in the Amerindian Act.

Looking at the same specific areas for the NRDDB Constitution as for the Amerindian Act, Table 2.11 reveals, unexpectedly, that processes of evaluation appear even more skewed in favour of the outside groups. The explanation for this latter point could be that, while each group is construed as evaluating twice, this represents a large fraction of the severely restricted GOG/NGO participation.

As for business and money (Table 2.12), construal of control in the Constitution is the converse of that in the Amerindian Act. Amerindians are five times construed as performer in money matters, but GOG/NGO never. Similarly, Amerindians are construed as conducting business 12 times, with themselves as overseer seven times and GOG/NGO never, whereas GOG/NGOs are only once construed as carrying out business, and this action is overseen by the NRDDB.

These analyses demonstrate that the NRDDB Constitution construes a far more active and authoritative role for Amerindians than the Amerindian Act

Table 2.10   Overseers and Beneficiaries of Actions, NRDDB Constitution

Performer	*Other as overseer:*		*Other as beneficiary:*	
	Constitution	*Amerindian Act*	*Constitution*	*Amerindian Act*
GOG	66.7%	0.6%	8.3%	17.3%
Amerindians	3.1%	37.9%	3.1%	4.9%

Background   71

Table 2.11   Participant Roles for Evaluate Compared between Amerindian Act and NRDDB Constitution

Performer	Total performer roles	Evaluate	As % of participant's total performer roles
GOG	12	2	16.7%
Amerindians	98	2	2%

Table 2.12   Performers in Money and Business, NRDDB Constitution

Performer	Total	Money (other-initiated)	As % of actions	Business (other-initiated)	As % of actions
GOG	12	0	0%	1 (1)	8.33%
Amerindians	98	5 (0)	5.1%	12 (0)	12.2%

does. In terms of the ability to choose and act for yourself, we can interpret the overseer role as demonstrating the power to choose the course of action and the performer role the power to act upon this choice. The beneficiary role implies someone acting on your behalf or in your interest. We can therefore reinterpret Tables 2.1 to 2.12 in terms of these three roles and whether they are filled by the local communities or outsiders, as in Table 2.13 below. Table 2.14, below, summarises the results for the two texts (out of a total of 210 processes in the Amerindian Act and 110 in the NRDDB Constitution).

The picture here would seem to be clear: the Amerindian Act construes the relationship between GOG and Amerindians as one of paternalism and cooptation, while the NRDDB Constitution calls overwhelmingly for local autonomy, but also for GOG/NGO to play the advocate's role for them in certain domains. However, the difference in legal status between the Amerindian Act and the NRDDB Constitution raises the possibility that any alternative construals of the Amerindian role in development they might display would not reveal an active bias towards one group, but would

Table 2.13   Relating Participant Roles to a Typology of Empowerment

Overseer	Performer	Beneficiary	Comparable power relationship
	GOG/NGO	Am	paternalism
Am	GOG/NGO		advocacy
GOG/NGO	Am		cooptation
Am	Am		local autonomy

72 Hybrid Voices and Collaborative Change

Table 2.14 Empowerment as Constructed in the Amerindian Act and the NRDDB Constitution

	Amerindian Act	NRDDB Constitution
paternalism	30 (41.1%)	1 (3.7%)[15]
advocacy	1 (1.4%)[16]	7 (25.9%)
cooptation	39 (53.4%)	2 (7.4%)
local autonomy	3 (4.1%)	17 (63%)
TOTAL	73	27

rather be a function of the different constraints on the different genres (Widdowson 2000:165) to which the two documents belong. For this reason Table 2.15 adds summary information from a third document, the 1996 Iwokrama Act. This document belongs to the same generic type as the Amerindian Act and deals with the same issue of the limits of autonomy on groups operating within sovereign Guyanese territory.

Table 2.15 shows that the statistics for the Iwokrama Act come somewhere between those for the Amerindian Act and the NRDDB Constitution, and in the crucial area of local autonomy the divide between the Iwokrama Act and the NRDDB Constitution, on the one hand, and the Amerindian Act, on the other, is striking. This all points to the conclusion that Iwokrama's contribution to development is construed by the government not in the same terms as they construe indigenous involvement in the Amerindian Act, but in terms closer to the level of involvement the communities of the North Rupununi construe for themselves through the NRDDB Constitution. This strongly suggests that differences between the Amerindian Act and the NRDDB Constitution cannot be explained in terms of generic constraints alone but that they also reveal fundamental differences between the stereotypical role of Amerindians in development as construed by the government, on the one hand, and their role as construed by the Amerindian communities of the North Rupununi, on the other.

Table 2.15 Empowerment as Constructed in the Amerindian Act, the NRDDB Constitution and the Iwokrama Act

	Amerindian Act	NRDDB Constitution	Iwokrama Act
paternalism	30 (41.1%)	1 (3.7%)	5 (23.8%)
advocacy	1 (1.4%)	7 (25.9%)	3 (14.3%)
cooptation	39 (53.4%)	2 (7.4%)	4 (19%)
local autonomy	3 (4.1%)	17 (63%)	9 (42.9%)
TOTAL	73	27	21

Background 73

The Amerindian Act might be seen as an attempt to fill the vacuum that modernism has produced within traditional authority systems and the attitude the government adopts towards the indigenous population within it hovers between paternalism and protectionism, as the analysis above demonstrates. This impression is reinforced in sections of the Act that bring out the often implicit construal of Amerindian identity and character that underlies the provisions of the Act. By its very title, "The Amerindian Act of Guyana", it construes the six distinct ethnicities it covers in essentially racial terms, undifferentiated amongst themselves yet inherently distinct from the rest of the population. Paragraph 2a defines the term 'Amerindian' as used within the Act as "any Indian who is a citizen of Guyana and is of a tribe indigenous to Guyana or to neighbouring countries" or "any descendant of an Amerindian". These terms carry a suggestion of antiquity and birthright, yet the paragraph adds "in the opinion of the Chief Officer", a government official, while Part II lays down strict rules for the registration of Amerindians and Paragraph 3 grants the Chief Officer the right to add, remove and change the boundaries of Amerindian districts, areas or villages; Paragraph 5.1 states that no non-Amerindian may enter an Amerindian area without the written permission of the Chief Officer. Paragraph 40f legislates for further state control in giving the Minister for Amerindian Affairs the right to make regulations "prohibiting any rites and customs which, in the opinion of the Minister, are injurious to the welfare of Amerindians". The extent of such control is made explicit in specific sections prohibiting the sale of alcohol to Amerindians (Paragraph 37); regulating the employment of Amerindians specifically as labourers (Part VII); and dealing with any non-Amerindian who "entices away or cohabits with the wife of any Amerindian" (Paragraph 41). This uneasy relationship between the government and the Amerindian population is emphasised in Paragraph 20a1d, where provision is made for the forfeiture of land rights by Amerindian communities who "have shown themselves to be disloyal or disaffected towards the State or have done any voluntary act which is incompatible with their loyalty to the State". These sections thus create a notion of racial purity mixed with corruptibility through an implicit construal of the Amerindian population as debauched, sexually fickle and best suited to manual work and as such in need of government protection.

In contrast the NRDDB Constitution construes the target population in primarily spatial terms, as is explicit in the name, and Paragraph 2, on the election of an Amerindian representative to the Iwokrama board, contains the only specific reference to Amerindians in the document. This contrasts not only with the government's stance, but also with other NGOs and regional and community-based groups working for Amerindian rights and development. This emphasis on space rather than race allows the Constitution to frame more inclusive activities. In language that superficially mirrors the act, but which in effect reverses the construal of agency, the NRDDB Constitution Paragraph 3 states that the Board's role within

74 Hybrid Voices and Collaborative Change

community development is to "facilitate and encourage . . . development initiatives", "to ensure that such initiatives provide benefits for and serve the interests of its constituent communities" and to "monitor the effects of the Iwokrama Programme and *all* other regional, national and international programmes" (emphasis in original). Similarly, while the Amerindian Act, in Part VI, establishes an "Amerindian Purposes Fund" to be "expended by the Chief Officer solely for the benefit of the Amerindians of Guyana", the NRDDB Constitution, in Paragraph 7, establishes a fund for "specific projects approved by the membership", a non-racial category.

Overall, while the NRDDB Constitution sets up conditions for community-based development within the North Rupununi, the Amerindian Act construes the indigenous groups within Guyana as racially distinct from the mainstream, yet ultimately under government control, as almost 'timeless' in their lack of development (Briggs and Mantini Briggs 2003:277) and as the passive recipients of government care and protection. However, merely to criticise the Amerindian Act for the "bad attitudes" it reveals would be a relatively futile act without considering the purpose it is intended to serve and its role within wider development practice. As suggested by its very title and by its strict categorisation of who counts as officially Amerindian, the Amerindian Act is essentially a racialising document; yet it is also very explicit as to the geographical areas that come under the act, listed and delimited within a detailed schedule. The Act is therefore an example of what Briggs and Mantini Briggs (2003, *passim*) call the "racialisation and spatialisation" of social issues. In the case these authors discuss, cholera outbreaks amongst the Amerindian population of Venezuela in the early 1990s, the indigenous population was consistently construed in distinctly racial and spatial terms as "unsanitary subjects" (Briggs and Mantini Briggs 2003:xvi) passive in the face of danger. This approach diminished the perceived threat to the rest of the population and legitimated state intervention while, conversely, appropriating the "cultural reasoning" of liberalism (Briggs and Mantini Briggs 2003:313) to enable the government and national press to blame the victims' distinctive culture for the state's ultimate failure in containing the epidemics. The mixture of autonomy and state control within the Amerindian Act and the implicit construal of "timeless" and "unsanitary subjects" have a similar potential in allowing the state to maintain significant control over the Amerindian population while drawing on cultural reasoning to abnegate its responsibility when the desired development is not forthcoming.

However, the NRDDB Constitution, to some degree, and related texts, to a greater extent, also call for a racialisation and spatialisation of development, as the focus on the North Rupununi or Region 9 as special cases and the references to Amerindian culture quoted earlier show. Similarly, both sides of the debate place the Amerindian population squarely within the greater Guyanese unity, as summed up by Uncle Henry, a community elder from Surama village: "We want the Government of Guyana to see Surama

Background 75

as an asset, not a liability". However, within the NRDDB and Region 9 texts the Amerindian population is construed as active in both formulating ideas and carrying them to fruition while their culture is represented in positive terms. The difference in perspectives is thus extremely significant: on the one hand, a population granted limited autonomy yet incapable of controlling itself and potentially culpable for its own economic deprivation; on the other, a population striving in word and deed to promote its cultural heritage within a modernising nation state.

An insight into the greater purpose of the Amerindian Act might be found in terms of Guyana's status at the time of its formulation as a newly independent republic seeking to establish its modern credentials. A useful comparison here is provided by the more recent and seemingly similar case of Slovenia, newly freed from Soviet domination yet seen as backward by the 'West' it seeks to join. Erjavec's (2001:724) article on media representation of discrimination against Roma in Slovenia talks of the country's need to create its own 'East' against which to contrast mainstream modernity:

> Words such as 'developed', 'cultural', have meaning only when contrasted with the notion of 'not normal'. Praising a culture as developed implies separating it from and elevating it above other cultures. It is not a surprise then that the elite in Slovenia needs an 'underdeveloped' ethnic group to contrast with its own society . . . [j]ust as the philosophers of the Enlightenment created the modern notion of a divided Europe by dividing it into the 'civilised' and 'barbaric' Europe.

However, the sociocultural situation in Guyana is more complex than this would suggest. According to Forte (1996b:8–9; cf. Briggs and Mantini Briggs 2003:198), since gaining its independence Guyana has needed a notion of 'the other' to break its dependence on its European past (and hence the vast majority of the population's history as slaves and bonded labour), and the 'Amerindian' has come to fill a symbolic role as Guyana's pre-colonial soul. However, if this construal is to be perpetuated, the 'Amerindian' must remain distinctly 'exotic' in relation to the 'Europeanised' majority. The result of the opposing myths of the Amerindian as at once the precolonial soul of Guyana as a nation and a benchmark of underdevelopment against which development on the coast is to be measured is that the Amerindians "are considered by other Guyanese to possess a non-Guyanese culture" (Sanders 1976:117) and are even "despised by the lower strata of Coastland society . . . and regarded paternalistically by the higher strata" (Sanders 1976:119). In order to sustain these opposing positions within the concept of an independent and single nation-state, it is necessary to create horizontal solidarities (Bernstein 2000:xxiii–xxiv) through myths of national consciousness, sustained by rituals, celebrations and emblems, and of organic integration, where each sector of society, despite imbalances in power, has its own value within the national whole. In sum, 'the Amerindian' needs

76   Hybrid Voices and Collaborative Change

to be construed as pure and timeless—and therefore potentially as 'backward'—yet organically contained within the new Republic's unifying myth of "One People, One Nation, One Destiny".

The Amerindian Act can be seen as establishing the complex interplay between Amerindian autonomy and central control necessary to maintain this duality, an attempt to fit the notion of Amerindian autonomy and development within the stereotypical schema (Gotsbachner 2001:730) of Amerindians as both undeveloped, and even barbaric, yet a symbol of Guyanese permanence. It goes some way to fulfilling these objectives through its allocation of control, officially granting the Amerindian population a level of legal autonomy while firmly reining in this freedom in practical terms, and through its implicit construal of Amerindians as, on the one hand, guardians of a timeless culture yet, on the other, as something approaching "unsanitary subjects", incapable of financial prudence, prone to drinking and adultery, and fit only for casual labour. Such a construal of corrupted grandeur corresponds to the West's depiction of 'the Orient' as a great culture gone to seed, unable to maintain itself, so that the West becomes the moral guardian of its riches (Said 1995:chap. 2). However, there are subtle differences arising from the external orientation of this latter case (Said 1995:21–22) and the need to construe 'the Amerindian' as internal to the Guyanese state. The Amerindian Act and the NRDDB Constitution can thus be placed within a framework of five (at least) possible 'development' ideologies in culturally diverse situations:

1. The Western-led Discourse of Development whereby underdeveloped nations are to be created in the image and likeness of developed nations and through the same means, separated only in time (Escobar 1995:5, see chap. 2).
2. A rejection of minority cultures by the nation-state, which sets out to distance itself from these groups through the use of negative cultural stereotypes and practical discrimination (as in Erjavec's analysis of Slovenia above).
4. Orientalism/colonialism, whereby powerful nations take it upon themselves to protect a once proud people whose cultures have fallen into stagnation (Said 1995).
4. Post-colonialism, whereby the newly independent country creates unifying myths in opposition to its colonial history, often drawing on the imagined histories of marginalised populations within the country. Unlike the Western Discourse of Development, the distinctness of the dominated group is emphasised, even while their place within an organic state is confirmed. This approach is similar to Orientalism/colonialism, only the subdued population is internal to the dominant state. This mixture of unity and autonomy allows the state to position its appropriation of the indigenous culture as a process of continuity, thus predating colonialism, while allowing it to abandon the indigenous group to its fate under the pretext of cultural reasoning.

Background 77

5. Local autonomy, or *cultural nationalism* (May 1999:25; 2001:78), whereby minority groups maintain their distinctive identity, focusing on the moral regeneration of the community while developing their culture through the same processes of hybridisation, assimilation and accommodation as majority cultures.

One role of the Amerindian Act can thus be seen as an attempt to create a postcolonial unifying myth while legitimating both state intervention and the underdeveloped position of the Amerindian population within it. Conversely, the NRDDB Constitution and similar documents can be seen as aiming for cultural autonomy within a diverse nation-state, the maintenance and development of a living cultural tradition as opposed to the 'poster culture' propagated by the government.[17]

CONCLUSION

Both outside commentators and community members themselves point to a system of development that has been led from outside and which has imported unsuitable and hence unsustainable practices into the community, practices that have further undermined both traditional activities and authority structures. This is not to claim that community practice was either perfect or ultimately sustainable in itself, but rather that traditional practices can only successfully evolve through the controlled assimilation of new practices if a connection is made between imported and existing forms of knowledge and when local authority systems are drawn upon to contest, validate and sanction new technologies. These are clearly discursive concerns, issues of voice; and innovative development fora such as the NRDDB provide crucial sites where the content of future development practice can be negotiated while new manifestations and alliances of power can be brought into being. Those responsible for the economic 'development' of the North Rupununi, however, have largely ignored meaningful collaborative discourse and imposed both material practices and authority systems from outside according to the dictates of an unresponsive ideological system. The result is that local communities have laboured under a communicative disadvantage in development discourse, a disadvantage that is both underpinned and perpetuated by the educational system and which has its roots in a racist and paternalistic ideology at the political level. In the following chapter I will trace the history of such development discourse and provide an analysis of discourse practice between Iwokrama and the local communities to suggest that the legacy of this paternalistic discourse continues to impose structural limitations on the potential for creating new voices even within such progressive spaces as the NRDDB.

3 Participatory Voice in Development Discourse

> *[Traditionally we] go out after football, we sit together and things would be discussed then, we don't have paper, we don't write these kind of things, and that is the effectiveness. The [Iwokrama-instituted] CEWs supposed to be prepared every time, at all time, to sit, chat to people: every time an opportunity is created, to discuss, to tell somebody about something. But you see what we've done . . . what we've done with the CEW programme, we have made it formal, we have made it more a Western system. So that is what you get: You've asked for this, and the people give you . . . they give you 12 hours' support and that's it.*
>
> Interview with Nicholas (NRDDB Meeting, Yakarinta, 19/1/02)

In this quote Nicholas highlights the problems inherent in attempting to exchange information through contrived channels of communication and the dangers of commodifying local practices. CEWs are local community members paid by Iwokrama to disseminate information throughout the region and to bring information and views from the communities into NRDDB meetings, and Nicholas's words suggest that the programme is not functioning as well as intended. Yet the very notion of a two-way flow of knowledge and the involvement of community members in disseminating dominant knowledge, as obvious as these ideas may seem today, represent a vast advance over the overbearing methods of the preceding generations of governmental and international development workers. In this chapter I will outline the *genealogy* (Foucault 1984:76–100) of current approaches to development discourse and illustrate through the analysis of a text from an Iwokrama-run Management Planning Workshop how the effects of this history, combined with the structural conditions described in the previous chapter, reverberate upon current NRDDB discourse relations.

THE ROLE OF DISCOURSE IN INTERNATIONAL DEVELOPMENT

According to Colombian anthropologist and critic of development Arturo Escobar (1995), the very notion of 'development' is a chimera, a discursive construction of the post-war industrial powers that distorted and reified the concept of poverty and created complex, self-contained and exclusionary 'rules of the game' for dealing with the resulting abstraction. Escobar is

Participatory Voice in Development Discourse 79

willing to give the benefit of the doubt to the generation of power brokers that initiated this process and to attribute their actions, at least in part, to a sincere if fundamentally flawed desire to see the rest of the world share in their abundance. This was the theme taken up by Harry S. Truman in his "Fair Deal" speech, the inaugural address to his second term as president of the U.S. in 1949 (quoted in Escobar 1995:3):

> More than half the people of the world are living in conditions approaching misery. Their food is inadequate, they are victims of disease. Their economic life is primitive and stagnant. Their poverty is a handicap and a threat to them and to more prosperous areas. For the first time in history humanity possesses the knowledge and the skill to relieve the suffering of these people. . . . I believe that we should make available to peace-loving peoples the benefits of our store of technical knowledge in order to help them realise their aspirations for a better life. . . . What we envisage is a programme of development based on the concepts of democratic Fair Dealing. . . . Greater production is the key to prosperity and peace. And the key to greater production is a wider and more vigorous application of modern and scientific technical knowledge.

The zeal with which this evangelising project was undertaken amongst the industrialised nations soon, however, turned to a fetishisation of increased technology and economic and political modernism, the supposed means of development, over the original goal "to relieve the suffering of these people". To more cynical modern readers this danger might be all too apparent even in the language of Truman's speech, yet the following extract, from a group of experts at the UN Department of Social and Economic Affairs in 1951 (in Escobar 1995:4) demonstrates how naturalised such discourse had become in the industrialised world, even to the extent that there was taken for granted a level of (other people's) social sacrifice which would be acceptable in order to impose these goals:

> There is a sense in which rapid economic growth is impossible without painful adjustments. Ancient philosophies have to be scrapped; old social institutions have to disintegrate; bonds of cast, creed and race have to burst; and large numbers of persons who cannot keep up with progress have to have their expectations of a comfortable life frustrated. Very few communities are willing to pay the full price of economic progress.

It is clear in discourses such as these that underneath the industrialised world's concern for the material conditions of the 'poor countries' lies a thinly veiled contempt for their ways of thinking and their social structures, which were perceived as the root cause of their problems and manifestly flawed when compared with those of the 'developed world'. For, despite the

80   Hybrid Voices and Collaborative Change

glaringly obvious fact that these yet-to-be-developed countries were beginning the race to modernity under vastly different entry conditions from those encountered by the already industrialised nations, the intent was:

> to bring about the conditions necessary to replicating the world over the features that characterised the 'advanced' societies of the time—high levels of industrialisation and urbanisation, technicalisation of agriculture, rapid growth of material production and living standards, and the widespread adoption of modern educational and cultural values. (Escobar 1995:3–4)

And if such fetishisation of the means over the end represented one degree of separation from the original intention of improving the living conditions of the poor, 'development' was to move one step further into the abstract as:

> The fact that most people's conditions not only did not improve but deteriorated with the passing of time did not seem to bother most experts. Reality, in sum, had been colonised by the development discourse, and those who were dissatisfied with this state of affairs had to struggle for bits and pieces of freedom within it, in the hope that in the process a different reality could be constructed. (Escobar 1995:5)

Following Foucault's (1972, 1984, 1991) genealogical approach to analysing the history of social constructs and institutions not as the description of a linear and intentional process but as an uncovering of the historical and social elements that created the complex conditions of possibility for the emergence of such constructs and institutions while largely blocking off alternatives, Escobar (1995:40–41) goes on to describe how a discourse of development was able to arise and take a firm grip of the minds of the international community:

> To understand development as a discourse, one must look not at the elements themselves but at the system of relations established among them. It is this system that allows the systematic creation of objects, concepts, and strategies; it determines what can be thought and said. These relations—established between institutions, socio-economic processes, forms of knowledge, technological factors, and so on—define the conditions under which objects, concepts, theories, and strategies can be incorporated into the discourse. In sum, the system of relations establishes a discursive practice that sets the rules of the game: who can speak, from what points of view, with what authority, and according to what criteria of expertise; it sets the rules that must be followed for this or that problem, theory or object to emerge and be named, analysed and eventually transformed into a policy or plan.

Participatory Voice in Development Discourse 81

In other words, official discourse moves ever further from the material conditions it originally surveyed as the texts produced become objects of analysis in their own right and, as these texts multiply, the discourse becomes increasingly self-referential and enclosed and so ever less accessible to local understanding and participation. This represents a process akin to what Edward Said (1995:92–93), in the context of colonial Western scholars defining and describing 'Orientalism' from their occidental towers, has labelled a "textual attitude": "a common human failing to prefer the schematic authority of a text to the disorientations of direct encounters with the human". And just as Orientalism had no need for oriental voices, neither was there room within development discourse for the participation of local actors from the countries to be developed who were, after all, by definition uncultured and uneducated within the perfectly circular and hermetically sealed discourses emerging.

The final result of such a process is a fixed division in the mindset of the external agencies between outside experts as all-knowing teachers and local communities as rather backward students. Half a century on from Truman's "Fair Deal" speech, in the specific context of the North Rupununi savannahs of Guyana, such a paternalistic attitude—the "infantalisation of the Third World as a child in need of adult guidance" as Escobar puts it (1995:30)—persisted in underlying the practice of government and international development organisations who, despite institutional demand for local consultation with the "objects of development", granted to these communities a status that hovered somewhere between audience and token participant (as demonstrated in the Amerindian Act). This seems to have been as true for Iwokrama in its early days as for other international, governmental and non-governmental organisations:

> Referring in particular to the initial consultation meetings of Iwokrama, many of the Amerindians from my host village have also noted that outsiders are willing to spend large sums of money to fly to the Interior to consult them and explain their purpose. However, despite the financial commitment, the unwillingness to dedicate the time required to develop a level of rapport as well as to ensure that issues discussed are truly understood has resulted in a continued problem in terms of dialogue and comprehension. (Hagerman 1997:172)

Iwokrama's attitude towards participatory discourse has changed considerably since those early days, but there is still a tendency to avoid more informal settings, as noted by Walter (Toka, 9/11/00):

> *Probably, like, I mean, Alicia and any one of them never come and really have a chat like how you be chatting, and they're not getting to hear what is my views and what is that one views about it . What we would have is, like, in workshops, we may have, like, short time*

82 *Hybrid Voices and Collaborative Change*

to kinda try to say what we want to really see how it, see how things work. And that wouldn't be able to cover all that—you know it wouldn't bring out the true sense, then. So, like, these kind of er chatting that we may have would kinda—you may hear more and get the point straight, like.

Hagerman's description of 'consultation' captures the vagaries of the term nicely, suggesting that the purposes to be 'explained' (an essentially one-way process) have already been decided back at headquarters and that the involvement from a community that does not fully understand the issues and with whom the developers do not know how to communicate effectively amounts to little more than a rubber-stamping exercise. Unfortunately, this is often exactly what has happened in all those undertakings around the world, from town-hall planning meetings to the granting of international oil concessions, that are described as taking place "after full consultations with the local community". The failings of such an approach are not lost, however, on local community members. As Nicholas (10/11/00) put it when I asked him if Iwokrama had mechanisms for hearing the local communities:

Well, they are working on that, I can see they are working towards it, but still like I said, erm, I still think Iwokrama is somehow like trying to bend people towards their . . . towards their agenda.

On the positive side, this is an area where, since those early days, Iwokrama has made its most innovative contributions to fostering sustainable social development as an integral part of its programme, while professional development organisations in general have been working to analyse their communication methods in order to develop spaces where community voices are enabled and encouraged to participate more freely and with greater purpose and autonomy. This need to *amplify* local voice (Cornwall 2002:8) is recognised by an increasing number of governmental and international organisation at two levels: (i) in improving methods for garnering local views on immediate local problems and (ii) in redefining previously unquestioned a priori concepts such as *poverty* through the testimony of the poor themselves. At the local level, the failure of existing methods of consultation and the need to improve these has been recognised by leading research and training institutions such as the UK's Institute of Development Studies (IDS). IDS fellow Robert Chambers succinctly captures the basic nature of this problem and the imbalance of knowledge/power it implies in the title of his critique on development practice *Whose Reality Counts? Putting the First Last* (1997). Chambers's main thesis is that bad inputs into development policy lead to failing practices because of certain entrenched beliefs and superficial analytical methods of the development set that are based on and in turn perpetuate dominant theories, universalist abstractions

Participatory Voice in Development Discourse   83

formulated in the ivory towers of development—the 'immutable movables' that Chambers describes as a "Model-T standard packages":

> Realities—the world as perceived and interpreted by individuals—are multiple but with commonalities. Human relationships can be seen as patterned by dominance and subordination, with people as uppers and lowers. Uppers experience and construct their realities and seek to transfer these to lowers. In normal teaching, adult realities are transferred to children and students. Normal successful careers carry people upwards in hierarchies and inwards in to larger centres, away from the poor and the peripheries. In normal bureaucracy, central authorities simplify, control and standardise. In normal top-down centre-outwards development, new technology is developed in central places by uppers and transferred to peripheral lowers. The resulting 'Model-T' standard packages often misfit diverse and unpredictable local conditions. Similarly, the transfer of procedures which require people to conform to fixed timetables frequently fail. Normal professionalism, teaching, careers and bureaucracy help to explain errors in development, but not fully how and why they persist so long without uppers learning. (1997:56)

Chambers's explanation for this persistence is given later:

> The upper rejects discordant feedback. He relabels the lower and redefines her reality for her. He seeks to transfer his reality. He wants it to be his reality that counts. What prevents him learning in this case is not professionalism or bureaucracy. It is his dominant behaviour, person to person. It is his power. (75)

As an antidote to the power relations that pervade interpersonal encounters in grassroots development, often reducing local participation to mere spectating, Chambers has been at the forefront of developing methods of participatory research and data-gathering that attempt to diminish the effect of the power differentials between researcher and researched, donor and recipient:

> As professionals have become more aware of errors and myths and of the misfit between the reality they construct and the reality others experience, some have sought and developed new approaches and methods in their work. Insights and developments in action-reflection research, agro-ecosystem analysis, applied social anthropology, farming-systems research and rapid rural appraisal (RRA) have contributed to the evolution of participatory approaches to learning and action, including participatory rural appraisal (PRA). PRA is a growing family of approaches and methods to enable local people to share, enhance and analyse their knowledge of life and conditions, and to plan, act,

84   Hybrid Voices and Collaborative Change

monitor and evaluate. Its extensive and growing menu of methods includes visuals such as mapping and diagramming. Practical applications have proliferated, especially in natural resources management, agriculture, health and nutrition, poverty and livelihood programmes. PRA approaches and methods present alternatives to questionnaire surveys in appraisal and research, and generate insights of policy relevance. Past dominant behaviour by outsiders goes far to explain why it is only in the 1990s that these participatory approaches and methods have come together and spread. (102)

At the macrolevel even the Word Bank, long scorned by radicals as a powerhouse example of a closed discourse community of the professional elite divorced from the realities of those it is supposed to 'aid', has been forced to redefine its realities, to reconsider what exactly it is supposed to achieve and the role of 'lowers' in defining this. Starting from 2000, with *Voices of the Poor: Can Anyone Hear Us?* (Narayan 2000), the World Bank produced a series of books that drew on testimony from marginalised communities around the world to interrogate, challenge and redefine some of the core concepts behind development, and in particular the concept of 'poverty' itself. In the foreword to the book (ix), Clare Short, then UK secretary of state for International Development, and James Wolfensohn, then president of the World Bank, summarise the new direction the book supposedly heralds:

> *Can Anyone Hear Us?* brings together the voices of over 40,000 poor people from 50 countries. The two books that follow, *Crying Out for Change* and *From Many Lands*, pull together new fieldwork conducted in 1999 in 23 countries. The Voices of the Poor project is different from all other large-scale poverty studies. Using participatory and qualitative research methods, the studies present very directly, through poor people's own voices, the realities of their lives. How do poor people view poverty and well-being? What are their problems and priorities? What is their experience with the institutions of the state, markets, and civil society?

To its credit, *Voices of the Poor* challenges textbook notions of poverty to come up with a multistranded and locally contingent understanding. However, it could be claimed that the approach is fundamentally extractive, mining the discourses of the poor for raw materials to be processed by professional development organisations as a finished product that bears the intellectual hallmark of the dominant institutions to whose largely predetermined policies and strategies they are made to fit. The notion of "voice" in the title of the World Bank's book is therefore a long way from the definition developed in Chapter 1 of local discourses that reproduce community experience, interpersonal relations and means of communication—the very

Participatory Voice in Development Discourse   85

same "[a]ncient philosophies" that, according to the 1951 UN Department of Social and Economic Affairs, "have to be scrapped; [the] old social institutions [that] have to disintegrate; [and the] bonds of cast, creed and race have to burst". Similarly, while Chambers's *Whose Reality Counts?* model goes further in involving grassroots participation in immediately practical concerns through the use of innovative interpersonal and descriptive techniques, it does not deal with the sustainability of the everyday decision-making processes of the community, and the very rapidity of the appraisal methods it promotes suggests that once the professional developers leave any locally based decision-making power is likely to go with them. As a result, although professional development workers have relinquished their previous infantilising/paternalist stance, they remain the advocates of those without voice and "spaces fostered as a way of amplifying marginalised voices may end up being filled by gatekeepers who speak for but not with those they represent" (Cornwall 2002:8).

Local voices may well have been amplified within the recommendations and publications of these groups, but the matrix discourses and the higher-level practices based upon them remain the construction of the international development elite, for in neither case have durable mechanisms been sought for the local communities to achieve within international development sustainable and autonomous voices that continuously redefine reality in their own terms and determine and carry out the appropriate practices to solve their own problems in improving their living conditions and in facing the twin juggernauts of globalisation and modernisation. As Norton et al. (2001:42) say with respect to both these approaches:

> The metaphor of 'voice' is powerful and communicates strongly with policy audiences for PPAs [Participatory Poverty Assessments, a development of Chambers' Participatory Rural Appraisal methods]. It may also have some problematic connotations. It can entail an implied claim that the results presented are the unmediated views of 'the poor'— when in reality all PPAs are a mediated research process, with a variety of different actors involved. Quotations and other devices which imply direct contact with opinions of poor people are selected—and the process of authorship is also framed within structures of power and authority which influence the representation.

In other words, what is lacking is a system whereby the 'poor' no longer need to cry out for outsiders to hear their voices, but rather use their voices on a day-to-day basis to control their own destiny.

If advocacy is the process whereby powerful, external voices are necessary to amplify local concerns, its uglier twin is co-optation, a situation in which external interests are pushed through, often for a price, by local agents using traditional power structures. This was a method perfected by Mexico's Partido Revolucionario Institucional (PRI) during their 64-year

86   Hybrid Voices and Collaborative Change

period in power. Increased government funding would be provided for social services in those indigenous communities that returned a unanimous pro-PRI vote using anomalous electoral practices that were allowed to continue under the pretext of 'traditional custom'. However, not only was such an allowance not granted to communities backing the opposition; it was also the case that the traditional practices themselves were not necessarily either old or indigenous, as Henríquez Arellano (2000:29; my translation) explains in his essay on the elections in Chiapas between 1991 and 1998, a period which saw the PRI challenged both in the jungle and in the hearts and minds of the populace by the indigenous Zapatista uprising:

> Much has been spoken in recent times about the importance of use and customs in the indigenous communities in Los Altos de Chiapas. However, these traditional practices have been transforming over time, and nothing is further from reality than the idea that the country's indigenous groups have remained the same throughout history.
>
> Indigenous groups in Mexico have lived in a constant relationship with national society, which, along with its own development, has obliged them to modify their traditional practices in order to adapt them to a changing reality. We might say that all the transformations that the so-called uses and customs have suffered are a result of pressure from external forces just as much as forces from within the communities themselves.

In this extract Henríquez Arellano also draws attention to the fact that in reifying select "traditional practices" for their own benefit the PRI's co-optive approach can be seen as an obstacle to autonomous indigenous development in a similar way to paternalistic approaches. What seems to be clear is that the three approaches to development discussed so far— paternalism, advocacy and co-optation—cannot provide adequate structures for local communities to have a meaningful and lasting voice in their own development. Such a voice would need to be autonomous and sustainable for several reasons, reasons that are not just idealistic but practical. The principle reason must be that every community undergoes development within a different set of entry conditions, a simple notion that seemed to be lost in the early evangelism of the post-war period with its visions of universal prosperity through a one-size-fits-all replication of Western industrialised structures. Such naivety (to be charitable) continues today in the simplistic championing of free markets and open borders from those countries that have already dominated the market and so altered categorically the conditions of possibility for 'emerging nations' to repeat the trick (to say nothing of the collective amnesia over the fact that the early globalising countries vaunt the desirability of a free market only after prolonged periods of the most sustained protectionism). An autonomous local voice within development discourse is therefore not only desirable in cultural

Participatory Voice in Development Discourse   87

terms, but a necessary basis for sustainable development that is not dominated by the fetishes of the international development elite, as demonstrated by the failings of such an approach outlined in the previous chapter. This means that there can be no single model for development and that the local community in each situation will have to redefine what the term means according to their own needs and conditions within the constraints and affordances of the structural conditions in which they operate. This is not to say that external input will not be helpful, or even crucial, in local practice, but that it will have to be *recontextualised* into terms that are relevant to and manipulable by the local community. Conversely, local systems and practices will have to be made to relate, in some way, to the global system within which local communities increasingly have no choice but to operate. In terms of discourse practice, this means fostering spaces where external expertise can be assimilated and local discourse systems—local voices—can be incorporated into the dominant discourses of development practice in distinct forms as appropriate to increasingly higher levels of control. This entails the production of hybrid discourse systems that speak to and from both communities of practice, making imported expertise relevant to local life and conditions while speaking to global practice in a local accent.

Many development practitioners have been involved in analysing local discourse practices with the idea that local voice is best understood as an unmediated and sustainable contribution to ongoing development discourse. These authors see "citizens not only as users or choosers but as active participants who engage in making and shaping social policy provisioning i.e. poor people as social actors with rights and agency . . . including rights to information and to involvement in decision-making over issues with implications for resources" (Cornwall and Gaventa 2001:1, 2, quoted in Hobley 2003:3). These approaches "underline the multidimensional nature of poverty" and the various forms of action needed to deal with the concept and seek to "explore the opportunities to develop such forms through an analysis of the power relations that need to be understood as part of any approach to support participatory governance" (Hobley 2003:4). Without doing justice to the complexities of the description and theoretical framework of these authors, the main thrust of much of this work can be summarised as attempts to create more open local discourse systems based on the belief that the mediation of grassroots voices, whether it be by professional development organisations or local power groups, amounts to controlling this voice and this group and so maintaining the status quo of power relations rather than allowing the underclass to forge new alliances to challenge existing authority structures and definitions of reality:

> the poor and their livelihood strategies exist within a network of power relations which have both positive and negative elements. What is clear is that they rarely enter into direct relations with the state, mainly they are mediated through patron–client relationships which

88 Hybrid Voices and Collaborative Change

act as gatekeepers to services and resources from the state. These relationships develop long-term dependency and short-term security and an aversion to challenging the structures that provide these elements of security (Blair 2003). For the weakest sections, they can only participate in such networks on terms which deprive them of independent voice and agency and reduce them to highly clientilist forms of dependency. "The pervasiveness of patron-client relationships serves to fragment and disunite such groups and prevent the emergence of horizontal, class-based solidarities which could be mobilised to defend and promote their interests" (Kabeer 2002). (Hobley 2003:19)

Much of the work of these authors is concerned with the structural conditions of local society that limit the emergence of local voices and the need to create alternative spaces in which these voices can be heard. This fundamental principle can be captured from the definitions of space, voice and choice as used in this discourse (listed in Hobley 2003:36):

Space: politically and socially constructed arenas in which individuals engage in decision-making and express their voice.

Voice: 'describes measures ranging from participation of people in decision-making and product delivery to lodging complaints, engaging in organised protest or lobbying, used by civil society actors to put pressure on public service providers to demand better service outcomes' (Goetz and Gaventa 2001:8).

Choice: describes both the right to exercise voice—(and therefore the obverse right not to)—and the provision of a diversity of channels through which voice can be articulated and responses delivered. The latter is significant in that it explicitly recognises that poor men and women are not a homogeneous group.

The description and analysis of the sociostructural conditions and discourse relations within local communities is therefore seen as a necessary first step in freeing up space for mobilisation strategies that create "an alternative social capital (building on the horizontal alliances) through which to transform the vertical ones, and to bring the poor into a direct relationship with the state through the principle of 'voice' . . . developing a collective identity and solidarity to counter the fragmentation and disunity engendered by their reliance on vertically organised and highly asymmetrical patron-client relationships" (Wood and Davies 1998, in Hobley 2003:30). However, Cornwall (2002:5) takes the problems of structural inequality further in suggesting that, even when spaces are created where the marginalised are able to participate, external social structures will continue to influence their ability to contribute their own perspectives within these spaces:

Participatory Voice in Development Discourse 89

The principles of institutional design or intentions motivating the use of participatory approaches may seek to create open, free, equal spaces or indeed may equate the use of such mechanisms with kinds of space. Yet issues of power and difference may not only undermine the very possibility of equitable, consensual decision making, they may also restrict the possibility of 'thinking outside the box', reinforcing hegemonic perspectives and status-quo reinforcing solutions.

This suggests that achieving participation in communicative events, while a step up from being merely audiences of the powerful, does not necessarily guarantee that grassroots voices are being expressed and heard. In fact, although *voice* is a very prominent word in all of these works, there is very little analysis of what the concept actually represents in real-time practice while the definition provided in the preceding suggests a notion of voice that is limited to a reactive range of speech acts contesting the impositions of outside forces. This falls well short of the definition developed in Chapter 1 and, in particular, fails to capture the idea of community voice as culturally distinct from outside voices rather than just an enhanced opportunity to participate according to dominant norms. Focusing on a quantitative increase in local contributions rather than a qualitative change in the discourse itself will not provide local communities with the necessary means of expressing themselves, and *amplification* of local voices is of little use if those voices are already distorted. In the remainder of this chapter I shall focus specifically on discourse within the NRDDB, its place within the wider history of participation in international development, and how this relates to the development of autonomous voice.

"YOU NEED TO LISTEN TO THE PEOPLE": EARLY DISCOURSE BETWEEN THE COMMUNITIES AND IWOKRAMA

Uncle Henry (Surama, Management Planning Meeting, 29/3/00) sums up the frustration felt by the local communities in the face of government-led paternalism:

> We want the Government of Guyana to see Surama as an asset not a liability.

For, while the communities are aware that the paternalism of the state has failed them, they do not seek to revert to the *status quo ante* of conventional authority and isolationism. On the contrary, there is universal recognition amongst the elders that the dramatic changes in their field of activity necessitate a realignment within the whole ideological system. As Nicholas says (9/11/00, Walter's House):

90 Hybrid Voices and Collaborative Change

The world is changing and we gotta find our place in it.

The community leaders do not want secession, but a level of autonomy that allows them to control and manage their affairs within the national context and to develop at grassroots level plans that are complementary to the national development strategies of the government: that is, the level of action which May (2001:77–80) labels *cultural nationalism*, and which largely corresponds to what I called *local autonomy* at the end of Chapter 2. Cultural nationalism subsumes Kymlicka's definition of minority rights (1995, in May 1999:25) as rights to:

> maintain one's membership in a distinct culture, and to continue developing that culture in the same (impure) way that the members of majority cultures are able to develop theirs.

Such an approach, while shunning the wholesale importation of exogenous methods, recognises the demands of modernity and the need to introduce a catalyst into the indigenous cultural dynamic—what Kymlicka might label an "impurity", the grain of sand that produces the oyster's pearl. Sam Bramley, speaking before national and international scientists and representatives from indigenous communities throughout Guyana at the Guiana Shield Conference (Pegasus Hotel, Georgetown, 4/12/00), put it like this (see Bartlett 2008 for a fuller account of this speech):

> *We have the community, you have the technology, why not join together for the great partnership that we are looking for?*

What Sam is calling for, then, is a recognition of community voices as legitimate, as having something to say and the right to say it. Such a move, recognising equality in diversity, would represent a cancelling out of the communicative disadvantage apparent in recent development discourse and institutionalised through the education system, as discussed in the previous chapter. While several NGOs and international organisations have taken up Sam's challenge, the local communities' principal partner in this enterprise has been Iwokrama.

The greatest success of Iwokrama's work in conjunction with the NRDDB is that their efforts have been undertaken in a spirit of collaboration as opposed to the disastrous paternalism of the government and private business. Andrew, a councillor and farmer from the village of Rupertee, is particularly enthusiastic about the more collaborative approach of groups such as Iwokrama and CIDA, the Canadian International Development Agency (Rupertee, 28/2/01; **A** is Andrew; I am **T**):

> **T:** *. . . when the outsiders come with their knowledge, how do you see them . . . what's their role in the community?*

Participatory Voice in Development Discourse   91

A: *Well, their role is that they're willing to contribute. They are not saying "Look, look, well we want you to do this." They present an offer. Okay, "Would you like, are you interested in so, so, so, so, we are willing to lend or contribute this article. With your consent." And that's what I like about the whole thing. Right, because now they are not forcing us into something that we do not know about. Right. But basically you carry out a little research there to find out first of all, okay, "Are you interested in this? And what are some of the things that you would need to have from us so that we can start?"*

Nicholas (Toka, 10/11/00), who is not slow to criticise when he feels it is appropriate, singles out Iwokrama's approach to communications and sees it as a model that other organisations should follow:

> *Iwokrama is doing an excellent job in that field because, like, Iwokrama right now actually is developing a system of communicating or trying at least to understand the way Amerindian people would think or how they communicate . . . so if Iwokrama could use that and effectively use it and could bring results, you would find that UNDP [United Nations Development Programme] and other NGOs might very well catch on.*

Similarly, Andrew (Rupertee, 28/2/01) considers that Iwokrama's outreach is based not on the banking method of development, but on a collaborative approach that draws on existing knowledge and practices:

> *Iwokrama contribute to this village uhm by like making us to understand the true uses of our resources. And also to educate us to know what and where is our boundaries of operations.*

Andrew cites the introduction of drip-feed irrigation systems as an example of this approach, and Uncle Henry (Surama Rest House, 6/3/01) is generally equally enthusiastic:

> *Well, one of the things which I know the communities have benefited from and they would continue to benefit from is the education, the outreach programme, the education. Because, as I said, since Iwokrama come, people are beginning to get aware of the value of their resources that we have and they are understanding that there is nowhere you can go. If you harvest everything, you destroy everything, then where would you go to get . . . ? So you have to start making an effort to try to save what we have now.*

Researchers from Iwokrama have also encouraged the study and application of methods learned from local communities in neighbouring Brazil, an

92 Hybrid Voices and Collaborative Change

approach that not only reconnects theory and practice to bring economic benefits, but in doing so also does much to enhance the prestige of local knowledge (Uncle Henry, Surama Rest House, 6/3/01):

What these experts from Brazil are doing with the arapaima [the world's largest freshwater fish and an endangered species], counting, it's like a census on the arapaima population they are going to be doing. People are very much enthusiastic and interested in it, people now want to go into fish farming, conservation, rather than poisoning and doing continuous overtrapping and these kind of thing. They are getting sensitive to the dangers of overharvesting. And things are picking up. They are getting to realise the mistakes we used to make.

However, the distinctive roles of the local communities in developing sustainable livelihoods for their own economic and cultural survival and Iwokrama as conservationists who do not depend for survival on the theories and practice they promote have at times proved less easy to reconcile. Gordon, Iwokrama's Senior Wildlife Biologist (Iwokrama Office, Georgetown, 24/4/01) neatly summarises the different approaches to conservation that must ultimately distinguish local communities and the scientists of Iwokrama:

I think in the early stages when I started working, what we did was we went out and tried to ask. The problem with asking is that even when you ask you create a framework of what is possible and what is not possible. And, yes, we have to do that because Iwokrama does have plans, and I think if we'd just gone out to the communities and asked them what they wanted, they would say, it might be something as simple as "We want more employment and we want it in such and such a way." Of course, Iwokrama doesn't do that, Iwokrama doesn't do employment, so it has to couch it and manage it and mould it, but if you look at the wildlife process, a lot of those concerns do come from the communities, but these may not be their major concerns. For example, if I was in the community, mine might be, you know, "What's going to happen to my kids, where's the schooling, where's this, where's that?", rather than "The environment's getting buggered up." And what you find is that in fact it weaves, goes back and forth like this, as you know, we're sitting here, we're thinking about the environment; they're there sitting thinking about jobs and opportunities.

Two corollaries to the needs-driven participation of the local communities are that many are too busy surviving to participate in development discourses, while those who do are likely to grab at whatever help is offered them (Nicholas, Toka, 10/11/00):

Participatory Voice in Development Discourse 93

Once you find a people that is poor, anything you actually give them, they're ready to grasp at it, but then sometimes that may not be the thing that they need, but just because of their poverty, they're saying it's an opportunity and they don't want to lose that opportunity. So, to avoid that, you need to come back to the people, right?

However, despite this tendency to accept gift horses without always looking too closely in the mouth, community activists attempt where possible to maintain a critical eye. Andrew (Rupertee, 28/2/01) shows a level of caution:

Everything is good to see but everything is not good to accept.

Nicholas (Toka, 10/11/00) similarly talks of a lack of trust and how he sometimes holds back local knowledge from outside researchers:

I'm a very suspicious Amerindian. You don't get everything from me [. . .] but if Amerindian would be allowed to do their own thing, I think then they would do a better job. [. . .] There's certain things, how to analyse these things, and that is why, when you take it outside to the white man, and they hear the white man analysing, they say "Wait, he gonna take something outta this." Then they start to retract. And we do need that kind of thing at this point in time, because we're talking about a people dying out.

This reluctance to pass on information to outsiders can be problematical. Those sponsored by Iwokrama to map Amerindian resources in the South Rupununi as a prelude to reclaiming land rights, for example, were only willing to mark down areas that they utilised without disclosing what they were used for, and Nicholas (Toka, 10/11/00) says how even he and Walter, as a result of their dealings with outsiders, are looked at with some suspicion when they go among the elders. Where Iwokrama has built up trust among the indigenous population, Gordon sees this as based on individual relationships rather than on trust of the institution, a relationship threatened by the constant changeover in personnel (Iwokrama Office, Georgetown, 24/4/01):

You're talking about the people initiating the discussions have to be the people who will be implementing policy. Because otherwise, what happens when you bring new people in is that they don't understand the things that happened before, they don't understand this dialogue that's been going on for years, and they immediately begin with a new dialogue.

Relating this changeover in personnel to deeper problems concerning the overuse of short-term consultancies throughout the international

94 *Hybrid Voices and Collaborative Change*

development sector in general, Gordon is scathing of what he sees as an old boys' network and what he calls "aid power" (Iwokrama, Georgetown, 24/4/01). This control of the superstructures of the development process and the indigenous reluctance to turn away assistance means that in practice the prioritising of issues and the pace of change are dictated by non-indigenous groups. When I put this to Uncle Henry (Surama Rest House, 6/3/01) he concurred that pressures on Iwokrama meant that they were forced to hurry processes that should have been allowed to mature at a steadier pace:

> *Yes. I think the problem with Iwokrama is time is against them and they are trying to get through their—(xx)—really, it took them a long time to get started, and now they are trying to catch up with time. Because there is a deadline to start being self-sufficient and sustainable. And they're trying to—that anxiety, like, you know, they're trying to kind of run, they've developed a momentum that is a bit too fast.*

While this process, a result of the need for immediate and quantifiable results, is understandable in terms of the pressures on Iwokrama from their international funding bodies, from the indigenous point of view it only takes control one step further away from the grassroots:

> *Well, they are working on that, I can see they are working hard towards it, but still like I said, erm, I still think Iwokrama is somehow like trying to bend people towards their . . . towards their agenda.* (Nicholas, Toka, 10/11/00)

Iwokrama's ultimate control over the NRDDB's agenda is explicitly stated in their Community Outreach Programme:

> Iwokrama will continue to facilitate workshops on wildlife in the North Rupununi as requested by the NRDDB *once the workshop subjects are considered to be consistent with the mission of Iwokrama.* (NRDDB and Iwokrama 1999:30; emphasis added)

Within those workshops they do facilitate, Iwokrama's control is also very noticeable and an in-depth analysis of this process follows at the end of this chapter.

The fact that Iwokrama can dictate the pace and direction of change to this extent is largely a result of the disequilibrium between Iwokrama workers and local participants in what Bourdieu (1977) calls their respective *cultural capital*. This refers to the social prestige adhering to particular groups and individuals as a result of such social factors as their wealth, their education or their position within official institutions. In Bourdieu's

Participatory Voice in Development Discourse 95

framework, to be developed in more detail in Chapter 4, speakers come to *embody* this cultural capital when they enter into discourse in diverse contexts, such that their words are seen to be *symbolic* of their cultural status and are afforded more respect than their content alone would merit. Bourdieu (1991) refers to this overvaluing of the discourse of those with more cultural capital as the *misrecognition* of the structural origins of their authority. In the case of the North Rupununi and similar contexts elsewhere, the largely one-sided discourse of development discourse and the history of 'top-down' control is likely to mean that the professional development workers, whose discourses carry *symbolic capital* in proportion to their social status, are accorded more respect than other community members (though I will take issue with this unidirectional reading in Chapter 4). This can lead to problems of advocacy, where it is Iwokrama rather than the communities who take forward locally formulated plans, or co-optation, where community efforts are controlled from within an Iwokrama-dominated framework. As described in Chapter 2, advocacy and co-optation differ from paternalism in that with paternalism the dominant group both decides upon and controls the course of development, leaving no room for community participation. However, both advocacy and co-optation are fraught with problems. The perception that local communities need a symbolically powerful advocate to validate their development plans stretches from the communities themselves to the Government of Guyana. Robert Thompson, local fishing expert and vice chairman of the NRDDB at the time of my fieldwork, has complained that community members, assuming that all progress must come from Iwokrama, wrongly attribute locally instigated development plans to Iwokrama. This is a textbook example of misrecognition in which the cultural capital already possessed by Iwokrama attracts to itself further symbolic prestige. This situation is mirrored in the government's attitude towards local knowledge and their willingness to accept shoddy mainstream research over more accurate local knowledge. As Gordon puts it:

> *I mean you've got people coming in and doing surveys of parrots and macaws using methods that are unintelligible, cannot be, well, from the scientific perspective they're in fact useless, they're all gobbledygook, basically, you come out with an estimate of how many parrots there are in the country based on seeing a hundred birds, then there are a million in the country. I mean, if you did that to any human population, people would laugh you out of the bloody room, but yet we do that and then we hide it in all the gobbledygook, in (wholesale) numbers. Nobody's going to read the numbers. But if you actually look at it, it says a hundred birds or so, and you're estimating two million in the country? From a hundred? I don't think so. I really don't think so. So where does this number come from? You might as well have pulled it out of your arse. However, nobody's going to ask that,*

96   Hybrid Voices and Collaborative Change

because this is <u>sci:entist</u> did it. The authority is there because the government (here??) agrees with the scientists, because they know science is good. Now, if Uncle Henry comes along and says "Excuse me, but I think that you should harvest 25 birds a year", and doesn't want to explain exactly why they think that, or if they did try and explain it, it would completely (out of) the books, it would be relevant to this thing, but it wouldn't be accepted. And that's what's wrong. Because the 25's probably much better than the middle of the—the effective number that's extracted from this thing with a model and a piece of shit here and a piece of crap there, 'cause that's all irrelevant.

However, at the level of immediate discourse between local communities and professional scientists, the converse can also be true in that Uncle Henry's approval of outside plans and his reformulation of them in local terms can carry significant weight in the local communities. The importance of this is discussed in Chapter 6, where an analysis of the linguistic strategies Uncle Henry uses to integrate imported and local knowledge is presented in some detail.

Advocacy, as illustrated here, relates to sections of the dominant group having ultimate control over the content of Development Discourse at the highest levels of policy-making. However, the petitioner–gatekeeper roles set up by the development process in its present form mean that this control often extended to the form of negotiations as the communities were obliged, particularly in the early days of the NRDDB, to meet Iwokrama representatives in contexts more familiar to Iwokrama. In practice most government officials spend little time in the Rupununi and what direct negotiations do take place are largely condensed into concentrated Western formats familiar to the international community rather than local methods, though efforts are being made by Iwokrama to hold discussions within community contexts and individuals such as Alicia, Gordon and Sara mix freely within the local communities and spend long hours chatting informally with their friends (though Nicholas, in the preceding, suggests this was not always so).

However, it remains the case that a large proportion of discussions between Iwokrama and the local communities is framed within non-traditional discourse structures. In these cases, the novelty of the institutional setting reduces the expectability of the content for local participants and familiar schemata can no longer be relied upon (Bremner et al. 1996:167; Kohonen 1992:20–21). The dominance of unfamiliar fora and the use of technical registers thus add to the more basic problem of having to negotiate in what for many is a second language. While in Iwokrama this might be considered a matter of expedience rather than intention, van Dijk (1997:21) points to the disempowering effects of such constraints when he says, of less benign contexts, that "the first set of strategies that are used to control public discourse as a means to exercise social power consist in controlling

Participatory Voice in Development Discourse 97

the parameters of the context". Deliberate or not, the question of control over the form and content of discourse relates once again to the need for appropriate structural conditions. Nicholas, in an interview from which the opening quote of this chapter is taken (NRDDB Meeting, Yakarinta, 19/1/02), describes how, in his opinion, the effects of institutionalised discourse go beyond the confines of NRDDB meetings themselves and into the communities as the Iwokrama-sponsored CEWs have adopted Western communication formats that have supplanted more appropriate local modes of communication:

> *and though it [local procedure] may not be something formal like this, here we would have to have our parliamentary procedure and all that kind of thing, and who stands first, who stands that, they sit down and they discuss, and that is the technique. And I think that is a system that we use, and we don't document that, but that is the system that we use to effect in Toka. And I'm telling you [that as a result of local methods of dissemination], the last two years, if there's 20 deer been killed in Toka, compared with what was killing before, that's a lot [i.e. a likely overestimate]. And the guys hardly would go out, and they find people try to utilise, you know, try to produce more and use more of the farm and actually (?had a go). And how did we disseminate that information? We go out after football, we sit together and things would be discussed then, we don't have paper, we don't write these kind of things. And that is the effectiveness, the CEWs supposed to be prepared every time, at all time, to sit, chat to people: every time an opportunity is created to discuss, to tell somebody about something. But you see how we've done . . . what we've done with the CEW programme, we have made it formal, we've made it more a Western system, so that is what you get: You've asked for this, and the people give you . . . they work for 12 hours, they give you 12 hours' support and that's it.*

Uncle Henry (Surama Rest House, 6/3/01) also appreciates the informality of community fora and emphasises how many more people are prepared to speak in these meetings than in the more formal NRDDB meetings:

> *It would be slightly different, because what you would find is that in the NRDDB meeting you would find very few speakers—just the head speaker, who might give you the presentation, and then you notice very few questions comes up, and if questions come, it would be two or three persons would be speaking the entire meeting.*

This demonstrates how external control of fora, made possible through the prestige afforded to international institutions and the resultant underestimation, or misrecognition, of the value of community practice, leads to a lack of integration of local and often very important, voices, with Uncle Henry,

98 *Hybrid Voices and Collaborative Change*

amongst others, complainsing that touchaus do not contribute nearly enough (Surama Rest House, 6/3/01). More drastically, as doctoral student Christie Allan put it to Iwokrama in a presentation of her research on indigenous knowledge (Iwokrama, Georgetown, 3/4/00, and see Allan 2002):

> There is a large sector of the community who do not want to be enlightened on the things that Iwokrama wants to enlighten them on.

Where there is participation, the reliance on communications fora more familiar to the aid organisations than to local communities means that there is a mismatch between community practice and the contexts in which community members are expected to operate. Combined with local participants' varying levels of competence in English and a failing by development organisations to relate issues sufficiently to grassroots concerns, this often entails a lack of understanding from the community in the double sense of comprehending the language used and empathising with the opinions put forward. Walter (NRDDB Meeting, Annai Institute, 4/11/00) refers to such a failure by Iwokrama to relate economic theory to community livelihoods at an NRDDB meeting:

> *And one of the things that I had realised at the SUA [Sustainable Utilisation Area] planning team was in—when we were in discussion of economics . . . and social, though we may have it in practice, we do not have it in theory, which made it a little bit difficult for us to have much of our inputs. You know what, if we could talk about, when you're talking about where which creek is, the rest of the participants would've . . . would be . . . they were quiet on that subject, or which tree is good for which creek. And when you're dealing with economics, you know, you're wondering what would be the economics of nibbi [a type of wood used especially in construction], what would be the economics of logging and I notice that the NRDDB participants, we're a bit dormant in those areas, and it's simply because of, we are not (from x like) most of the participants that attended there.*

This lack of understanding of abstract terminology, despite an intuitive grasp of the concepts in local terms, leads to a lack of participation, even from the touchaus. As Walter put it to me when I raised this issue with him (Toka, 8/11/00):

> *Why they don't contribute is because they don't understand.*

The vicious circle of dependence again becomes clear: Lack of understanding leads to lack of confidence and so on to increased prestige for outside experts. This helps to create the idea held by many community members that external resources are inherently superior and so confirms for them the

Participatory Voice in Development Discourse 99

need for outsiders to take the lead in such communicative fora, a process that is demonstrated in detail below. The ultimate outcome of this process is that the development organisations themselves, often unconsciously and against their better natures, accept their enhanced prestige at face value and fail to consult with the communities at all or bypass community elders when consulting at grassroots level. As Walter (Toka, 9/11/00) puts it:

> *As I was saying to Iwokrama, they think that, erm, they prefer to have a social scientist to do the work for them, because they feel that we are incapable of doing it. But they should learn from their experience of, now, the last, for the past six months or so the social scientists were working with the CEWs and so forth, and they ain't getting anywhere. And where we could do the same work, give us your plan, what is it that you need, what you expecting, and we gon do it.*

Similarly, Nicholas (Toka, 10/11/00), amongst others, makes the point that traditional knowledge is undervalued with respect to book learning:

> *Though you're doing your part here, you're not getting your part coming back from Iwokrama. What I would expect at the end of the day is that we should be able to have boys that are actually, though they don't have a degree or anything in biology or, you know these kind of thing, that they would be able to actually operate practically on a par with these people, with the academics. You have a doctor come. That doctor, he's got a certificate, he gets so many U.S. [dollars] per day, but this poor man comes, then they give him a thousand five hundred [Guyanese dollars: about five pounds in total] and they say that's good enough, because that's good pay in Guyana. A thousand five hundred is not good pay in Guyana, because that is why the public service is fighting for more salary. [. . .] Cause they [the local experts] got the practical, you [outsiders such as myself] got the academic, so . . .*

As I was leaving Guyana, however, Iwokrama was beginning to use local experts as consultants and to pay them appropriately.

In words echoing the failings of institutionalised education outlined in Chapter 2, Uncle Henry (Surama Rest House, 22/6/02) claims that agricultural workshops are rendered virtually redundant through their emphasis on theory over practice, book learning over local knowledge, and institutional modes of knowledge transfer. Despite having undergone such training "about a hundred times", Uncle Henry concludes that:

> *after it's finished now, it's a dead end. There's nothing now till you put on the ground. Teaching the indigenous people about that background, they know they are not—their education, and most of them when they go, whatever notes they have, they don't go back to it. Because to*

100   *Hybrid Voices and Collaborative Change*

> *them it's no use going back to those notes, because they have nothing to practise with, you know, to try, experiment with. But you put that and you start up, I told them, "Start a plot of land, and experiment with that [. . .] what we want you to do is do a two-acre plot." For people see the real way of land preparation, how you plant, how you . . . what plant husbandry is, how many times per week you goes to your farm, how you deal with weeds, how you deal with insects, when the harvesting time come, how you harvest, how you dry out, how you select or grade, and then how you would store.*

Walter elsewhere compares the imported format unfavourably to traditional modes of transmitting information with their connection to local practice and a two-way flow of ideas and expertise (Toka, 8/11/00):

> *A day is not too long, but, as I said, if you don't get anything in a whole day session, it gets boring. [Tom asks if there would not be a similar problem with the traditional format.] It wouldn't be a problem now, because of the two-ways flow of activity. This is not from the Makushi perspective I was talking [earlier], this is like everyday living now, why and how a person can be active in a workshop, and why it can be boring. If you and me did a workshop and we, you talk, I talk, but how would it look you talking all the time and me concentrating on just what you say? It get bored.*

These shortcomings in practically based communication can occasionally be magnified into a total lack of consultation, as when Iwokrama unilaterally overruled an NRDDB election process or planned an aerial walkway over the forest without negotiating with or even informing the NRDDB. These failings in the Iwokrama approach are attributed by one Makushi elder to researchers "becoming Guyanese" and acting in the paternalistic manner of the government and other coastal Guyanese towards Amerindians:

> *Guyanese Coastlanders have a culture "We know best, we know it all", and we the Amerindians don't know nothing.*

There is a real danger, then, that Iwokrama workers at times replicate the paternalist approach of previous international development ideology, as described by Redford and Sanderson (2000:1363):

> It is not uncommon for top-down political coalitions to assume the role of speaking for the poor without showing that they actually do. The world of nongovernmental organisations and umbrella organisations speaking on behalf of indigenous or voiceless peoples in the forest can make superior claims to advocacy only if they can truly represent the populations they defend.

Participatory Voice in Development Discourse 101

Such factors are examples of the *vox nullius* approach to Amerindian perspectives that typify coastal Guyanese attitudes and seem, to some extent, to detract from Iwokrama's own ideals, so that the advocacy and co-optation that international aid structures almost force upon them are at times uncomfortably close to the paternalistic attitude of the government. In the following analysis of an extract from an Iwokrama-sponsored Management Planning Workshop I will discuss the effects on discourse between the local communities and Iwokrama of the structural conditions described in Chapter 2 and the history of development discourse, including previous experiences of discourse between the communities and Iwokrama, described in this chapter. In particular I will consider the extent to which difference perceptions of the prestige of the participants, the *orders of indexicality* that are effects of such historical conditions, force unwanted interpretations on the actions of the Iwokrama representative and lead to a breakdown in communications.

IWOKRAMA-DOMINATED DISCOURSE

Text 3.1 comes from the Management Planning Workshop referred to above, organised by Iwokrama as one of a series of events in different locations which were aimed at training local participants in a holistic approach to development based on a systemic exploitation of community resources. The overall strategy was to integrate community experience into a general procedural framework used by development organisations internationally. The design encouraged participation from locals in an exchange of knowledge and ideas and so, in theory, is a response to the standard one-way flow of information that Walter criticises as boring. Similar workshops took place in several communities over a period of some weeks, with Text 3.1 coming from the workshop in Toka run by Gordon and Sara from Iwokrama. The general format was a presentation of the theory to the entire group from the Iwokrama representatives, followed by discussions in two smaller groups, with the two groups reporting back and comparing notes in the evenings. Each of the smaller discussion groups comprised around a dozen participants from the community and an Iwokrama representative to facilitate discussion. The facilitation role included stimulating and maintaining the flow of discussion and the writing up of salient points on a flipchart. Although the format was relatively flexible, ultimate control over the turn-taking character of the event lay with the facilitators. The reporting-back sessions were more or less jointly constructed by Iwokrama and local participants, though the Iwokrama representatives remained the focal points of the discussions. Throughout the tone was friendly and relatively informal, particularly in the discussion groups. Text 3.1 is taken from one of the discussion groups. The Iwokrama representative here is Sara (**S**), the designer of the workshop

102 *Hybrid Voices and Collaborative Change*

programme, and amongst the participants are two of the most prominent members of the local community, introduced above, Walter (**W**), later to become chairman of the NRDDB, and Nicholas (**N**), village pastor and ex-touchau. Nicholas and Walter are extremely aware of the conditions of Amerindians in Guyana at the close of the twentieth century, as has been demonstrated by the various quotations I have drawn on in this book so far, and both are fluent and articulate speakers of English. Walter, however, is a native Makushi speaker, having learned English chiefly at school, while Nicholas was raised as a native English speaker on the coast and has a largely passive knowledge of Makushi. The discussion group took place in a classroom of the village school with the facilitator standing at the front of the class with a flipchart at hand and the remainder of the participants seated on school benches. At this point in the management planning exercise Walter is to take on the role of facilitator, previously played by Sara, as an exercise in skills-transfer. The importance of the event in terms of community control over development issues is not lost on Walter, who refers to this at various points. In Walter's words (lines 31–33 in Text 3.1), this exercise provides Toka with the chance of:

31 (xxx) identifying what we could do right away, could do right away, like then, right?,
32 what we could do, what we can. .what is. .what we are <u>cap</u>able of doing. .by
33 ourself.

Similarly Walter emphasises that:

57 Sara is not
58 going to do it for us anymore. .we've got to do it for ourselves.

And even more explicitly:

66 Actually, it's a. .a. .a s-. .a
67 step for us in this community to show er if we have the potentials at doing it. .because
68 later on that. .later on we're going to do all the. .the 27 that we have listed yesterday.
69 Right? We're not going to depend on Iwokrama for er. .come and do this any more,
70 but we'll have to do it for ourselves. Remember this is not for Iwokrama, this is for
71 the people in this village.

In lines 31 to 33 Walter takes great care with his choice of words, changing from "could" to "can" to "are capable" (which he stresses). The choice of "are capable" emphasises the notion of skills existing within

Participatory Voice in Development Discourse 103

the community waiting to be tapped, in contrast to the rejected 'can' and 'could', which suggest less agentive and less immediate possibilities respectively. The issue of existing community ability is echoed elsewhere in Walter's talk, as in his "we have the potentials" in line 67. For Walter, then, control over discourse formats such as the workshop represents a display of ability and a step towards community control over decision-making. Moving through Text 3.1, however, there emerges a pattern whereby control of the discourse, after being passed ceremonially to Walter, shifts back, over several stages, from Walter to Sara. These stages are analysed sequentially as:

I.	Lines 1–11.	Preamble.
II.	12–27.	Handover.
III.	28–121.	Walter's confident presentation.
IV.	122–157.	Walter's growing unease.
V.	157–182.	Sara's concern for Walter.
VI.	183–212.	Sara's guiding of the process.
VII.	213–275.	Sara's taking over of the process, reformulating work done by Walter in stage III.

I shall follow each section first with an objective glossing of the text and then with a more subjective interpretation of what the section reveals with respect to the temporary and long-standing roles of the different participants. I will finish the chapter with a discussion of my interpretations in light of the background to NRDDB discourse provided in these opening chapters and develop a model of authority in language which contextualises the discourse within the wider sociocultural framework. This model will be used as a basis for analysing later texts in which the 'top-down' control that ultimately imposes itself on the discourse of Text 3.1 is effectively subverted in various ways by speakers from the local communities.

In Stages I and II (ll.1-27) Sara introduces the topic of water management to be developed later on and relates it to the workshop process so far (3) and what is expected to follow (3–4), restating the whole purpose of the workshop (4–7) in terms that emphasise Toka as the agents of their own development (5–6) and Iwokrama as no more than facilitators (7). Once the local participants seem to have no objections to this arrangement, Sara is able to initiate the next stage (12), which is to have Walter take over her role as facilitator. Sara does this indirectly, checking that Walter is "in shape" (16), and Walter agrees to take over (17). Sara and Walter then between them get Vanessa to take over the role of writing up brief notes on the discourse, mixing a direct summons and a command (20&21) with an indirect suggestion (25). Another prolonged period of off-the-record discussion (26) brings this phase to a close, and Sara takes the initiative in reopening the process (27).

104   *Hybrid Voices and Collaborative Change*

Text 3.1   Management Planning Workshop, Toka Schoolhouse, 19/3/2000

Transcription conventions are given on page **xiii–xiv**.
I and II: Preamble and Handover.

```
 1 S:  The second thing is is whether or not we want to continue with drinking water,
 2     (xxxxxxx). Now (xxxxx) topic of discussion, where do we go from here. (xxx).
 3     What=what is, what kind of thing you've put together so ↑far and what is the
 4     future. .next steps of activity. (xx) remember, this is just the beginning, it's a (?step)
 5     assessment. Of (x) developing a management plan. .erm, what does T-. .what does T-
 6     want to do. .and to what extent would you like to. .continue to have Iwokrama involved
 7     in. .in. .in facilitating it. And in. .in building capacity to to (xx).
 8     ((data omitted))
 9 S:  Okay, so you're prepared to finish off the water. [Okay.]
10 W:  [I feel] the whole point (xxxx).
11     ((unclear background discussion))
12 S:  I wish. .I was hoping that maybe you could (xx) do it (to the other xx room).
13     Just kind of get one person to do what er . . . what. .er er I was hoping (?to be)
14     facilitator and one (person xx) to do the planning (xxxxx). Yeah?
15 W:  Okay.
16 S:  Right, Walter, you in shape for this?
17 W:  A'right.
18 S:  (Or we could) try . . .
19 W:  (xxxxx).
20 S:  (xx) did you want (xxx). So we need. .two other people . . . Vanessa. .Nicholas . . .
21 W:  VANESSA! COME NOW! °(xxxx)°.
22     ((shuffling)) (12s)
23     Come here and do some writing.
24     (9s)
25 S:  Here, Vanessa, (you could do with this pen).
26     ((mumbling)) (50s)
27     So . . .
```

Interpretation of Stages I and II

While this section of discourse allows Sara and Walter to work together, and leads to Walter becoming the focus of the event, it is Sara who has provided the *raison d'être* for the exercise and established both the content and the structure, moving the process along from preamble to handover and from handover to Walter's presentation. Thus, while Walter now has the floor, both the field of activity and the interpersonal roles within the workshop have been established within Sara's terms and as under her ultimate control. While this relationship is to be expected, given that Sara has been invited by the local community to give the workshop, it potentially sets Walter up in the contradictory roles of facilitator and evaluee simultaneously.

In Stage III (ll.28-121) Walter begins his presentation. He sums up the nature of the management plan and emphasising the importance of this to the village (28–38). He also suggests that this is not just a dry run, but

Participatory Voice in Development Discourse   105

III. Walter's confident presentation.

28 W: Right. .erm. .right. .start talking about drinking water problem. The erm (shortfall here),
29   right? There was three activities or key sections (xxxx).
30   (11s)
31   (xxx) identifying what we could do right away, could do right away, like then, right?,
32   what we could do, what we can. .what is. .what we are capable of doing. .by
33   ourself. .(xxx) for own water. .uh, and we talk about. .and one of the. .why we choose
34   this here because it was more important than any other thing else. So, er. .we started
35   off by the well, but this one here should be worked on the fixed current. .well for
36   short-term access. And with this here now. .this is what, this is what they call
37   activity . . . and er . . . the method. .or the way of doing=working this out right is through
38   the management. .plan. .is using these thi:ngs. .Right?
39   (23s)
40   And this is what we were actually doing yesterday afternoon . . . with. .er. .we could do
41   this one here and said what is the proposed solution. .and er. .for each solution, (check).
42   We said. .what you think would have been the best thing? How you (?go about) by
43   doing this thing here, right?
44 S: Right.
45 W: But those this. .how does this fit with the problem, go within all the other areas of
46   natural resources? Now . . . when we doing that thing there, how. .how is it going
47   to. .affect the creek or. .affect the people or affect the animals. .and so forth? Right?
48   So when we planning all of those things, looking at . . . we looking at how it would. .er
49   (?pump up) the creek then, or the fishes in the creek, if it would disturb your fishes in
50   the creek, or if it would disturb the animal, or if it would disturb the bird, or if it
51   would destroy. .we looking at all the thing around you here. You understand? But,
52   when we say that. .we have a problem with the creek=is that it filling up, if we could
53   use the sand from the creek now. .we have the (xx) sand (xx), but this is so small. .and
54   it wouldn't show no kinda change like, i. .in the creek, that is whether it will be. .close
55   up with sand. So, this is a. .(concluding stage),< that is why the action (xxxxxxx)
56   through all of these stage here.> We have 1, 2, 3, 4, 5 . . . just to do one of it. Okay?
57   All these thing here. And now. .what we doing this morning is that they not. .Sara is
58   not going to do it for us anymore. .we've got to do it for ourselves. We did this one
59   here? Yesterday?
60   ((noise of flipchart))
61   And now we doing this one here.
62   (p)
63   Okay?
64   (p)
65   And, er, while we talk now, using this thing here, remember . . . using this method and
66   as we come up with ideas Vanessa is going to write it for us. Actually, it's a. .a s-. .a
67   step for us in this community to show er if we have the potentials at doing it. .because
68   later on that. .later on we're going to do all the. .the 27 that we have listed yesterday.
69   Right? We're not going to depend on Iwokrama for er. .come and do this any more,
70   but we'll have to do it for ourselves. Remember this is not for Iwokrama, this is for
71   the people in this village.
72   (2s)
73   So shall we go ahead?
74   (p)
75   Let me check off this one.
76   (39s) ((a little mumbling))
77   Let everything fund. .funded reserve . . . reservoir
78 N: (Matty[1] Guyana, Guywa) help us?

(continued)

106 Hybrid Voices and Collaborative Change

```
 79  W:  (/Gaan²/ with) Guywa?
 80  N:  (Let it be with) Guywa.
 81  W:  How we doin that? Two or one? It's one we got to do first.
 82  N:  Why you can't do all two one time?
 83  W:  Think you can do it? If you think you could ma:nage it?
 84  S:  Uh-uh.
 85  W:  (xxxx). Now |what Sara was saying| earlier is that we finish off with this here
 86  N:              |You gotta (x x x x x)|
 87  W:  and then we er. .when we finish we go then to the way forward. Unless we could
 88       do all two one time, way forward (and everything).
 89       (4s)
 90       Well let us see how we feel. .let us give it a try if we could er do all two at one time.
 91       (2s) ((muted muttering))
 92       Not po:ssible.
 93  ?:   °(xxxx)°
 94  W:  One you dealing with Guywa and next thing you dealing with the British High
 95       Commission.
 96       (5s) ((muttered interchange between ?N and ?S.))
 97       So, what . . .
 98       (5s) ((muttering continues))
 99       Now how does this fit with the problems, goals, and all the other areas of natural
100      resource, socioeconomic issues or interests to do other activities? How would
101      this. .when we're going about doing this, how would it affect (xx), how would it
102      affect all of these thing here= =logging, fishing, ecotourism or . . . agriculture?
103      Garbage disposal, education, sustenance et cetera.
104  N:  (xx pick up xxx see what copying, na?)
105  W:  Uh?
106  N:  I don't think I actually get the idea here.
107  S:  It's right behind them. °°(xxx)°° Uhm . . .
108      (3s)
109  N:  Right, now I can see them.
110  S:  °Okay.°
111      (4s)
112      Remember this wasn't numbered like that, right? It just went down the. .the ↓list.
113      (9s)
114  N:  So uh. .how does this fit in with the problems?
115  W:  Wanna get fixed current wells for easier and safer use by children and others.
116      (3s)
117      We do the same thing with this one (here)?
118  N:  (??This what we don't understand.)
119      <<rustling of papers >>
120      (12s)
121      ((mumbling)) (61s)
```

an opportunity to discuss pressing problems (31–34). Once he has allowed
this to sink in (39) he contextualises it with respect to earlier work (40–43),
with Sara's encouragement (44), and goes on to illustrate the aims of the
workshop to link the cause, effect and repercussions of individual activities throughout the village ecology. This is done with particular reference
to the subject in question, drinking water (45–57). After early disfluencies

Participatory Voice in Development Discourse 107

such as restarts (32, 33&37), pauses and fillers (32–38), this develops into a long and coherent stretch of discourse with the one significant silence (39) apparently part of its design in that it allows time for consideration and potential feedback and provokes no signs of disfluency in Walter when he next speaks.

After going over the method, Water attempts to get the process underway (58–66), once again emphasising the importance of Toka doing this for themselves (66–71). However, there is no definite response for 39s (76), and Walter effectively responds to this by narrowing the topic of water to the specific question of the reservoir (77). Nicholas responds, introducing new considerations regarding the role of the Guyanese Water Authority (Guywa) in the process (78–82). Walter suggests this is a separate issue (81) which might make the process too complicated for the participants (83), and Sara backs up this assessment (84). However, Walter seems willing to give it a try (85–91) until he thinks through the practicalities and rejects the idea (92–98). Walter then returns to his earlier topic of water and the reservoir and relates the issue to the wider system, in line with the aims of the workshop (99–103). Again he is interrupted by Nicholas (104–118), who asks for clarification of what is being discussed, particularly in relation to the integrated approach of the workshop. Sara twice intervenes (107&110–112) to explain how the process works with respect to the written list (112). At this point (117–121) Nicholas states that he doesn't follow what is going on. Walter is unable to respond and there is a longish pause followed by prolonged background muttering.

Interpretation of Stage III

Not surprisingly, this section shows Walter taking up his combined role as facilitator/evaluee a little warily (28–38), contextualising his position in terms of the activity's importance to the community, on the one hand (28–34), and on the other in terms of adherence to Iwokrama structural norms (36–38) and their practice the previous day (40–43). Sara's following 'Right' (44) can thus be interpreted as either a sign of encouragement or as an 'official sanction' of Walter's approach, the first in a series of such ambiguous inputs. Walter is soon into his stride, and his understanding and description of the systemic nature of the process behind the management plan, particularly lines 40–43, 45–56 and 99–103, are accurate, clear and concise. Walter shows skill here in glossing the concept of integrated management behind the workshop (45–46) in terms of the particulars of everyday Makushi life, drawing connections between the expansion of the creek and animal and human welfare (46–51) and suggesting that the sand removed might be put to use elsewhere (51–55). Clearly the thinking behind the process presents no difficulties to Walter; however, the workshop process itself is not so straightforward. After reiterating both the importance of the process to the community and its adherence to Iwokrama norms

108 *Hybrid Voices and Collaborative Change*

IV. Walter's growing unease.

122 W: Right.
123   (3s)
124   Remember (?how it is) that the longest we chose this one here. .and er. .before we go
125   into this we said this was much easier using this method here. After we use
126   this. .generally a. .(thirteen. .thirteen) a. .method. .method (x) we come up with this
127   here. And what we doin now is. .we we said could tackle these two=we do these
128   two at one time. .using the same thing.
129   (6s)
130   So how would this . . . I think we should take one of them °here and leave this one.°
131 ?N: °(xxx).°
132 W: How you think this would now. .affect or how good this would be like? Would
133   it be the same thing for this (a) fixed current well for easiest and safe use by children
134   and others?
135   (3s)
136 ?S: °°(either way)°°
137 W: It would be much easier if we have this. .er. .you=the well down there with a
138   nice. .reservoir at that point. You have the pipes going all around and. .so forth.
139   ((muttering)) (6s)
140 N: If you get this, the fish would take advantage of the situation and break free.
141   And it would meet . . . what would be the expectations of government, which is
142   to bring what more water we can into close reach of . . . within. .close proximity
143   of members of the community.
144   (11s)
145 W: Rainwater fresh at the ho:me. Is that what we saying?
146 S: °(xxx ?tea. . . . .)°.
147 W: Uh?
148 S: °°(xx)°°
149 W: Remember we talk about this here, right? Yesterday, the tank and the pipes
150   going down and then getting taps going into every house. .er. .probably we get er
151   showers and. .flush toilets and so forth. Right?
152   ((mumbling and rustling of papers)) (14s)
153   The second phase here. .(the goal). .for poor people, water, using reservoirs. .over
154   current. .potable water. . . . .potable water. . . . this reservoir, over current well.
155   (8s)
156   (xxx), when you get a big help (motor transport) and . . . all the rest . . .
157 S: Walter, you managing okay? (xxx)

(55–71), Walter throws the issue of the well open to the floor. The long
pause that follows seems appropriate at this point, but when no response
is forthcoming Walter makes a further attempt to elicit input, which is
taken up by Nicholas. This initiates a prolonged exchange between Walter
and Nicholas on the nature of the process (78–86, resuming in 104–118).
Despite Walter's attempt to override Nicholas's objections, taking advantage of the temporary authority of his role as facilitator (81), Nicholas,
who is Walter's equal in terms of local standing, again queries the nature
of the process (82) and Sara intervenes to clarify matters in Walter's favour
(84). There is thus a situation developing where Walter is being forced to

Participatory Voice in Development Discourse 109

justify the *process*, as opposed to the *content* of the workshop, in the face of Nicholas's objections. This is hampering his presentation of the work at hand and drawing Sara into the role of final arbiter, as becomes clearer in the following sections.

In Stage IV (ll.122-157) Walter is less fluent than previously, with shorter, more broken stretches of speech, while what he does say is less clear in aim, displaying numerous pauses and fillers (124–128, 137, 138&150–156) and repetitions and restarts (126, 127, 130, 137&153–156). He begins with a justification of the process in terms of previous discussions with the floor (124–128), which he then relates to the immediate topic, and invites the floor to contribute their opinions (132–134), reiterating the need to tackle one aspect at a time (130). After a short pause with no response from the floor (135), Sara begins to offer what would appear to be an evaluation of the options introduced by "either way" (136), but Walter overrides Sara in a further attempt to open up the floor, expanding on his previous explanation of the options (137–138). This provokes a general reaction (139) and Nicholas then gives his (in parts enigmatic) response to the proposal (140–143). However, the floor once again fails to take up the points made (144&155), although Walter repeatedly attempts to draw them in (145–156). In his efforts to open up discussion at this point Walter summarises and clarifies Nicholas's previous comments (glossing "water" with "rainwater" and adding that it will be "fresh"), seeking confirmation that this is what the floor seeks through an explicit reference to the joint construction of the discourse by floor and facilitators, "Is that what we saying?" (145). He also calls on the floor to consider previous joint discussions on the topic (149) and twice actively solicits contributions with "right?" (149&151). Finally, he lists several potential areas of discussion (153–156). Despite these efforts, and what sound like attempts by Sara to lighten the situation (146&148), the presentation begins to lose coherence and Walter's input becomes increasingly disjointed (149–151, 153–154&156), with comparatively long pauses (139, 144&155) and mumbling from the floor (152). The increasing disfluency prompts overt concern from Sara with "Walter, you feeling okay?" (157), a comment which mirrors the earlier comment preceding Walter's participation:

16. S: Right, Walter, you in shape for this?

Interpretation of Stage IV

Overall, we can see in this section a disruption in the flow of the discourse and, as will be seen later, this begins the process whereby Sara takes over the proceedings from Walter, who is clearly becoming increasingly uncomfortable in his assumed classroom-style role standing in front of the other local participants as the focal centre of the process. This tension between Walter's habitual standing in the community and the unaccustomed

110 *Hybrid Voices and Collaborative Change*

temporary role he now finds himself playing also seems to affect participation from the floor as community members fail to respond to his prompts for contributions, such as the increasingly urgent lines 145–156. The only community participant willing to contribute is, in fact, Nicholas, whose contributions remain largely concerned with challenging the process. In the previous section Walter had responded well to one such intervention (78–86), but that section finished with Nicholas again making a challenge (104–118). This section begins with Walter responding to defend the process (122–130), which he has built up as tremendously important for the village, and attempting to involve the rest of the participants. Apart from Nicholas's contribution, however, no one from the floor takes up the discussion. Breaks open up in the discourse which would not seem overlong or intrusive in a situation where the facilitator's presentation is confident and no one doubts their control over the situation, yet in this case they might be interpreted as difficult. As no contributions seem to be forthcoming from the floor, Sara attempts to relieve the tension in the situation on

---

V. Sara's concern for Walter.

```
157  S:  Walter, you managing okay? (xxx)
158      (18s)
159      (xxxx). It's extra.
160  N:  (xxxxxxx) in that situation [it (magnifies the situation)]
161  S:                             [Okay, we can do the first one]. .(in a
         minute) . . . And
162      then you can [(see that)]
163  N:               [(The thing with Guywa is)] Guywa adjust the whole
         situation, you
164      know?
165      (48s) ((a little background muttering))
166  S:  A'right . . . What is it?. .No, Vanessa, you're not off the hook. Come back.
167      (9s)
168  W:  We're talking about >the current fix. .well. .there<=
169  N:  =This thing got more detail (now there than then).
170  S:  Do you want to erm . . . to come closer together and just sit among yourselves
171      and do your own writing? In that small group rather than using this
172      classroom style? (5s)
173      Walter? You're not feeling so good, huh? CAN SOMEBODY . . . ? Do you,
174      do you want to sit and [rest and] have somebody [else to do this?]
175  W:                         [D'you want something?]
176  N:                                                  [(That'll do nicely.)]
177  W:  You want to say something?
178      (7s)
179  S:  All right, if everybody sit together, Walter's not feeling so well. If we sit
180      together maybe it would make it easier. °Rather than standing up in front of
181      everybody.°
182      ((quiet exchange between S and ?W)) (14s)
```

Participatory Voice in Development Discourse 111

three separate occasions (136, 146–148&157), the last of these through an overt expression of concern for Walter. Sara's question (which I've repeated below) sets the tone for the following section.

Stage V (ll.157-182) begins with Sara following her overt expression of concern for Walter (157) with attempts to rearrange the format (161) and setting (166, 170–171, 173–174&179–181). Although this intervention is framed in terms of Walter's plight (157), Walter has neither overtly expressed his ill ease nor suggested a change in format, and he does not respond to Sara's question but attempts to carry on with his presentation without any of the suggested changes. Sara continues to voice her concern, however, and there seem to be two separate discourses running in parallel here, with Walter and Nicholas (in a reversal of his previous stance) attempting to discuss the issues surrounding the water supply (168) and the role of Guywa (163) while Sara performs an independent series of speech acts centred on the mechanisms of the workshop as a process and the discourse as performance. As a result of this mixed focus the section displays far more interruptions (169) and overlaps (161, 163, 175&176) than previous sections.

Interpretation of Stage V

We can see in this short but tremendously important section how Sara's concerned intervention makes overt Iwokrama's authority with regard to control over the workshop process and hence the fact that Walter's temporary role as facilitator is embedded within the community's longer-term role as beneficiaries. This relationship was clear in the setting up of the exercise and has been latent throughout the discourse thus far or expressed through tokens of encouragement such as "okay" from Sara, which, although relatively unintrusive, point to her role as 'evaluator'. In this section and the end of the previous section, Sara has in fact been initiating a parallel discourse to Walter's in terms of tenor, through interrupting him and speaking over him (157, 161&174); of mode, through shifting from his decontextualised use of language (149–156) towards more immediate Commentaries (157, 166&170–174) and calls for Action (161–162&179–181); and of field, through ignoring the topic under discussion to focus on Walter's health (157, 173–174&179–181) and the workshop as process (161–162, 166&170–171). This resetting of the *register* of the discourse (the realisation of field, tenor and mode, introduced in Chapter 1 and discussed further in Chapter 6) reaches its culmination in lines 179–181, where Sara takes it upon herself to speak on Walter's behalf and so sets in motion the process by which Walter becomes increasingly marginal to proceedings and Sara regains control over the discourse, first guiding the process more overtly (section VI) and then resuming complete control (section VII).

In Stage VI (11.183-212), despite Sara's concerned attempts to change the format, Walter returns to the immediate topic and again attempts to draw

112   *Hybrid Voices and Collaborative Change*

VI. Sara guides the process.

183 W: Okay, the goal for the short term, why don't we say it is that er the potable water
184   using the reservoir over current well will bring water right to your home.
185   (4s)
186 N: It would make water more accessible (then). .°(in the community).° With easy
187   access.
188   (4s)
189 W: Lighter work for the women?
190 S: Wh. .where are you? Number two? What was. .where are we? Positive-negative?
191   (8s)
192 W: °See, that could be the first.°
193   ((faint background discussion)) (4s)
194   °We get number three (xxxxx). Probably getting a . . . °
195 S: °Which (xx) you want to do?° So: . . . how does it work, (what are its goals)?
196 W: Try and look at the positive and negative of er. .of the water down here now.
197   Now, wha. .what we've taken about positive is the good things that this will do, and
198   the negative is the bad things. .will happen, like. Uhm, if there is |any]
199 N: [They've] done
200   number one, whole. I wanna know what that thing mean: "potable water using
201   reservoir over current well".
202 S: How would you like to say it? ((slightly irritated?))
203 N: No, I wanna know what it means.
204 S: Say what you want to say and I'll write it down. ((irritated?))
205   (4s)
206 N: Does it mean. .to be getting (brought here)?
207 S: Okay. .let. .tell me what to [write.]
208 N: [(that's what)] . . . (that's what I was going to say now, we
209   an't) set up a dam. It would make the water more. .near a point where you could
210   access it more easily, <and that would meet the requirement of the
211   community> . . . when it comes to accessing the water . . . So that's (all).
212   (7s)

---

in the floor by summarising the discussion so far and throwing it open to
question (183–184). Again this leads to comments from Nicholas (186–187),
which, after a short silence (188), Walter once more glosses and seeks to confirm through his rising intonation (189). However, Sara interrupts and again
attempts to focus on the workshop as a process (190). This time Walter picks
up on Sara's lead into matters of process (192–194). However, Walter shows
hesitancy (193) and uncertainty (194) and Sara interrupts again, forcing the
pace by defining the questions to be tackled at this point and relating them
to the process framework (as defined by Sara) (195). Walter responds to the
task, also providing a clear gloss on "positive" and "negative" (196–198),
but Nicholas interrupts and once more questions an aspect of work "already
covered" (199–201). This draws an irritated response from Sara (202), who
has become a more overtly active facilitator by taking over Vanessa's writing-
up role and who, instead of answering Nicholas's request for clarification,
asks him to clarify things himself. There are two more such exchanges (203–
204&206–207) before Nicholas responds to his own request for clarification

Participatory Voice in Development Discourse   113

(208–211). This section again displays a high frequency of interruptions (190&195) and overlaps (199&208) as interpersonal roles are reorganised and subject matter is negotiated.

Interpretation of Stage VI

Having re-entered the process as an active participant in the previous section, expressing her concern over the material setting and Walter's discomfort, Sara now begins to intervene more directly, first prompting Walter (190, 195, 202) and then taking up an overt position of control (204, 207). This display of ultimate authority over the proceedings shifts control over the discourse away from Walter as temporary facilitator and back to Sara, despite a burgeoning dialogue between Walter and Nicholas (183–189). This is apparent here in two ways. Firstly, Walter cedes to Sara's reflexive discourse on the process itself, something he avoided in the previous stretch of discourse (196); secondly, once Sara has succeeded in focusing attention on the workshop as process, she immediately moves beyond questions of the material setting to once again redefine the register of the discussion. She does this in terms of field, by changing the topic (195); tenor, by reversing the exchange structure (202); and mode, by emphasising the role of the written medium (204–207). Once back in control, Sara attempts to force the pace of the discourse as process, and seems impatient with Nicholas's backtracking. Sara's requests that Nicholas rephrase what is being entered on the flipchart might represent a genuine attempt to keep the discourse on local terms, yet the two direct imperatives (204&207) show who is ultimately in charge of the process.

This section contains a series of interventions from Sara aimed at keeping the workshop as a process 'on course' and these interventions, along with her earlier attempts to rearrange the physical format of the workshop (166–181), highlight what appears to be a fundamental difference of approach between the Iwokrama representatives and local participants as to whether the workshop is a practical exercise intended to discuss pertinent issues with a view to resolving them or simply the presentation of a working model that draws on local issues as exemplars of problems in the development process but which is not concerned with resolving them during the workshop itself. This difference in perspectives would seem to imbue the remainder of the text as Sara repeatedly attempts to steer the workshop as a process along a preordained path while the local representatives seem anxious to resolve practical issues as they arise. From here on in Walter's contributions come as if from the floor rather than as facilitator, a role now entirely played by Sara.

At the beginning of Stage VII (ll.213-275) Sara reintroduces the activity in hand (213–214), relates it to work done earlier in the workshop (221) and emphasises the importance of the process and the systemic linkages within the local ecology (216–217&223–225), thereby duplicating Walter's

114 *Hybrid Voices and Collaborative Change*

VII. Sara takes over process, reformulating work done by Walter in Stage III.

```
213 S:   Okay, so. .so the activity . .is. .to do what? >To get a reservoir. .set up. .in the
214      village?< Right? That's the activity?
215 N?:  Yeah.
216 S:   °Right.° And then. .how does that fit with. . . . with all these other things in terms of
217      of agricultu:re, health, and all of those. .is the next thing you're talking about? Makes
218      it more accessible, makes it easier . . . maybe healthier, those kind of stuff, right?
219      So. .so, let's just back up. So, you wanna ↑do . . . ↓three.
220      (15s)
221      And remember this from yesterday. .the various points we've built, right?
222      (5s)
223      Right? And re. .re . . . and so. .that's one, it is "How does it ↑fit with other things in the
224      village?", and you're saying it makes it more accessible an' easier. So . . .
225      (6s)
226      Any other . . . things [to go with]
227 N:                         [Safer], it was safer.
228 S:   Sa:fer. ((writing it down?))
229 W:   °(xxx) safer (xxx).°
230 S:   (xxx).
231      (9s)
232 S:   Because drinking water is such a straightforward thing, these two collapse into
233      one basically. I mean 'cause it's not like you're talking about lo:gging or. .or cutting
234      down trees to do agriculture, right? So 1 and 2 would. .
235 N:   Less time taken to. .t= =for your water.
236 S:   °°Yeah. 1 and 2.°° Less time taken to acquire (our) water. So, less labour,
237      right?
238 ?:   ((grunt of assent))
239      (14s)
240 S:   Mm-hmm. Anything else?
241      (6s)
242 W:   Encourage agr. .kitchen gardens.
243 S:   Encourage agriculture, right?
244      (20s)
245      °Anything else?°
246 W:   Is it okay that hoping they erm. .a flush toilet system (xxxxx)?
247 S:   In the future?
248 W:   °Mm-hmm.°
249 S:   But that's not meant to be activity right now? (Eh,) the activity right
250      now is to find somebody to fund . . . the reservoir. .and the pipes. .to certain points,
251      right? So, potential future . . . so that's potential.
252 N:   I think maybe we should put that part.
253      ((W and N mutter a while)) (12s)
254 S:   We have. .you talked about this yesterday, activity (xx). How it's going to each
255      ↑home and. .and. .
256 N:   We could have taken it from under. .easier access, °(xxx)°.
257      (12s)
258 S:   (What about other) sanitation, Walter? Flush toilet system, (?sanitary towel)
259      system. (This is to put under) positive=
260 N:   =We don't see water in the home as something that should be automatic.
261      ((mumbling from floor)) (16s)
262 S:   They would get what?
```

(continued)

Participatory Voice in Development Discourse   115

263	((further mumbling, with N's voice suddenly becoming prominent.)) (6s)
264 N:	. . . not a necessity, you could collect (more than) water from outside). I mean,
265	which can happen,
266 S:	[Could everyone]
267 W:	[When we] talked about the flush toilet, it was the. .around the nearby
268	well. .(xxxxx). Nearby homes to the wells, because of er. .(away then from) the shit-
269	juice bringing into the wells and the water stream.
270 S:	Right. So it links (xxxx). Sanitation, right?
271 W:	Right.
272 S:	We also talked yesterday about ecotourist things. .having better water supply. So
273	that if we collapse . . . in here we could do one and two together, kind of collapse it
274	in. .okay? So . . .
275	((mumbling leading to laughing, especially from N)) (23s)

earlier efforts. As she assumes control, Sara at first only rhetorically asks for feedback (216–217), immediately providing her own answer (217–218) and drawing her own conclusions about how to build on this (219). This does lead her actively to encourage participation from the floor in choosing the topic of discussion (219, 221&226) and allows time for responses to be forthcoming (220, 222, 225&231), with Nicholas (227) and Walter (229) duly obliging on the third occasion. Then Sara returns to the process itself, suggesting ways of saving time by condensing tasks (232–234). Nicholas's utterance (235) might be a response to this, saying that the suggestion will leave less time for water, but is taken as input to the debate on water itself, which is thus reintroduced (236–237). Sara again solicits responses from the floor, on any aspect of the process, with "anything else?"(240&245), and allows the time necessary for this (239, 241&244). This pays off with two contributions from Walter (242&246). Walter's "Is it okay . . . ?" (246) demonstrates how far he has formally ceded control to Sara, who then goes on to re-orientate the activity according to the prescribed process—as she sees it (249–251). This causes a reaction from both Walter and Nicholas (252–253) and Sara seems to return to the topic in hand (254–255), with Nicholas contributing this time (256). After a further pause (257), this time with no response forthcoming, Sara introduces the topic of sanitation (258–259), which encourages further participation from Walter and Nicholas as well as discussion on the floor (260–269). Sara sums this up (270) and extends the topic into new areas, again suggesting condensing topics (272–274). The section ends with discussion on the floor turning into a joke (275)—about ecotourists and "shit-juice", no doubt.

Interpretation of Stage VII

This section shows a decrease in the rate of interruptions and overlaps and, though these still occur (227, 235, 256, 260&267), they tend to display a continuity of discourse as opposed to the oppositional nature of

116 Hybrid Voices and Collaborative Change

the interruptions and overlaps in the previous two sections. In line 227 Nicholas is supplying an answer that predicts the full form of Sara's question in line 226, with Sara echoing and writing up the answer provided. In line 235 Nicholas similarly seems to be predicting a point Sara is making as evidenced by Sara's positive evaluation, echo and development of his contribution. Further evidence of the collaborative nature of this section is provided by the repeated use of discourse markers aimed at the cooperative flow of discourse such as "right?" to elicit evaluation (214, 218, 221, 237&270); rising intonation calling for clarification or confirmation of specific points (214, 247&262); "anything else?" to elicit further contributions (240&245); a polar question (246); and a wh-question (262).

The section again demonstrates how emphasis is laid on the process at the expense of content, with Sara attempting to condense separate issues and to re-orientate the discussion towards funding after Walter has introduced the topics of agriculture and flush toilets: "But that's not meant to be the activity right now?" (249). This emphasis would appear to go counter to attempts by Walter and Nicholas throughout to use the workshop as a forum for solving actual problems and not just as a trial run (cf. 31–34), something I observed on several occasions during my fieldwork when community participants devoted great amounts of time to resolving questions from the floor, often running into the evening, even when these were not directly related to the ongoing flow of discourse. Control of the topic is also an issue when Sara introduces sanitation (258), which is later treated as if it arose spontaneously from the floor (270), and more importantly when Sara twice makes the unilateral decision that some topics are simpler or less important than others and can therefore be condensed—an imposition of outside presuppositions.

This section works successfully in terms of facilitator–floor interaction, with Sara speaking fluently and encouraging participation (219, 226, 240, 247, 258, 262, 270). However, this success is achieved at a cost, as it is clearly now Sara, as the Iwokrama representative, who is in control of the situation, directing information flow (216–218, 223–224, 254) and overall structure (232–234, 249–251, 258–259, 272–274). Walter accepts and seems more comfortable with this state of affairs, acting as a member of the floor in a similar role to that of Nicholas, his equal in the community. The clear break from Walter's performance as facilitator that this section demonstrates is emphasised by Sara reintroducing the activity from scratch and going over some of the work earlier done by Walter in discussing the linkages in the management plan and the relevance of previous work during his confident presentation. Such repetition potentially creates the impression that Walter's contribution was either a trial run or a misfire and that now the real thing is getting under way, with Sara's role as evaluator consequently enhanced. In fact, Walter explained to me some time later (Toka, 9/11/00) that he had been aware that Sara was taking over but that he was caught between facilitating and contributing from the floor and, feeling

Participatory Voice in Development Discourse   117

that the format did not allow him to combine these roles, he was not too unhappy at Sara resuming the facilitator role.

This section is very important in that it shows a successful period of dialogue, as demonstrated by the relative fluency of the exchanges, but it also highlights that within the NGO-based workshop format this was achieved only through the outside-facilitator/local-floor opposition that this whole exercise was supposed to break down. Sara's retaking of the floor and leading of the discussion are no doubt appropriate personal reactions to the growing unease of Walter's presentation and are the natural resources of workshop facilitators in the NGO format, aimed at maintaining the pace of the discourse and adhering to preset goals and schedules; however, they are not conducive of the type of two-way participation Iwokrama is seeking and do not appear to be appropriate for skills-transfer to the local community. This is particularly unfortunate bearing in mind Walter's high hopes for this process and the relevance he has attached to it in terms of the community's capacities and associated prestige.

DISCUSSION OF TEXT 3.1 IN THE WIDER SOCIAL CONTEXT

While Iwokrama's intentions generally, and in the Management Planning Workshop specifically, may be to realign the relations of power that have historically underwritten discourse in development, as outside professional development workers sanctioned by the Government of Guyana they carry with them the baggage of this history, including their own history of discourse with local communities and the paternal attitude inscribed in the Amerindian Act. An awareness of these long-standing power relations is likely to colour the attitudes of the various participants in different ways and to affect their contributions to the discourse accordingly, no matter the temporary roles and relations that are formally established as part of the official purpose of the event. As van Dijk (2008:72) says:

> Speaker/writers and recipients by definition have different models of the same communicative event; such differences may lead to negotiations about the shared aspects of their context models, but also to misunderstanding and conflict.

Clearly it would be wrong to attempt to read the minds of the various participants in Text 3.1; but it would also be unreasonable to discuss the shifts of *footing* within it (Goffman 1974, 1981) as if these were consequences of the text in isolation, divorced from the previous experience of the participants and their knowledge and expectations of each other and of the event (for a discussion of this question, see Schegloff [1999a, 1999b] and Billig [1999a, 1999b]). In the workshop, therefore, it would not be

118   *Hybrid Voices and Collaborative Change*

unreasonable to suggest that, no matter how much Iwokrama speakers attempt to background the unequal power relations between themselves and the community, these are always latent in the context as a level of expectation from the community that they will be lectured at and have the scope of their discourse constrained to suit the aims of the historically dominant group. In this particular instance, the fact that the workshop was instigated and designed by Iwokrama workers is likely to reinforce these expectations, as will the schoolroom setting, given the history of banking pedagogy described in Chapter 2. There is always the danger, therefore, that a misplaced or misconstrued word from one of the speakers will bring these background expectations to the fore and that, as a result, local participants will react by reverting to long-standing *frames* (Goffman 1974) for interpreting the discourse and their role within it.

Text 3.1 contains inherent tensions as it is simultaneously an exercise in self-management and a discussion of community issues, and there are several points at which the tension between these two goals come to the surface. For example, when Sara intervenes to focus on the mechanisms of the discourse, interrupting discussions on specific issues, she temporarily reframes the discourse as a workshop, over which she ultimately has control, rather than as a discussion of community issues, an area in which the local speakers possess relevant knowledge and authority. This occurs at several points in the text before Sara actually takes over control of the workshop at line 213 (see lines 136, 161–162, 170–174, 179–180 and 190), and corresponds to a different emphasis on process and practice generally from development workers on the one hand and the local community on the other within NRDDB–Iwokrama discourse. As suggested by Gordon (see Chapter 2), local participants are only secondarily worried about issues such as the sustainability of the environment after more immediate concerns such as feeding their family. For such participants practice is clearly going to be more important than process. On the other hand, development agencies are themselves the objects of stronger structural forces, coming under great pressure from their funding bodies to produce quantifiable results at a steady rate if they wish to secure future funding (Chambers 1997:66). This can result in an emphasis on getting through one process and on to the next, an approach which at times rides roughshod over more qualitative targets and means of evaluation. A very concrete example of this within wider development practice is the building of wells, where meeting or surpassing a target is often taken as the measure of success and considerations of whether the wells are appropriately situated or even functioning at all can be left behind.[3] In terms of discourse, Iwokrama is at times guilty at the microlevel of overloading presentations with information (Bartlett 2002) and at the macrolevel of moving ahead with projects before they are properly understood by local participants. Apart from fostering misunderstanding, the emphasis on external processes places Iwokrama in the position of experts and local communities as trainees.

There is thus a momentum building up within Text 3.1 towards Iwokrama control, though this remains only an undercurrent for the first half of the text. However, this parallel discourse means that whenever Sara utters what from her perspective are words of encouragement or assistance for Walter (as in lines 44, 84, 107, 110, 146 and perhaps line 148), it is possible that these are heard as evaluations of Walter's performance within the workshop format, so foregrounding the teacher–pupil/knowledgeable–unknowledgeable roles that the workshop was designed to overcome. This may be seen by local participants as a means of Sara reclaiming control over the discourse as a whole. The tension between the two discourses comes to a climax in section VI when Sara intervenes to enquire about Walter's health and to rearrange the format of the workshop in order to assist him; it is after this explicit if temporary shift to management of the workshop as the focus of attention that the facilitator role passes to Sara and Walter gradually retreats to the floor.

To finish this chapter I will focus on line 157, as this appears to be what sets the change of control in motion, though the analysis would account for section VI as a whole:

157 S: *Walter, you managing okay?*

We can analyse this utterance in terms of the wording Sara uses and the *position* that she adopts with these words, or which she is perceived to take up, in relation to the ongoing discourse as part of a longer history of relations. This relationship has been formalised in Positioning Theory (Harré and van Langenhove 1999) through the model of a *Positioning Triangle* (Figure 3.1).

This Positioning Triangle represents the idea that at any given point within an evolving *storyline* a speaker uses an appropriate discourse act[4] to take up a position, establishing an expectation of reciprocal rights and obligations with their interlocutors. This act of *subject positioning* immediately becomes part of the context as it is absorbed into the storyline, altering its influence upon the continuing cycle.

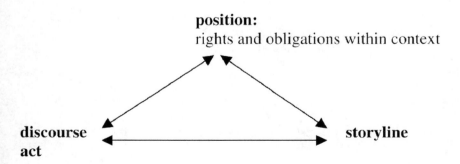

Figure 3.1 Positioning Triangle (adapted from Harré and van Langenhove 1999).

120   *Hybrid Voices and Collaborative Change*

Positions:
Walter's rights as facilitator;
Sara's obligations as co-worker.

Acts:	**Storyline:**
Asking if Walter is okay	Walter appearing ill at ease
to show concern.	while facilitating discussion;
	history of egalitarian discourse between
	Iwokrama and NRDDB.

Figure 3.2   Positioning Triangle of Sara's intended real-time positioning?

Analysing line 157 from Sara's point of view we can suggest, given Iwokrama's overall egalitarian approach to interpersonal relations in all NRDDB events, that her act represents nothing more than a sign of empathy with a co-worker who is struggling in a difficult situation, as set out in Figure 3.2.

From the community perspective, however, the storyline might be rather different, given their experience with external agencies and the cumulative effects of Sara's previous interventions. As a result, her intervention here, and in particular her choice of words, *"Walter, you **managing** okay?"*, might well seem to be the realisation of a very different triangle in which Sara is questioning Walter's ability to act as facilitator[5] (Figure 3.3).

Such an understanding would be natural given the long-term social structures, both in Guyana and the development paradigm in general, in which the discourse is embedded, and once such a misunderstanding occurs (and goes unnoticed) older traditions than Iwokrama's egalitarianism take over the proceedings. In response, Walter falls back on a role with which he feels more comfortable: being a prominent contributor from the floor, a role akin to that of elders within the more open discourse systems of the local Makushi population, held after sports and church and with a far less clearly demarcated boundary between floor and chair.

Positions:
Sara/Iwokrama as leaders:
Walter as trainee;
Iwokrama's right to lead the process;
Community obligation to listen.

Acts:	**Storyline:**
Sara retakes control over the proceedings	Iwokrama representatives as expert
by questioning Walter's ability	scientists teaching new knowledge
to manage and speaking for him.	to Amerindians.

Figure 3.3   Positioning Triangle of local interpretation of Sara's positioning?

Participatory Voice in Development Discourse 121

Viewed in these terms, the disruptive effect of Sara's interventions are not so much a result of her taking up an inappropriate position as of the *limitations* placed upon her by her status within the longer-term history of relations between the local communities and outside development workers. Similarly, Walter's move to the floor is not so much a *volte face*, contradiction or retreat from his earlier overt position of showing the capabilities of the local community within the imported discourse paradigm as it is a recourse to an alternative role through which he can instantiate his community-based knowledge and authority, a retrenchment that allows him to guide the proceedings as best he can given the unintentional, though seemingly unavoidable, realignment of positions.

In my analysis of Text 3.1 I have largely focused on the effects of the background, as outlined in Chapters 1 and 2, on the unfolding of discourse. I have suggested that this background can affect the way in which particular discourse acts are taken up and the effect this can have on the discourse as a whole as a consequence of the tension between long-standing and temporary relations between the participants. I have referred to the different roles the participants can play within different storylines and the different prestige, or *symbolic capital*, they are afforded. In the following chapter I will discuss the concept of symbolic capital in greater depth and in particular I will discuss the variability of such symbolic capital within different contexts, or *marketplaces*, adhering to different *orders of indexicality*, and expand the Positioning Triangle as a model in order to incorporate these ideas and to take into account the importance of voice in establishing positions that reflect different forms of symbolic capital for different audiences.

4 Local Prestige, Local Power

> *Yeah, well, of course there is a lot of differences. Because naturally I believe not everything they say is good. Again, not everything they say is bad. Because—so what we do, we make a suggestion here, "Okay, we are glad for the advice, but this is how we know it. Because from our past experience, this is how we . . . are (x) now." If we were not sustainable, I think we could've been find ourselves in a very lacking way now, not having so many things. But up to today's date, we still have a variety of things that we can have to show you, or to show many more people: "This is our (x)". This is the reason why I say we stick with our own way of life.*
>
> (Andrew, Rupertee, 6/3/01)

In my analysis of Text 3.1 in the previous chapter I suggested that Sara's status as professional development worker meant that, though it was not her intention, control over the Management Planning Workshop reverted to her when her words of encouragement and facilitation were misunderstood by the local audience as negative evaluations of Walter's performance and as interventions aimed at reclaiming the floor. We can say, then, that Sara's status imbued her words with the power to control the discourse while Walter, despite his position as a local elder, was unable to translate this authority into power. In this chapter I will consider in more detail what it means to have control over discourse and the relationship between a speaker's social position and their use of language in attaining this control. This discussion is based on Bourdieu's (1977, 1990a, 1991) concept of *symbolic capital*, the embodied prestige that speakers carry with them as a result of their social position and which lends authority to their discourse over and above what is merited by the content alone. I will go on to suggest that, while Bourdieu's framework offers a useful starting point, it simplifies the concept of power in discourse by reducing it to a struggle over speaking rights in which those with the most symbolic capital, realised in discourse through the arbitrary features of an *authorised language*, win out over those with less. I will modify Bourdieu's framework to accommodate a broader understanding of symbolic capital and to provide a fuller account of the relationship between a speaker's social position, the array of linguistic features they employ in discourse and the orientation of their audience towards these features. I will then analyse three interviews with differently positioned participants within NRDDB discourse as a means of revealing the symbolic capital they implicitly appropriate to themselves within the discourse of local development and the relationship between these types of symbolic capital and the overall social context as described in Chapters

Local Prestige, Local Power   123

2 and 3. These analyses will then provide the basis for an idealised model of collaborative power in discourse, as opposed to Bourdieu's competitive model, as a heuristic framework for analysing interactional discourse from NRDDB meetings in the following chapters.

SYMBOLIC CAPITAL

Bourdieu (1991) labels as *cultural capital* non-monetary but socially advantageous attributes such as level of educational, institutional position, class membership and ethnicity and describes how relative status in a particular discourse context is a function of the speakers' *embodiment* of these cultural advantages as *symbolic capital* and the association of the language variety they naturally command with their social position. Bourdieu (1977:651–653) considers this mastery of the *authorised language* within a specific field an essential part of a speaker's linguistic competence, so expanding on what he sees as artificially restricted views of competence within linguistics (by which he means Saussurean and Chomskian linguistics). Thus, for Bourdieu (1977:652), "[i]t follows from the expanded definition of competence that a language is worth what those who speak it are worth, *i.e.* the power and authority in the economic and cultural power relations of the holders of the corresponding competence." This concept is clearly connected, at an individual level, with Blommaert's notion of *orders of indexicality*: the idea, introduced in Chapter 1 and to be discussed further here, that the voices of different social groups are hierarchically ordered in terms of the prestige they are afforded. Importantly for Bourdieu's position, the relationship between social position and the *authorised language* that distinguishes powerful speakers is an arbitrary one:

> There is a whole dimension of authorised language, its rhetoric, syntax and vocabulary, and even pronunciation, which exists purely to underline the authority of its author and the trust he demands. (Bourdieu 1991:76)

Thus Bourdieu (1991:75) compares the Latin of the cleric and the abstruse terminology of the lawyer to the ermine robes of the judge, as mere symbols of authority within their field. Despite the arbitrary nature of this authorised language, however, those within a speech community come to see it as "the only legitimate" form of speech within a specific field as a result of a long process of socialisation and coercion within institutions such as the state, the church and the school, whose representatives benefit from the continued *misrecognition* (Bourdieu 1991) of the arbitrary language as inherently authoritative. As a result, those who possess the authorised language are in a position to exert control over those who do not; or, as Bourdieu (1997:652) puts it:

124 Hybrid Voices and Collaborative Change

> The integration into the same 'linguistic community' (equipped with coercive instruments to impose universal recognition of the dominant language . . .) of hierarchised groups having different interests, is the precondition for the establishment of relations of linguistic domination.

The hierarchisation of these different groups is seen as a function of "the size of their respective capitals of authority" (Bourdieu 1977:648) within a *marketplace* defined by "the social conditions of the production and reproduction of producers and consumers" (Bourdieu 1977:651). Control over discourse is achieved by speakers matching their symbolic capital with the authorised language in a zero-sum game in which those whose language displays most authority win out. The specific form of this domination is described by Bourdieu and Wacquant (1992:57–58), who speak of "the balance of symbolic forces" determining:

> for the most part who can cut somebody off, ask questions, speak at length without being interrupted, or disregards interruptions, etc., [and conversely] who is condemned to strategies of denegation . . . or to ritual refusals to answer, or to stereotypical formulas, etc.

While accepting Bourdieu's basic premises that power in language can be defined as a level of domination that is disproportionate to the content of a speaker's discourse alone and that this can be theorised in terms of the relationship between a speaker's embodied cultural capital and specific features of their discourse, this brief outline of his theory reveals several key assumptions with which I take issue and which are central to a full analysis of the relationship between power and language. These assumptions, which I shall discuss in turn, are: (i) that domination over discourse is purely a matter of controlling speaking rights; (ii) that the balance of speakers' symbolic capital in any given discourse is a function of the size of their respective capitals within a single hierarchical ordering within society; and (iii) that the relationship between a speaker's social capital and the linguistic features that realise this capital in discourse are arbitrary and hence purely symbolic. After discussing an alternative perspective on these key features of Bourdieu's framework, I will then discuss the idea that symbolic capital is a shifting resource open to strategic manipulation.

Control over Participation and Meaning

Bourdieu and Wacqant's view of domination as control over participation is echoed within CDA by Fairclough, who states that "power in discourse is to do with powerful participants *controlling and constraining the contributions of non-powerful participants*" (2001:38–39; emphasis in the original). Such power, however, is relatively futile unless it is in the service of a

Local Prestige, Local Power   125

deeper and more lasting control over meaning, as in Holmes and Stubbe's (2003:3) perspective:

> There are many ways of defining power. From a sociological or psychological perspective power is treated as a relative concept which includes both the ability to control others and the ability to accomplish one's goals. This is manifest in the degree to which one person or group can impose their plans and evaluations at the expense of others. A more anthropological and social constructionist perspective extends this potential influence to embrace definitions of social reality.

Chouliaraki and Fairclough (1999:102–104) take a similar stance in emphasising that control over participation is a very limited power without control over perceptions of reality. In response to the limited definition provided by Bourdieu, and in contrast to Fairclough's earlier formulation above, they point out that that the construction of a worldview and the legitimation of this construction through the control of proceedings are two separate aspects of power and that influence is a question of the interplay between the substance of the discourse produced and the style with which it is imposed. The approach to be developed here is that control over participation in discourse is at the service of imposing definitions of reality through configurations of representational meaning, interpersonal strategies and means of communication: the field, tenor and mode of discourse that between them instantiate a locally appropriate voice.

Types of Symbolic Capital and Alternative Orders of Indexicality

Bourdieu (1977:651) introduces the metaphor of the *linguistic marketplace* to make the point that: "Discourse is a symbolic asset which can receive different values depending on the market in which it is offered. Linguistic competence [in Bourdieu's expanded definition] . . . functions in relationship with a certain market." In other words, while a speaker's symbolic capital is a relatively stable resource, it is of no value until it is converted into the currency of the local marketplace (Bartlett 2009). We have seen above Bourdieu's (1977:651) claim that the values of the marketplace are a result of "the social conditions of the production and reproduction of producers and consumers" and that an integral part of this process of production and reproduction are a linguistic community's "coercive instruments to impose universal recognition of the dominant language", or, in the broader terms discussed in Chapter 1, universal recognition of the dominant language as most prestigious within that community's order of indexicality. Bourdieu (1977:652) cites the educational system as one such "coercive instrument", and we can add to that the obvious examples of political, legal and religious institutions, particularly if we assume that coercion includes (promised) rewards as well as (threatened) discipline. Bourdieu (1977:652) goes on to

126 *Hybrid Voices and Collaborative Change*

claim that "[i]n order for one form of speech among others . . . to impose itself as the only legitimate one . . . the linguistic market has to be unified" as "integration into the same 'linguistic community' . . . of hierarchised groups having different interests, is the precondition for the establishment of relations of linguistic domination". The failing in Bourdieu's theory, and in his subsequent analysis, is that he seems in practice to equate the same "linguistic community" with "a unified market", so missing the important idea that a single linguistic community can be *polycentric* (Blommaert 2005:171–172, 231), composed of many diverse marketplaces formed by simultaneous yet diverse "social conditions of the production and reproduction of producers and consumers" (Bourdieu 1977:651) and including diverse "coercive instruments to impose universal recognition of the dominant language" (Bourdieu 1977:652). Thus, while Bourdieu (1977:647–648) recognises that symbolic capital operates in relation to specific fields, each with their own marketplace, he fails to account for the fact that within a single field there may be different marketplaces at play, each with their own hierarchy of power and their own order of indexicality, with speakers competing to promote the values of the particular marketplace in which their symbolic capital is dominant. Bourdieu's framework also misses the point that such relations of cultural capital operate in mundane fields such as football, cooking or DIY, fields in which it is not the coercive instruments of the state and church that determine the authorised language but within which the recognition of lived experience and past expertise imbue the speaker with as much prestige as the superficial features of the language they use. Within an intercultural context, such as the NRDDB, the potential for a proliferation of relevant fields, each with their own distinctive marketplace, is heightened. For example, the specific form of symbolic capital a speaker holds, even within a single field of discourse, such as local development in the North Rupununi, may relate to different types of authority (as a scientist, a professional development worker or local elder) that stem from different sources (academe, the government, the community) and which therefore operate within different marketplaces inasmuch as they exert control over different members of the marketplace (academics, lay public, congregations, community members) or even over different aspects of each audience member's complex identity. Moreover, even if we accept that there is competition both within and between these marketplaces for control over discourse, Bourdieu's view that different speakers will necessarily have "different interests" in broader social terms is unduly pessimistic, an idea I will develop at the end of the chapter.

Arbitrariness

Identifying contextually powerful language implies looking at the different sources of symbolic capital within a particular context and relating these to the linguistic means through which they are instantiated, and to do this we must go beyond the universal arbitraries of power suggested by Bourdieu's symbol of the judge's ermines for two reasons: Firstly, because clerical collars and mortar boards might be in play within the same field, as discussed above; and, secondly, because the authorised language includes not only surface phenomena such as peculiarities of syntax and pronunciation, but also "rhetoric" as Bourdieu (1991:76) himself suggests. While for Bourdieu "rhetoric" would appear to imply cosmetic loftiness of style, it can be expanded to include all the features of *voice* discussed in previous chapters and grouped under the categories of field, tenor and mode, features which display *indexical order* (Silverstein 2003, in Blommaert 2005:74), being related in a non-arbitrary way to the social background of speaker and audience. Thus, within a locally appropriate voice, the field of discourse relates to the lived experience of the community, the tenor draws on established social relations amongst them and the mode reflects their customary means of passing on information. In this view linguistic marketplaces are not simply abstract relations of value, but are determined by the values that specific audiences bring with them to any communicative event, and these are related in non-arbitrary ways to the field, tenor and mode of the discourses that unfold in these events.

Power as a Shifting and Strategic Resource

I have suggested that while symbolic capital may be a relatively permanent resource, the ability to convert capital into power is dependent on the relationship between speakers, relations which are varied and immanently variable and which operate within even the most mundane of contexts. For example, I will attribute more authority to a friend's opinions on football if this friend plays football regularly or if they have demonstrated themselves to be knowledgeable on the topic in previous conversations. That is to say that I grant my friend a degree of prestige in this area and, as a result, their words are likely to have more power over me than those of less qualified speakers, no matter how coherently and eloquently these are expressed. This means that prestige is also open to strategic manipulation. For instance, my football-savvy friend may find himself being ignored in a group conversation and so change the topic to football in order to increase his prestige within the group at that time. In certain contexts it could even be the case that the particular issues being discussed are not the prime object of the conversation but the relative social positions that the topic affords the different participants. This is a view that squares with Bourdieu's conceptualisation of power in discourse as competition over control, but which allows for collaborative as well as competitive strategies. For example, official conversations may well be prefaced with a stretch of small talk in order to minimalise the difference in status between the participants and so facilitate the smooth running of the specific matter in hand. Of course, such a realignment of interpersonal positioning is generally the

128 *Hybrid Voices and Collaborative Change*

prerogative of the speaker who is in control of the primary discourse; however, it is a strategy that is open to the 'subordinate' speaker as well, and in some cases there is a reversal in the normal relative social status of participants, as when at a student party a student might talk about their studies to a lecturer in order to put them in their 'comfort zone' in an environment where they are the odd one out.

This idea of the shifting nature of symbolic capital can be illustrated through a brief analysis of Text 3.1 and the drift in control, over both participation and meaning, from Walter to Sara. In my analysis of Text 3.1 I suggested that when Sara intervened in the management workshop process her words carried with them the weight of previous discourses between the local communities and outside agents, including previous encounters with Iwokrama representatives. As has been discussed earlier, however, it would be more accurate to say that this weight was not in the words themselves, but in the relationship between the words spoken, the speaker and the audience. Within the specific context of Text 3.1 Sara's cultural capital as a professional development worker affords her a certain prestige, or symbolic capital, before the local community, and this imbues her words with a degree of authority beyond that which might be expected in terms of their content alone. Had Sara's exact words been uttered by somebody else they would have carried different import; similarly, had Sara uttered the same words in front of a different audience, with different experiences and expectations, then they may well have been taken up in a different way. However, in analysing Text 3.1 I suggested that Sara's words were open to more than one interpretation or, in the terms of the *Positioning Triangle* discussed in the previous chapter, could be read against the background of more than one storyline. I suggested, therefore, that there was a tension between one storyline, in which Sara was drawing on Iwokrama's more recent egalitarian approach to discourse in order to position herself as a co-worker with the local communities, and a longer-term storyline, based on previous encounters, in which Sara could be seen as representing the authoritarian and paternalistic approach of outside agents historically. And within these two storylines, as will be argued in more detail in Chapter 6, different orders of indexicality are in operation: Within the egalitarian storyline local voice is in many ways equal to Sara's professional voice; within the authoritarian storyline, her professional voice carries more prestige than Walter's local voice. This is to say that Sara embodied at least two forms of symbolic capital, either of which could be foregrounded in the minds of the community as the discourse proceeded. These two capitals differ significantly across a number of parameters. While her long-term capital as a professional development worker placed her in a position of relative authority over the communities as a default condition within official development, her capital as a sympathetic co-worker could be trumped by other forms of local capital, as will be illustrated in Chapters 5 and 6. Sara's capital as a co-worker was therefore an altogether more fragile attribute than her capital

Local Prestige, Local Power 129

as a professional and it required strategic manipulation, such as setting up Walter as facilitator in the Management Planning Workshop, in order to maintain it. Far from being a constant state, therefore, embodied symbolic capitals can fade in and out of prominence in relation to the unfolding discourse, sometimes by accident, sometimes as a result of the short-term goals of different speakers. And as these embodied symbolic capitals shift in and out of prominence, they affect control of the discourse, as demonstrated by the difference between the function of Sara's various interjections as encouragement and facilitation, and their actual uptake (in my analysis) as a means of intervening in the discourse to retake control. Thus we see a shift in relevant storyline, as perceived by the audience, resulting in a shift in the symbolic capitals in play and a resultant shift in tenor relations. Similarly, we see a shift in control over meaning as, once the shift in storyline has taken place, it is left to Sara both to determine what is relevant to local development and to define the meaning of these concepts. There is thus a shift in the field of discourse as well as in the tenor (and the importance of mode as a variable in voice will be developed in Chapters 5 and 6). However, while Text 3.1 illustrates that significantly different positions are at least potentially open to Sara, this is not to say that all positions are open to all speakers, as such short-term possibilities are severely restricted by long-term social conditions and relations. In the context of the discourse of local development in the North Rupununi, for example, the history of development within the region generally and the attitude of the Government of Guyana, as legally enshrined in the Amerindian Act, are structural conditions that affect the potential for the *emergent* relations (Sealey and Carter 2004; Blommaert 2005:chap. 5) established within discourse.

In this section I have outlined Bourdieu's theory of symbolic capital and "the economics of linguistic exchanges", as his 1977 article is entitled, linking this to Blommaert's concept of orders of indexicality introduced in Chapter 1. I outlined in brief what I see as shortcomings in the theory and made appropriate modifications in order to accommodate these differences in understanding. These can be summarised as follows: (i) that domination over discourse is a matter not only of controlling speaking rights, *but also of controlling meaning*; (ii) that the balance of speakers' symbolic capital in any given discourse is a function of both the type of capital they embody and "the size of their respective capitals of authority" within a *multiple* hierarchical ordering within society; and (iii) that the relationship between a speaker's social capital and the linguistic features that realise this capital in discourse are *not arbitrary, but related to the social background of the community in systematic fashion*. This relationship is captured in the concept of *voice*.

I finished by suggesting that a corollary of the immanent variables of the marketplace is that power is a shifting, and hence strategically manipulable, feature of discourse and I illustrated this briefly through some mundane examples and a further analysis of Text 3.1.

130   *Hybrid Voices and Collaborative Change*

In the following section I shall develop the Positioning Triangle introduced in the previous chapter in line with added theoretical insights from this chapter as a prelude to an analysis of some of the different symbolic capitals likely to be in play within NRDDB discourse.

FROM POSITIONING TRIANGLE TO 'POSITIONING STAR OF DAVID'

As should have become clear in the previous section, the basic Positioning Triangle described in Chapter Three represents a fiction somewhat akin to the notion of an idealised speaker-hearer in that it appears to give speakers free rein in adopting whatever position seems most advantageous to them against the evolving storyline and ignores the constraints imposed by the structural conditions of the historical context. As a model of discourse in action the Positioning Triangle masks three assumptions: first, that the speaker possesses the symbolic capital to take up the desired position with respect to the storyline; second, that the speaker has control over, and the right to use, the linguistic means of realising the desired position, referred to as the *code*; and, third, that a specific audience will correctly interpret the speech act, accept the code employed as appropriate to the context and recognise the position taken up as a legitimate contribution from that speaker to the ongoing storyline. This is clearly not always the case. For example, one of my students cannot come to the front of the class and proceed to lecture their peers, no matter how eloquently they speak, as they lack the appropriate symbolic capital. Likewise, although my everyday middle-class and predominantly English accent is effective in giving a lecture, when ordering a pint in an Edinburgh pub I employ a different way of speaking to overcome the stigma attached to my usual code within that specific marketplace. For others less proficient in the vernacular, however, such code-switching is not possible.

In sum we can say that while a speaker's cultural capital may be a relatively stable attribute, this capital does not translate automatically into *power* as the ability to get things done. Power, while it may always be a latent attribute of different speakers, can only be realised in practice (i.e. an effective position taken up) if the speaker has the appropriate symbolic capital within the specific marketplace and competence within the appropriate code, constraints which were missing in the original Positioning Triangle. We can therefore impose a second triangle of symbolic capital, code and marketplace over the original Positioning Triangle to model these constraints within a *Positioning Star of David* (see also Bartlett 2008, 2009):

While in general terms the variables of symbolic capital, marketplace and code can be said to place constraints on the positions open to different speakers, from an alternative perspective they can be viewed as potentially recalibrating the acts, positions and storylines that are already in play

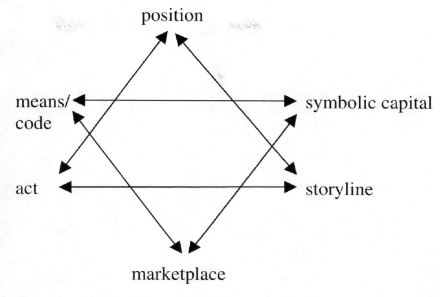

Figure 4.1 A 'Positioning Star of David'.

within a given discourse. Taking this perspective, we can say with regard to Sara's utterances in Text 3.1 that the conjunction of her embodied capital as a professional development worker with the particular marketplace constituted by members of the local community meant that alongside the storyline of equitable collaboration there was a latent storyline of outside domination of local development issues. Within this alternative storyline, the wording she adopted in encouraging Walter, in conjunction with the specifics of the local marketplace, led (in my analysis) to an interpretation of her act as an evaluation of Walter's performance rather than a sympathetic enquiry about his well-being. And the conjunction of Sara's capital and the wording she adopted realigned her position relative to Walter as one of authority rather than solidarity, which, in accordance with the latent experiences and expectations of the audience, reframed the storyline in such a way that the workshop element of the Management Planning Workshop became foregrounded over the management planning aspect, with a resultant shift in the order of indexicality in operation. As this analysis shows, in starting and finishing with reference to the storyline, though it could have started and finished with any part of the figure, the elements of the Star of David model do not operate in simple sequence, but act cyclically and in a mutually constitutive fashion.

Such an analysis of Text 3.1 illustrates the potentially disruptive effect of the different elements captured in the Star of David model. However, as has been suggested by the example of the lecturer at the student party, the model also captures the potential for different features to be used strategically in

132 *Hybrid Voices and Collaborative Change*

order to realign relations of symbolic capital, in that example through the introduction of alternative fields that legitimate different voices. Such disruptions or strategic manipulation can come about in various ways. While the analysis of Text 3.1 focused in particular on the interpersonal elements of the interaction between Sara, Walter and the other participants in the Management Planning Workshop, the conception of voice I outlined in Chapter 1 simultaneously comprises the discourse features of field, tenor and mode, and in the following two chapters I will analyse texts in which local speakers realign ongoing discourses through the manipulation of these three features in isolation and in conjunction. Before such analysis, however, I will attempt to categorise some of the different forms of symbolic capital that are likely to be in play within the discourse of development on the North Rupununi. This will enhance the idea, introduced above, that the different symbolic capitals in play in a given context can be used collaboratively rather than in competition with each other. I will then sketch out a rough model for such *collaboration* within the specific context of the NRDDB. This model will be used in the following chapters as I analyse further discourse between the local communities and Iwokrama, interactions in which local representatives can be seen to be more confidently asserting their positions, drawing on their own embodied capital through the use of appropriate community voices.

AN ANALYSIS OF THE APPROPRIATION AND ALLOCATION OF SYMBOLIC CAPITAL

In order to gain a greater understanding of the various forms of symbolic capital operating within the discourses of local development on the North Rupununi, in this section I analyse descriptions of the development process from three key participants, each occupying a very different structural role within that process: Andrew Martins (28/2/01), a local farmer; Uncle Henry (6/3/01), a community elder with wide experience of dealing with external agencies who was instrumental in setting up the NRDDB; and Gordon Wilson (24/4/01), Iwokrama's chief wildlife biologist, who was also a key figure in setting up the NRDDB. These interviews were originally carried out in order to obtain a range of perspectives on the history of development in the region, and they have been mined as a source of content for my background chapters. In the present chapter, following the principle discussed above that it is not just what you say but how you say it that is important, I shall analyse the three interviews in terms of the authority with which the three speakers discuss local development in spontaneous talk with an outsider. Based on this analysis I shall draw some conclusions as to the kind and degree of symbolic capital the different speakers appropriate to themselves within the field of local development. The analyses are based on the following assumptions: (i) that the symbolic capital of different participants

Local Prestige, Local Power   133

will derive chiefly, though not solely, from either their knowledge in specific fields or the positions of authority they occupy within the different communities; and (ii) that these two sources of symbolic power can be respectively instantiated in discourse as the right to offer opinions and suggestions concerning local development and the right to determine the responsibilities of others within this process. Grammatically, the principal ways of expressing these rights within narrative are through mental projections, such as THINK, KNOW, WISH and BELIEVE, each with their own degree of certainty; and through the use of modal verbs, such as MUST, SHOULD and COULD, each with their own degree of obligation or certainty. There is thus some degree of functional overlap in that both mental projections and modality can be used to assign degrees of certainty to a proposition, and this will be reflected in the analysis. Given the realisational relationships between symbolic capital and mental projections and modality, I shall present a comparative analysis of the three interviews in terms of the type and number of mental projections and modals used by the three speakers in order to gain a rough idea of how the different speakers implicitly appropriate to themselves different types and degrees of knowledge and authority, and hence the symbolic capital associated with these, with regard to the development process. It should be noted, however, that the context of these interviews is very different from the 'real world' of development discourse in action and as such represents a very distinctive *marketplace*. While my status as an outside researcher clearly imposed constraints on the discourse, I did not really represent a 'competitor' in the field, and we can therefore treat the positions of the three speakers as having been taken up *in idealis* and, as such, only a point of departure for an analysis of the symbolic capital they display *in realis* in the texts analysed in later chapters.

I had met all three interviewees several times before and the interviews followed a semi-structured schedule in as informal a manner as possible. This approach focuses attention on one particularly broad topic and ensures speakers stay close to the same material while allowing each to develop the topic in the direction most relevant to them. I interviewed Andrew outside his house as he took a break from work, Uncle Henry outside the Rest House in Surama, and Gordon in the resource room of the Iwokrama offices in Georgetown. Each was therefore in their own environment at the time of the interview. I attempted to lead as little as possible in the interviews, preferring to follow the speakers' own directions and to develop these, only returning to the schedule either when the conversation had dried up or it seemed to me that we were no longer discussing the issue at hand.[1] While it might be argued that the widely different responses elicited by the semi-structured interview technique create texts that are not directly comparable, the more relevant point for the purposes of these analyses is that this looseness of structure allowed each interviewee to focus on their own particular conceptualisation of the development process with the result that the texts reveal the speakers' spontaneous appropriation of authority more

134   *Hybrid Voices and Collaborative Change*

accurately than would be achieved through either the artificial similarities of fixed interviews of the randomness of totally free and unconnected discourses. Moreover, the analyses themselves compensate for the level of free variation between the texts in that they consider only clauses referring directly to the development process.

My analysis is primarily based on a quantitative comparison of the key features of mental projection and modality produced by the three speakers. Clearly such a quantitative analysis will present only the dry bones of the three interviews, so I shall first provide and comment on a brief extract from each speaker which I think gives an authentic impression of their different voices. The quantitative analyses can be compared to the statistics of a sports match in that they cannot convey the dynamics of the match itself but instead provide an insight into underlying patterns that may have been missed in the excitement of watching the match itself. Extending the metaphor, the extracts that follow are the Match of the Day highlights, deemed to be reflective of the game overall, but highly selective. The first extract (Text 4.1, below) comes from Andrew, and was prompted by my asking him how an understanding of new concepts had been enhanced in the community (**A** is Andrew; I am **T**).

An interesting feature of Andrew's positioning with regard to community development here is that he redirects my question about communication and the transfer of information towards the effects of the collaboration between the local communities and Iwokrama on farming practices (11) rather than on the mechanisms of such communication, an emphasis which is maintained throughout the interview as a whole. We can interpret this as Andrew maintaining a field of discourse (farming rather than organisation) and a mode of discourse (an emphasis on Accounts of concrete events with occasional Conjectures) that between them facilitate an interpersonal context, or tenor, in which he feels qualified to make an evaluation of the development process according to his embodied capital as an expert in the realities of local farming practice—that is, within the field of local framing practices, Andrew's style of discourse ranks higher in the associated order of indexicality than it might within other fields. It could, of course, be argued that my line of questioning, based on my own appraisal of Andrew's relative expertise, was at least in part responsible for this focus; but in the extract it is fairly clear that this shift was initiated by Andrew, and that this stands in contrast to the other two interviews, as will be illustrated below. This demonstrates the importance of what Halliday and Hasan (1985:39) call the *configuration* of discourse variables, the alignment of field, tenor and mode that are viable in specific situations. The particular nature of Andrew's symbolic capital is thus realised through the interpersonal elements of the lexicogrammar[2] that he draws on, including his use of modality and mental projections. Here Andrew often talks about what HAS TO (18, 30, 43, 52&70) be done, using objective modality to present the obligation as arising from external sources rather than through his own evaluation,

Local Prestige, Local Power 135

Text 4.1 Interview with Andrew Martins, Outside Andrew's House, Rupertee, 28/2/01

1   *A:* *Uh. .we. .we. .we. .we . . . for instance, like how we are operating now, when we have*
2   *the meeting, okay*
3   *T:* *The meeting with . . . ?*
4   *A:* *Yes.*
5   *T:* *With the experts, with the=*
6   *A:* *=No, no, no, no. The meeting with the leaders here in the community. [T: Yeah.]*
7   *Right. Okay this is what we . . . because of this, because of that. Then we carry on*
8   *the spot in the field work. And there now (again) we=*
9   *T:* *= You pass on the knowledge.*
10 *A:* *Right. "Well, this is the actual spot, this is the experience that we're going to share*
11   *here now. You do. .are interested in . . ." Now, from our record, with this farming*
12   *business, it seems that the garden and the poultry is going to have a*
13   *shining . . . uhm . . . result. From what, and from the amount involve, becau—what I*
14   *notice is that there seems to understand now what were the lots, family. [T: Mm-hmm.]*
15   *And by, let's say, keeping away the participation in this venture, that would*
16   *contribute to the failures of that, or whatever. By moving, like how we are moving*
17   *together, this is what we accomplish; this is ours. All right? So, as we concluded*
18   *work today and then we've got to burn it and then clean it up and then plant it, we*
19   *can very well expect (p) beyond our—the minimum, about, say, a thousand pounds*
20   *or more. Because there'll be more. [T: Yeah?] Right, let's . . . I just like to*
21   *minimise the quantity.*
22 *T:* *And will that supply you for half the year? That will keep you for half the year?*
23 *A:* *Well, it depends to the amount of production that we will have in the time.*
24 *T:* *Oh, so you might produce more [A: more] more chickens, yeah?*
25 *A:* *So, you know, it's a very interesting piece of work. I feel real satisfied about the*
26   *whole turnout. The whole turnout—we started Monday and we finished today.*
27 *T:* *Three days?*
28 *A:* *Three days, yeah.*
29 *T:* *The whole community contributing?*
30 *A:* *So this was a very good sign. And they know for sure, well, they don't have to look*
31   *for feed either way, we're looking to supply our own feed.*
32 *T:* *Yeah, very good.*
33 *A:* *We can move on with our projects. Likewise, that is what we will be doing. To*
34   *make the most (xx responsible) from east, west, north, south. One from there, one*
35   *from there, one from there. This is your part.*
36 *T:* *So they all look after their own [A: Right.] area?*
37 *A:* *[x] recognise their responsibility.*
38 *T:* *Did you have a grow corn before?*
39 *A:* *Yeah, we grow corn here. Uhm, but actually since this part of the project started,*
40   *we never really started this . . . (dig) this stage, in planting our own seedlings. I*
41   *mean feeding. [T: Right.] That was one of our uhm findings. And (I said) . . . ,*
42   *investigating the whole failures of this whole thing, I said, "This has really failed.*
43   *And this is why it failed. And let's see how we've got to do it.*
44 *T:* *You failed because you didn't start from the seedlings?*
45 *A:* *Seedlings.*
46 *T:* *How did you start before? What did you have before?*
47 *A:* *Well we had, like, directly from Georgetown.*
48 *T:* *Right, so you didn=*
49 *A:* *=Georgetown supply and supply and supply. We've kind of been dependent on the*

(continued)

136 *Hybrid Voices and Collaborative Change*

Text 4.1 (continued)

50 *way, right? And you know, you know what is it when you depend for someone, at*
51 *the time when you expect supplies, "Man, look, I would've come, but something*
52 *wrong was up. I had to go to Canada [T: U-huh u-huh.] or somewhere, and, you*
53 *know, things*
54 T: *And the chickens can't wait. [A: Right.] Yeah.*
55 A: *So we just (had x x). So, looking at it from the (xxx), you know what? Let's*
56 *everybody feel free to go to Canada, whichever way, we have (big thing) over here,*
57 *let's use it. [T: Right.] Let us . . . use it for what and make things happen, what we*
58 *wants to see happen.*
59 T: *How would you say that UNICEF, UNDP and these people, how did they help with*
60 *this, was it through advice, or through money, or organisation? What was the*
61 *main . . . how did they help most? [A: Ehmmm.] The outside organisations, how did*
62 *they help in producing this project? Was it with advice, or with scientific*
63 *knowledge, or . . . ?*
64 A: *Particularly, with the garden part of it, CIDA has contributed a method of like*
65 *(xx) produce.*
66 T: *Oh, okay, right.*
67 A: *Apart from the drip irrigation is (the bad like) wasting water, you know, on the*
68 *beds, when you use a spraying can, the water seems to be spilling all over, but with*
69 *the driplet you direct it to the plants. Added to it, they also teach you the methods*
70 *of, like, mulching, when you can mulch, why you have to mulch. They also teach*
71 *you about planting various species of plants that is called windbreaker, that is to*
72 *ease the pressure of the wind when the plant is young.*

---

as would be the case with the subjective modality of modals such as MUST or SHOULD. Likewise, Andrew uses CAN here in its dynamic sense (33, 19[3]&70) to point to the community's abilities rather than to express modal evaluations of what is theoretically possible (what I have labelled the "no obstacle" sense in Figure 4.2 below). Where Andrew does use subjective forms is in the expression of what the communities can EXPECT (19) and what they WANT (58) to happen. Summarising Text 4.1, we can say that Andrew outlines what he sees as past failings in local practice and offers a summary of present and desired benefits to the community from Iwokrama's input, stressing that such benefits are contingent on the local communities understanding what it is Iwokrama have to say (10–11, 41–43, 64–65&67–72). Delving a little deeper, we can say that Andrew draws on his symbolic capital as an experienced farmer with a good understanding of local issues that enables him to offer his professional evaluation of the results of collaboration and to express his wishes for future benefits, but that he cedes authority to Iwokrama in terms of the new knowledge that is introduced and does not talk of benefits to Iwokrama as a result of the collaboration. The discourse position Andrew adopts can thus be said to correspond with his social position within the community and within NRDDB as a grassroots practitioner rather than as part of the NRDDB 'hierarchy'. This does not mean, however, that he cedes all authority to local elders and

Local Prestige, Local Power   137

professional development workers such as Uncle Henry and Gordon, *pace* Bourdieu. He does, in fact, offer very definite opinions; however, in doing so he adopts a voice that focuses the symbolic capital at his control within those areas where it carries most weight.

The following extract (Text 4.2), from my interview with Uncle Henry, illustrates a very different voice, a voice which draws on Uncle Henry's unique standing as a community elder with extensive knowledge and experience of outside expertise and practice. Uncle Henry's standing and its repercussions on his discourse will be discussed at length in Chapter 6, but they are evident in the following extract, which was prompted by my asking him what he thought the communities had benefited from Iwokrama being in the area (**UH** is Uncle Henry; I am **T**).

A notable contrast between Uncle Henry's discourse here and Andrew's in Text 4.1 is that, although my line of questioning was very similar, Uncle Henry discusses both specific local issues and problems of resource management in general, as opposed to Andrew's singular focus on the specific

---

Text 4.2   Interview with Uncle Henry, Surama Rest House, 6/3/01

 1 **UH:** *Well, one of the things which I know the communities have benefited from and they*
 2 *would continue to benefit from is the education, the outreach programme, the*
 3 *education. Because, as I said, since Iwokrama come, people are beginning to get*
 4 *aware of the value of their resources that we have and they are understanding that*
 5 *there is nowhere you can go. If you harvest everything, you destroy everything,*
 6 *then where would you go to get . . . ? So you have to start making an effort to try to*
 7 *save what we have now. [T: Okay.] And then they are learning and . . . they are*
 8 *seeing, at least you have some of those rangers, even if they don't continue to work*
 9 *with Iwokrama, surely they would be able to get a job with any other organisation*
10 **T:** *So they have the training, which they can take with them.*
11 **UH:** *With the training they got.*
12 **T:** *And what would you say, what has the—what has the community got to offer*
13 *Iwokrama? What do they get from you that they can't get from anyone else?*
14 **UH:** *Well, Iwokrama has benefit a lot from our knowledge of the resources, the*
15 *reproduction period, and even though they are not very accurate, but it is there,*
16 *somewhere near accurate, [T: Mm-hmm.] and Iwokrama has benefited from that*
17 *because from those workshops we have done, people look at them, the reports and*
18 *so on, I mean what we've done in three years, people said it might take 15,*
19 *20 years to do it.*
20 **T:** *It's amazing the amount of work. So those two, that's—how do you see these,*
21 *Iwokrama as the modern scientific, well the modern, Western knowledge, if you like,*
22 *and you have the traditional knowledge that you've developed over centuries, how*
23 *do you see these two acting together? Do you think they can work together?*
24 **UH:** *Well, this is a comment I made when we went, after a board meeting, it was then*
25 *Dr. Jagan, Cheddi Jagan, before he died, we went to his office and we had a short*
26 *discussion where he was asking questions (and these things), and one of my*
27 *comments was "I hope", and I am still hoping, "that the scientific technology of*
28 *today and the indigenous knowledge, if they can be blended together, I think we can*
29 *get something going".*

138 *Hybrid Voices and Collaborative Change*

gains for community practice. This demonstrates a difference in both the field of his discourse, as communications systems and the workings of the ranger system rather than changes in farming practice, and the mode of his discourse, as theoretical Generalisations in conjunction with specific Accounts. This movement away from the concrete and the immediate opens up for Uncle Henry a different range of tenor variables that manifest his own particular symbolic capital. Unlike Andrew, Uncle Henry has a marked tendency to use CAN in its modal sense to suggest what he personally thinks is theoretically possible—the "no obstacle" usage (5&28 in this extract). However, he also employs the dynamic sense of CAN, and there is a particularly salient blending of the two uses in the closing lines (27–28), which can be paraphrased as Uncle Henry suggesting that if the two communities *are able* to fuse "scientific technology" and "indigenous knowledge", then there should be *no obstacle* to them "get[ting] something going" together. Notably, Uncle Henry's first-person use of THINK (28) that projects the second CAN clause appears not so much a pseudo-modal expression of probability as an expression of personal evaluation. And in projecting this whole interpersonal complex through a personal expression of HOPE (27), we might go still further to say that Uncle Henry is not just evaluating the process here, but sanctioning it. This point will be developed below in my discussion of the quantitative analysis and in Chapter 6. Summarising Text 4.2, we can say that Uncle Henry describes development as much more of a two-way street than Andrew does, with a personal evaluation of the need for local and external expertise and the potential benefits of collaboration for both sides. Though Uncle Henry's discussion of benefits accruing to Iwokrama was specifically prompted by my questioning, the willingness with which he expands on this point and his very explicit reference to his own role in establishing relations between the two groups and his discussions with Cheddi Jagan, the president of Guyana at the time, demonstrate that this is an opinion that he holds strongly and that he feels more than entitled to expound upon. In these terms we can say that Uncle Henry is willing to draw on, and emphasise, his symbolic capital both as community elder and as someone with prestige in professional and government circles, and that this is manifest in the configuration of field, tenor and mode that define the voice that he adopts.

The third extract, from Gordon, occurs at a point where we were discussing consultative processes between the local communities, Iwokrama and the Government of Guyana (**G** is Gordon; I am **T**).

In Text 4.3 Gordon gives his evaluation of methods of communication and technology transfer between the local communities, Iwokrama and the Government of Guyana . In this way, the field of discourse is broadly similar to the extract from Andrew; however, the mode of discourse is rather different in that Andrew provides Accounts of how outside scientific expertise has been successfully incorporated into local practice while Gordon discusses hypothetical improvements (Conjectures) to the

Local Prestige, Local Power 139

Text 4.3 Interview with Gordon Wilson, Iwokrama Offices, Georgetown, 24/4/01

 1 G: *So that there needs to be, as if like, there needs to be a consultative process. But n-*
 2 *this is not consultation in the terms of what the government might think of*
 3 *consultation, this is not just "Look, I'm going to go and do this and explain it to*
 4 *you", this is actually much more complicated. This is "I think I want to do*
 5 *something like this, what do you think?"*
 6 T: *And this is an everyday consultative [(xxxxx)] maturing at their own rate?*
 7 G: *[This is an everyday]*
 8 *Yeah, yeah. [But we don't have a system.] That's part of the problem. The*
 9 T: *[At this distance?]*
10 G: *problem there is the question of whether or not you need to manage from*
11 *Georgetown or you should be managing from Annai. And my view, I think in the*
12 *long term, and this is one of the recommendations that came out from the one of*
13 *the reviews that we had, maybe in both reviews, mid-term reviews, is that we need a*
14 *centre in Annai, close to the community so that we can actually co-manage.*
15 T: *Just with one person there? Several people there? Half the staff there?*
16 G: *I would say that anybody doing any work there [needs to be . . .] Yeah. Need to be.*
17 T: *[Would be based in Annai?]*
18 G: *But then there are also, because of co-management structures there are*
19 *communication needs here too. [T: Yeah.] But then we're suffering from the same*
20 *fundamental problem that the government does: it's centralised so you have the*
21 *government sitting over on one side, and then all the way over here, that's where*
22 *you're actually doing, this is where the (marital????) impacts are, I mean you've*
23 *got a set of people around there that are going to be impacted, and what we're*
24 *doing is ending up (xxx) ease, because it's so difficult to communicate who's*
25 *making the decision here, and then by and by maybe telling some people what we*
26 *decided later on. But we did this in all the programmes. I mean, we look at*
27 *different kinds of decisions and then the decision-making process is not one of this*
28 *lot sitting down with that lot to make a decision what goes on here, what happens,*
29 *it will vary substantially, sometimes the things come from here*
30 T: *(Xxxx), but how does that work? So how would that happen? That's Iwokrama,*
31 *okay . . .*
32 G: *Well, I think in the early stages, but again this is very complicated, 'cause I think in*
33 *the early stages when I started working, what we did was we went out and tried to*
34 *ask. The problem with asking is that even when you ask you create a framework of*
35 *what is possible and what is not possible. And, yes, we have to do that because*
36 *Iwokrama does have plans, and I think if we'd just gone out to the communities and*
37 *asked them what they wanted, they would say, it might be something as simple as*
38 *"We want more employment and we want it in such and such a way." Of course,*
39 *Iwokrama doesn't do that; Iwokrama doesn't do employment, so it has to couch it*
40 *and manage it and mould it, but if you look at the wildlife process, a lot of those*
41 *concerns do come from the communities, but these may not be their major*
42 *concerns. For example, if I was in the community, mine might be, you know,*
43 *"What's going to happen to my kids, where's the schooling, where's this, where's*
44 *that?", rather than "the environment's getting buggered up". And what you find is*
45 *that in fact it weaves, goes back and forth like this, as , you know, we're sitting*
46 *here, we're thinking about the environment, they're there sitting thinking about*
47 *jobs and opportunities, I mean this is very generalised, but then it sort of leads*
48 *back and forth, until you finally get to something like the Development Board or the*

(continued)

140   *Hybrid Voices and Collaborative Change*

Text 4.3 (continued)

49	*Aquarium Fish Programme, or the, rather for the Arapaima Programme (Jarvis*
50	*can xx arapaima), but for this to happen you need to have this constant*
51	*communication and, and I think this is going to be a really big problem, people,*
52	*and we've already seen this, the people that start this have to be the people that*
53	*end it. Not end it. Because if you bring in somebody new here, the whole thing*
54	*starts again.*

---

communications systems in order to align local expectations with what Iwokrama is willing and able to provide. In doing so Gordon sets himself up as an advisor with a special understanding of the issues and of the expectations of all those involved in local development and how these can be accommodated through effective communications. This position is manifest in his talk through the use of direct speech in which he vocalises, as if in their own terms, what he sees as community and government perspectives on development (3–5, 38&43–44), and through a very high usage of the modal NEED TO (1, 10, 13,[4] 16, 19&50) as a means of evaluating existing failings and potential means of repair. Gordon's positioning as an advisor in some ways parallels that of Uncle Henry, though there are significant differences here as well. Both, for example, talk of the potential for improved collaboration and preface many of their comments with a first-person use of THINK (11, 32, 36&51 in Gordon's extract) that stresses the element of personal evaluation. However, while Uncle Henry talks of the existing potential for action within the community and what further actions are open to them, Gordon stresses existing problems and their necessary means of repair.

From the preceding analyses it can be seen that Gordon's talk has elements of both Andrew's and Uncle Henry's discourse as well as important differences from both. This can be explained in terms of the relative positionings of each speaker within the local development process. Like Andrew, Gordon is an expert on methods of cultivation, including farming and fishing; however, whereas Andrew's expertise is locally and practically based, Gordon's is more an external and theoretical expertise. This means that the two speakers share a field of expertise but that their capital within this field is of different sorts, each of which legitimates specific positions that will be realised through language in different ways. Similarly, while both Gordon and Uncle Henry have authority as advisors, Uncle Henry's authority derives from his position as a community elder and Gordon's from his position as a professional development worker with external expertise. This brings us back to the two elements of symbolic capital highlighted above, knowledge and authority, and how the different sources for each of these and the different combinations of each as embodied by different speakers will have significant effects on discourse practice in terms of what positions are legitimate for different speakers to take up within different marketplaces and the means in which these positions are realised as discourse acts.

Having provided a feel for the different voices of Andrew, Uncle Henry and Gordon in the context of local development, I will now present a more representative quantitative analysis of their use of modality and projections and make further suggestions as to the symbolic capital each speaker appropriates to themselves through the tenor of their discourse. To do this it will first be necessary to present a fuller description of modality and projections and to set up a network of sense relations within each so that the different speakers' uses can be compared at different levels of generality.

Modal Analysis

The use of modality is indicative of the truth-value a speaker imputes to propositions or to the degree of obligation that they assign to the carrying out of an action. These two facets of modality correspond to the two elements of symbolic capital identified earlier, knowledge and authority. When addressed to an interlocutor in dialogue, therefore, the use of modality generally represents the negotiation of interpersonal status between speaker and hearer; in third-person narrative, however, it might be more accurate to state that the modalities employed represent the degree to which the speaker claims knowledge and authority over the issues being discussed. To use certain modalities consistently throughout a discourse is therefore to claim for oneself the symbolic capital necessary to take up a particular position of knowledge or authority within that particular field of discourse.

As with the analysis of processes and participation in the Amerindian Act in Chapter 2, the first step in the modal analysis was to create a network of those modal forms actually occurring within the interviews. These were categorised according to their discourse function rather than their more general lexicogrammatical meanings, and the network of relations is presented in Figure 4.2. The specific modal forms used are given for each end-term and examples of each category are given in Appendix 2 in order to clarify the meaning of the descriptive labels. The categories I have employed differ from those often used within CDA, especially those based on SFL descriptions, as the concept of modality frequently remains underanalysed in such studies of language and power in terms of the relationship between the modal used and its discursive function. In general SFL-based studies fail to go beyond the broad logic-based division into *deontic* and *epistemic* modality (in SFL terms *modulation* and *modalisation*, respectively). This approach leads to a lumping together of such different speech acts as offers and commands within the deontic category and so loses analytical power. Categorising modals as expressing *either* obligation *or* possibility also misses the possibility that certain usages blend the two modalities to create more complex meanings. This can lead to the poor analysis of modals such

142   *Hybrid Voices and Collaborative Change*

as SHOULD and CAN (see Bartlett 2000). In the following sentence, for example, "should" expresses neither a degree of knowledge nor of obligation alone but a position which seems to contain both and more:

Taxis from Cardiff should cost no more than £10.

Such usage can be analysed as expressing 'expectations' as one subcategory of what is 'appropriate'. Labels such as 'expectations' and 'appropriate' avoid the a priori divisions of formal logic through the use of more socially oriented glosses and so reveal an interplay of knowledge and obligation ("what usually happens is right") that provides greater analytical insights into speakers' use of SHOULD. Thus, while the network of modal use presented in Figure 4.2 retains the categories 'possibility' and 'obligation', uses of SHOULD are placed within a new category, 'appropriate', subdivided into the more delicate options of 'correct action' and 'expectation'. Similarly, 'permission' becomes a category of its own in Figure 4.2, rather than being analysed as a weak form of obligation as it is in SFL-based studies. Within the network as a whole, the inclusion of subclassifications for all types of modality introduces relevant distinctions for the discussion of authority that would be lost in a less delicate analysis, as with the use of CAN to signal that the speaker sees "no obstacle" to a course of action as a subcategory of 'possibility', a point already discussed and taken up again below.

There is a related tendency in quantitative analyses based on grammatical descriptions from SFL to undervalue the effect of context on the social implications of discourse acts. In such analyses, repeated use of high- or low-force modals as linguistic items, as with the high obligation of MUST or the low probability of COULD, is often correlated with high or low degrees of social power held by speakers. This is not always the case, however, as low-force modality, for example, is often employed by high-status speakers in a specific type of sociolinguistic balancing act. This is a phenomenon that is widely accepted in qualitative approaches such as Interactional Sociolinguistics, and the failure of quantitative methods to capture such subtleties has led to criticisms of a widely perceived tendency within CDA to "fix on some particular linguistic feature . . . and assign it ideological significance without regard to how it might be understood" within the actual context of interpretation (Widdowson 2000:166). Developing this point, I will suggest in the analysis that follows that those with high degrees of symbolic capital are in a position to use a low degree of modality to make a point as their symbolic capital will amplify the import of any such usage.

Analysis that correlates degree of force with symbolic capital also fails to distinguish the effect of different forms of symbolic capital on modal use (Bartlett 2004, 2006). To give a simple example, speakers producing 13 examples of high epistemic modality through MUST and no examples of its deontic use would be considered as showing the same degree of authority as those producing two epistemic and 11 deontic examples of the same modal. Such an analysis would clearly miss the important distinction between speakers' symbolic capital that is derived from their knowledge and that which is derived from their institutional authority. There is therefore a need both to correlate the degree and type of modality used by different speakers and to treat with caution the assumption that high force reflects high symbolic capital if we are to uncover more complex patterns of modal use and what they tell us of the interpersonal relations that exist between speakers.

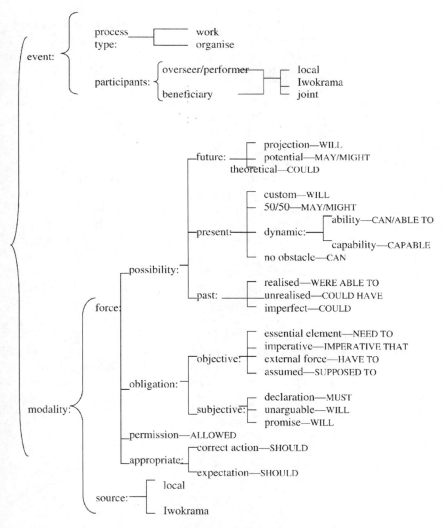

Figure 4.2 Network of modal use in interviews with Andrew Martins, Uncle Henry and Gordon Wilson.

144 *Hybrid Voices and Collaborative Change*

Beyond analysing the degree and type of modality employed by different speakers, it is also important to consider the nature of the processes over which they assert their modal authority and another significant feature of the network in Figure 4.2 is that it includes the type of process that is modalised and the role of the different participants within each process, so providing a more detailed account of the scope of authority each speaker assumes. Processes are distinguished according to whether they relate to either 'organisation' or 'work'; participants within the modalised process are labelled as 'local', 'Iwokrama' or 'joint'; and the degree of participation lumps together 'overseer' and 'performer' and distinguishes this category from that of 'beneficiary'. In this way the analysis brings out important distinctions, already alluded to above, concerning not only the degree and kind of authority the different speakers appropriate to themselves, but also over whom they claim such authority and in what subcontexts of the development process, as well as the extent to which they see each other as either being responsible for or benefiting from different activities. Figure 4.2 also includes the original source of the modality, as either 'local' and 'Iwokrama', to allow for those cases where the modality is attributed to people other than the speakers themselves.

Drawing on the broad distinctions discussed above, Table 4.1 shows the total number of instances of the modal expression of possibility, obligation, permission and appropriateness for the three speakers interviewed. The two final columns add the subdivisions of appropriateness, 'expectation' and 'correct action' to the figures for possibility and obligation respectively in order to provide categories corresponding more closely to epistemic and deontic respectively.

As might be expected given his status as community elder, Uncle Henry uses a higher percentage of obligation modality than Andrew, and this difference is increased once their uses of SHOULD are considered. In Uncle Henry's case there is a need for caution, however, as several of his uses of MUST are reports of the government and Iwokrama's positions. While his willingness to impute modal use to these sources, and to challenge it, as he does, is surely indicative of his own personal standing, it cannot be equated with his personal use of modality. Gordon's use of obligation modality lies between that of Andrew and Uncle Henry, while his use of

Table 4.1 Division of Modals by Superordinates

	Total	poss.	as %	oblig.	as %	approp.	as %	poss. + expect. (epistemic)	as %	oblig. + correct (deontic)	as %
AM	63	40	63.5%	20	31.8%	3	4.8%	40	63.5%	23	36.5%
UH	64	34	53.1%	24	37.5%	6	9.4%	34	53.1%	30	46.9%
GW	150[5]	68	45.3%	52	34.7%	30	20%	69	46%	81	54%

SHOULD to signal appropriateness is far higher than the use of either of the other speakers. And once Gordon's use of SHOULD is included within the standard deontic/epistemic split his percentage of deontic uses is markedly higher than that of either local speaker. The use of SHOULD to signal correct action is therefore crucial in differentiating Gordon's modal use from that of the local speakers, and I shall return to this when analysing other features.

Table 4.2 looks a little more deeply at the use of the major modals of obligation used by the speakers: NEED TO, HAVE TO and MUST.

The first point of interest here is that Gordon, who would be considered the most powerful speaker in analyses focusing on his cultural capital and his role as gatekeeper between the local communities and international assistance, never signals obligation through MUST, a marker of high subjective obligation generally taken as a sign of interpersonal power within CDA. Secondly, within what can be labelled objective modals, in that they imply obligation from external forces rather than the speaker's imposition, though they also carry overtones of this,[6] both Andrew and Uncle Henry use HAVE TO far more frequently in relative terms than Gordon. One possibility is that Uncle Henry and Andrew are more willing to deal in absolutes than Gordon, as both MUST and HAVE TO express high modal force. Moreover, if we consider Gordon's high use of SHOULD, we see that he is in no way reluctant to present subjective judgments; it is rather that he tends to phrase them through the suggestion of correct actions rather than as direct fiats. Similarly, Gordon compensates for his relatively infrequent use of HAVE TO with a very high use of NEED TO, which can be considered as equally forceful. Where NEED TO differs from HAVE TO is that it relies more on personal evaluation of shortcomings rather than the suggestion of unnamed external forces that HAVE TO carries, and as a result it allows for a greater degree of human agency in accepting or rejecting the proposal. It is thus closer to a suggestion form than HAVE TO. Overall, then, Gordon makes considerable use of modality, though he prefers to steer clear of strong directive forms in favour of suggestions, while Uncle Henry and Andrew use more directives. They also have a strong tendency towards identifying problems as a result of external forces (through HAVE TO) where Gordon sees problems in terms of shortcomings or appropriateness

Table 4.2 Modals of Obligation by Speaker

	Total	NEED TO	as % of total	HAVE TO	as % of total	MUST	as % of total	Other
AM	20	4	20%	11	55%	3	15%	2
UH	24	5	20.8%	12	50%	5	20.8%	2
GW	52	31	59.6%	18	34.6%	0	0%	3

146 *Hybrid Voices and Collaborative Change*

Table 4.3 Modals of Possibility by Speaker

	Total	Future	as % of total	Present	as % of total	Past	as % of total
AM	40	13	32.5%	23	57.5%	4	10%
UH	34	3	8.8%	29	85.3%	2	5.9%
GW	68	26	38.2%	39	57.4%	3	4.4%

(through NEED TO and SHOULD), both of which suggest potential remedy, as befits a status as a scientific advisor.

Table 4.3 shows the division of modals of possibility according to time frame. The contrast in usage in this respect is between Andrew and Gordon, on the one hand, with a sizeable minority of future forms (largely projections with WILL[7]) and Uncle Henry, on the other, with an absolute emphasis on present forms. Looking at these present forms in greater detail there are clearly more delicate differences at work here, as shown in Table 4.4.

Again the major contrast here is between Uncle Henry, on the one hand, with his emphasis on CAN to signal 'no obstacle' usage, and Andrew and Gordon, on the other hand, with their emphasis on 'dynamic' ability through CAN and BE ABLE. This split can be explained in terms of Andrew and Gordon's heavy involvement in the concrete issue of cultivation and what the communities are capable of achieving as compared with Uncle Henry's position as community elder with responsibility for authorising any potential developments.

For all the speakers, possibility is primarily situated in the present, yet whereas Andrew and Gordon also make extensive reference to future possibility, Uncle Henry largely avoids such reference. This could be explained if we regard the strong use of future possibility by Andrew and Gordon in terms of their roles at the cutting edge of development on either side of the local–professional divide, Gordon as a research scientist and Andrew as a farmer. In this interpretation, there are resonances among the two speakers' expressions of future possibility, their dynamic use of CAN and their expressions of obligation. Andrew's position as a farmer involved directly

Table 4.4 More Delicate Present Possibility

	Total	custom	as % of total	50/50	as % of total	Dynamic	as % of total	no obstacle	as % of total
AM	23	2	8.7%	1	4.3%	11	47.8%	9	39.1%
UH	29	0	0%	4	13.8%	6	20.7%	19	65.5%
GW	39	2	5.1%	2	5.1%	20	51.2%	15	38.5%

Local Prestige, Local Power 147

and personally in development is captured in his conjunction of HAVE TO to identify external obstacles and dynamic CAN to identify the community's abilities in order to project possible outcomes. Similar, but crucially different in some respects, is Gordon's position as research scientist and his intense involvement in the social development programme. In this role Gordon identifies shortcomings within the existing set-up through NEED TO and suggests solutions to these through SHOULD before mirroring Andrew in projecting outcomes based on an assessment of abilities. A very different picture emerges in the case of Uncle Henry and his overwhelming expression of present possibility and the predominance within this of CAN to express 'no obstacle'. In fact 29.7% of Uncle Henry's *total* modal use in this text is accounted for by this one usage. At the risk of overstating the case, this use of CAN functions as a judgment in both the physical and moral order, stating that something is allowable on the grounds that it is physically possible: It is the *nihil obstat* that simultaneously validates ideational truth and interpersonal acceptability. The following example of CAN (in bold) seems to capture this duality of possibility and permission, but I should stress that not all instances are as clear-cut:

> And, er, I think one of the things that we should encourage is to allow them to put it over in Makushi. Even, I mean, they can't read and write, but they have very good memory collection. They **can** put it over in Makushi and people would take notes, we have scribes who take notes and these things.

'Permitting' processes to go ahead on the grounds that they are theoretically possible simultaneously establishes and manifests Uncle Henry's credentials as an expert voice in matters practical and moral, as befits a community elder. It also demonstrates his power over Iwokrama in that his *nihil obstat* is as crucial to their efforts, continued funding and livelihoods as it is to the community. Andrew's symbolic capital, in contrast, relates purely to his local knowledge of the difficulties faced within the communities and their capabilities for dealing with them rather than to any moral authority. However, any unsatisfactory distinctions grassroots activists such as Andrew make between what has to be done, what can be done and what is likely to happen will also ultimately affect Iwokrama's prospects. Gordon's symbolic capital is different again, springing from specific external knowledge that allows him to identify problems within the system and to make suggestions to remedy them. Indeed, it is the authority that comes from Gordon's external knowledge that allows him to make suggestions rather than bald declarations of what "has to" be done.

Examining the different use of what in SFL are traditionally called high, median and low force within modality (Halliday 1994:91), the results suggest two challenges to standard CDA analyses of language and power: that the correlation of high modal force to high status is not as straightforward as suggested, or else the social analyses of power within society underlying

148 *Hybrid Voices and Collaborative Change*

Table 4.5 Modal Force by Speaker

	Low			Median			High		
	Oblig.	*Poss.*	*Total*	*Oblig.*	*Poss.*	*Total*	*Oblig.*	*Poss.*	*Total*
AM	0	4	4	3	9	12	14	0	14
UH	0	0	0	6	3	9	17	0	17
GW	1	4	5	29	23	51	18	0	18

such correlations are simplistic. I suggest the truth contains a little bit of both. Table 4.5 shows the force of the different speakers' modal use. Not all modal forms that appear in the texts are included, but only those traditionally labelled for force within SFL. Low obligation, for example, is realised by CAN for permission; median obligation by SHOULD for correct action; high obligation by HAVE TO for external force; and MUST as a subjective declaration. Low possibility is realised by MAY/MIGHT for 50/50 chances and potential; median possibility by projecting WILL; and high possibility by MUST and HAVE TO, though there are no tokens of these uses in the texts. A quick look at the table shows that Gordon overwhelmingly uses median force (though the inclusion of NEED TO would alter this distribution) while Uncle Henry uses mainly high force and Andrew uses high and median roughly equally. I will return to this point below.

Table 4.6 compares the three texts in terms of the percentage of their total modal use represented by CAN or CAPABLE to express 'dynamic modality', CAN to express 'no obstacle', NEED TO as 'essential element', HAVE TO as external force and SHOULD as correct action. The highlighted boxes bring out the important points discussed thus far: Andrew's high use of dynamic CAN; Uncle Henry's high use of no obstacle CAN; and Gordon's high use of SHOULD and NEED TO and his low use of HAVE TO.

Turning briefly to the question of who is the driving force in the collaboration between the local communities and Iwokrama and who are the beneficiaries, Table 4.7 demonstrates the point, made earlier, that Uncle

Table 4.6 Distinctive Tendencies in Modal Use by Speaker

	Dynamic		*No obstacle*		*Essential element*		*External force*		*Correct action*	
	Total	*As %*	*Total*	*As %*	*Total*	*As %*	*Total*	*As %*	*Total*	*As %*
AM (n = 63)	11	**17%**	9	15%	4	7%	11	17%	3	5%
UH (n = 64)	6	9%	19	**30%**	5	8%	12	19%	6	9%
GW (n = 151)	20	13%	15	10%	31	**21%**	18	**12%**	29	**19%**

Local Prestige, Local Power 149

Table 4.7 Allocation of Involvement, Uncle Henry and Gordon

		UH		GW	
Obligation	Beneficiary	Ag/In		Beneficiary	Ag/In	
Local	8	L	7	14	L	7
		I	0		I	7
		Jt	1		Jt	0
Iwokrama	12	L	7	4	L	0
		Iw	3		I	4
		Jt	2		Jt	0

Henry sees Iwokrama as benefiting significantly more than Gordon does from this collaboration (in terms of the processes over which he exerts modal authority at least), and also that he sees the local communities as being agentive in processes that benefit both groups. Gordon, in contrast, sees the local communities as the prime beneficiaries, with responsibility for these benefits equally shared between the two groups, while Iwokrama is solely responsible for those processes that he sees as to their own benefit. This demonstrates a marked difference between the two speakers' positions with regard to the purpose of their collaboration and also with regard to the scope of their symbolic capital within the development process.

In terms of how the different speakers allocate the overseer/performer role across the categories of work and organisation in those processes over which they exert modal authority, Table 4.8 shows that Uncle Henry construes the local community as equally responsible for each category, a position compatible with the "local autonomy" approach to empowerment in Table 2.1, discussed further below, while both Andrew and Graham see the local communities as primarily concerned with organisation. This skewed distribution also suggests that Uncle Henry, as a community elder, feels more entitled to demand work from the community than the other two speakers. In terms of the processes in which Iwokrama is the overseer/performer, Andrew's use of modality suggests that he sees Iwokrama in a predominantly organisational role while both Uncle Henry and Gordon see Iwokrama as equally involved in work and organisation. This would reflect the difference in Andrew's position as a grassroots member of the NRDDB, from which he sees Iwokrama's responsibilities as primarily advisory, and Uncle Henry and Gordon's positions as members of the NRDDB 'hierarchy', within which they share awareness of Iwokrama's responsibilities in carrying projects through to completion. However, it can also be seen that both Uncle Henry and Andrew use modal authority far less than Gordon in processes with Iwokrama in the overseer/performer role as compared with processes in which the local

150   *Hybrid Voices and Collaborative Change*

Table 4.8   Allocation of Organisation and Work by Speaker

		AM	UH	GW
Local as overseer/performer	Organise	20	**21**	23
	Work	10	**21**	10
Iwokrama as overseer/performer	Organise	8	2	43
	Work	1	3	48
Joint as overseer/performer	Organise	14	13	24
	Work	8	4	2

communities fill this role. Gordon, conversely, construes Iwokrama as overseer/performer twice as often as he does for the local communities. This suggests that all the speakers see their authority over action as primarily related to their own communities, though Gordon is more willing to allocate responsibility to his out-group than either Andrew or Uncle Henry, again reflecting his position as external advisor.

The following brief section turns to the different speakers' use of projections of affect and cognition as they relate to discursive power in order to complement and extend the analysis of modality and capital offered here.

Projection Analysis

As with the analysis of modality, the first step in the analysis of projection was to identify and systematise the forms appearing in the three interviews, categorised in Figure 4.3. These are divided into two broad categories of affect and cognition, with more delicate categories provided for each. The specific verbs used are given for each end-term and examples of each category are given in Appendix 3 in order to clarify the meaning of the descriptive labels. The network also includes the categories of Senser and projected participant to enable more delicate analyses in terms of who is involved in the projected processes and to allow for those cases where the speakers report the perceived projections of others:

Table 4.9 shows the ratio of affect to cognition mental projections for the different speakers. The figures here suggest that Andrew uses relatively more affect process types than the other two speakers, though the figures are small. As affect covers hopes and desires this would seem to reflect Andrew's symbolic capital as a farmer, in a position to make demands of the development process without holding a particularly strong personal influence within it. More unexpected figures come up, however, in analysing the division of cognition into knowledge and opinion, as in Table 4.10. What is initially surprising here is that Gordon, whose symbolic capital is underwritten by his scientific knowledge, shows the lowest ratio of knowledge to opinion. This finding resonates with the figures in Table 4.11, which show

Local Prestige, Local Power 151

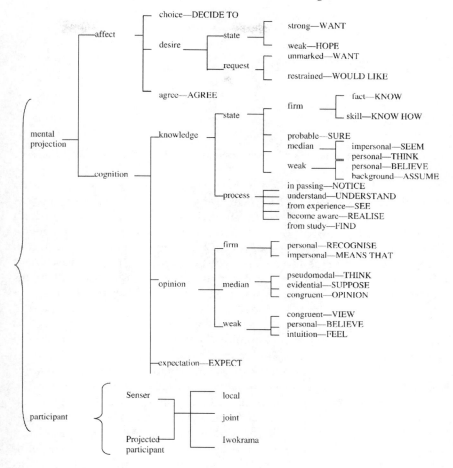

Figure 4.3 Network of projections in interviews with Andrew Martins, Uncle Henry and Gordon Wilson.

Table 4.9 Affect and Cognition by Speaker

	Total mental Processes	Total Affect	as % of mental	Total Cognition	as % of mental
AM	24	7	29.2%	17	70.8%
UH	25	5	20%	20	80%
GW	92	16	17.4%	76	82.6%

152 *Hybrid Voices and Collaborative Change*

Table 4.10 Subdivision of Cognition by Speaker

	Total cognition	Total Knowledge	as % of cognition	Total Opinion	as % of cognition	Total Expectation	as % of cognition
AM	17	12	70.6%	5	29.4%	0	0%
UH	20	9	45%	7	35%	4	20%
GW	76	28	36.8%	47	61.8%	1	1.3%

that Gordon states his views with less force than either of the other two speakers.

Overall, an analysis of cognitive projections shows that Gordon, rather than projecting concepts as known, overwhelmingly gives opinions, the great majority of which are median in force. In fact, 40.2% of all Gordon's mental projections, cognitive or affective, express median opinions. It might be expected that Gordon would deal in facts rather than opinions and in firm opinions rather than weak ones; however, recalling his extensive use of SHOULD to offer suggestions rather than stating firm obligations, it seems possible that the ability to give opinions, and of median rather than strong force, is in fact a result of Gordon's knowledge-based capital and not a contradiction of it. In this sense, suggestions of appropriateness, as opposed to declarations of obligation, and opinions on states of affairs, as opposed to statements of fact, are very similar speech acts in that they carry force as pronouncements in direct proportion to the embodied symbolic capital of the speaker. This suggests that projecting ideas as personal opinion is not always a form of hedging that reflects lack of confidence, but might well be related to a strong sense of self-belief (as suggested in the qualitative analysis of the extracts from both Gordon and Uncle Henry's interviews in the preceding). Whereas Andrew, for example, relies on what he has concrete evidence for, through HAVE TO and KNOW, Gordon introduces his own personal views of reality, particularly through SHOULD and THINK clauses. Andrew appears, thus, to present realities beyond his control, while Gordon is actively negotiating and construing his own realities.

As we saw above with regard to modality, Uncle Henry is closer to Andrew in using the strong forms HAVE TO and MUST rather than

Table 4.11 Force of Knowledge and Opinions by Speaker

	Total Knowledge[8] and Opinion	Total Firm	as %	Total Median	as %	Total Weak	as %
AM	14	7	50%	5	35.7%	2	14.3%
UH	11	3	27.3%	7	63.6%	1	9.1%
GW	68	15	22.1%	46	67.6%	7	10.3%

Local Prestige, Local Power 153

SHOULD. In terms of mental projections, however, Uncle Henry is closer to Gordon in using median force, suggesting that he can rely on his stature within the community and his mix of local and imported knowledge to give his opinions their due weight. However, while Gordon presents his own views in a seemingly weaker fashion than do the other speakers, he takes the liberty of presenting the mental projections of others a total of 23 times (see Bartlett [2003] for further details and examples), something Uncle Henry does only twice and Andrew never. This would seem to suggest that Gordon's knowledge-based capital not only enables him to present his own version of reality but to construct and present reality as it is for others and this mirrors his relatively high modal use in construing the actions of others, as shown in Table 4.8 and analysed there as reflecting his status as external advisor.

CONCLUSION: DIFFERENCES IN SYMBOLIC CAPITAL AND THE POTENTIAL FOR COLLABORATION

I started this chapter with a discussion of Bourdieu's concept of *symbolic capital* and his suggestion that within a given field of discourse the speaker who embodied the most symbolic capital within that field would be able to dominate the discourse as a process through their mastery of the *authorised language* that is an arbitrary symbol of authority within that field. In these terms a discourse event is a linguistic *marketplace* in which those with the greatest symbolic capital have the greatest purchasing power as their discourse will carry a weight that is disproportionate to its content. Expanding on Bourdieu's notion of the linguistic marketplace, I suggested that within any given situation there might be a tension between different possible storylines, each with their own hierarchies of symbolic power and orders of indexicality, and that there is potential slippage between these different storylines as the discourse progresses. I then went on to suggest that, rather than there being a single symbolic capital attached to a field such as local development, there are in fact different types of capital related to the positions of different speakers within the field, such as experienced local farmer, community elder and certificated expert. These positions are conjunctions of various oppositions, such as knowledge versus social position, local versus external and experience versus education, and are realised in practice through the configuration of field, tenor and mode that comprise each speaker's unique voice. And these features are far from arbitrary as they foreground the area of expertise of each speaker, their social relationship with their audience and the accustomed means of transmission within their community (this last to be illustrated in greater detail in the following chapters). In these terms, the workings of the linguistic marketplace are not simply a function of the relative weight of the speakers' embodied symbolic capitals, as in Bourdieu's formulation; rather, the

154 *Hybrid Voices and Collaborative Change*

audience themselves become an integral part of the marketplace, as they will attach different weight to the discourse of different speakers, recalibrating the order of indexicality that is in operation, as a function of their own background and the specific field of discourse at any point in time, as demonstrated with the slippage in storylines in Text 3.1. And, as with the slippage between storylines, there is an ebbing and flowing of these different voices in a sustained discourse, comprising as it does many subfields that between them constitute the general field of discourse. Following Bourdieu, we can assume that within each subfield there is a competition for authority; however, over the discourse as a whole, there is likely to be an interplay between the different types of authority displayed, each with its own specific purpose, and these different authorities have the potential to be used in collaboration rather than in opposition, particularly if there is a common interest at stake—or, at least, compatible interests. From this perspective discourse can be simultaneously competitive and collaborative, and even the competitive features can be subsumed within a collaborative whole. In seeking to further the collaborative potential of discourse and the empowerment of marginalised groups, therefore, we can look for both commonalities across the discourses of the two groups and fault lines in the discourse of the dominant groups that can be exploited, a theme I will return to in Chapter 7.

To conclude: A corollary of Bourdieu's conceptualisation of symbolic capital and the linguistic marketplace is that there is a zero-sum competition for dominance in which the winner takes all; in my expanded conceptualisation, however, the existence of different capitals, each with a specific function and domain, means that the symbolic capital of different speakers can be employed collaboratively towards a common goal. The analyses of this chapter have suggested that three different, and complex, types of symbolic capital were at work in the narratives of the three speakers, each related upwards to the speaker's social position within the development process, and downwards to their use of linguistic features in constructing an appropriate voice. In the present chapter I focused on the interpersonal elements of these voices, as construed through the use of modality and mental projections. At the grassroots, practical end of development is Andrew Martins, who largely orients to development process in terms of goals, through high objective modality (HAVE TO), the expression of desires (WANT), and through the identification of the dynamic capabilities of the community (CAN) in achieving these goals, so projecting likely future benefits (WILL). At the other extreme, as a professional development worker and certificated scientist, is Gordon. Gordon, too, considers dynamic capabilities and projects outcomes, but he is concerned not so much with identifying objective goals as with identifying shortcomings in the process (NEED TO), expressing explicitly personal opinions (THINK), and making suggestions (SHOULD). In contrast to Andrew's use of high modality, which counterbalances his status as a grassroots member of the NRDDB,

Gordon's median opinions carry weight in proportion to his certificated knowledge and his position within the NRDDB 'hierarchy'. Mixing elements of both discourses is Uncle Henry who, like Andrew, draws on local knowledge to state what has to be done, yet, like Gordon, expresses explicitly personal opinions that derive their force from his status as local elder and member of the NRDDB 'hierarchy'. Unlike either Andrew or Gordon, however, Uncle Henry's unique status means that, rather than projecting future results, he can determine what is conceivable, with his high status in the community underwriting his use of CAN to simultaneously define what is practically possible in relation to Andrew's HAVE TO and what is permissible in relation to Gordon's SHOULD. In other words, Uncle Henry's status permits him to pronounce the *nihil obstat* on potential activities, as appropriate within the *local autonomy* approach to empowerment in Table 2.1. This potentially collaborative interaction of different types of symbolic capital is represented in diagrammatic form in Figure 4.4.

As an example of the interplay of these types of symbolic capital, we can look again at the extract from Andrew that provided the epigram for this chapter:

Yeah, well, of course there is a lot of differences. Because naturally I believe not everything they say is good. Again, not everything they say is bad. Because—so what we do, we make a suggestion here, "Okay, we are glad for the advice, but this is how we know it. Because from our past experience, this is how we . . . are (x) now." If we were not

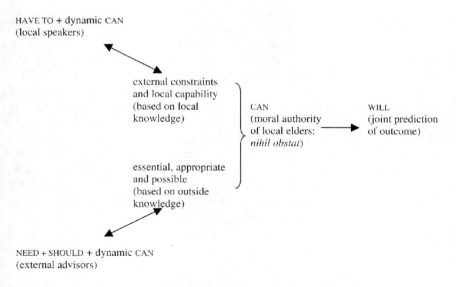

Figure 4.4 Interaction of different modes of power based on analysis of modality and projection.

156 *Hybrid Voices and Collaborative Change*

sustainable, I think we could've been find ourselves in a very lacking way now, not having so many things. But up to today's date, we still have a variety of things that we can have to show you, or to show many more people: "This is our (x)". This is the reason why I say we stick with our own way of life.

This extract shows how Andrew values the knowledgeable input of outside experts yet feels free to accept or reject this advice in relation to his own position as an expert in local production (and note his use of THINK here to express personal opinion within his specialist field), an expertise developed through an accumulation of past experience that translates into symbolic capital in a marketplace where this experience is recognised, that is to say, both known and acknowledged.

The analyses of the three interviews offered here represent only a small sample of discourse. And even if similar results were found from a larger sample, the model of collaborative power in Figure 4.4 would represent only a heuristic device for analysing further discourse within the Star of David model, developed above, and to be considered against the social and discourse background outlined in Chapters 2 and 3. Moreover, the positions taken up by Andrew, Uncle Henry and Gordon were achieved in an artificial and relatively non-threatening context, and thus represent the positions they adopt *in idealis*; it remains to be seen if and how they are able to adopt such positions *in realis*, that is to say, in the nitty-gritty of genuine discourse.

Between them the linguistic analyses of this chapter and the social and historical background presented in Chapters 2 and 3 represent a means of 'triangulating' with the analysis of interactive discourse and the interplay of symbolic capitals that I present in Chapters 5 and 6. In these following chapters I compare and contrast the failings of the Management Planning Workshop as a contrived exercise in the redistribution of power with the successful discourse strategies employed by skilled Amerindian speakers, including a more experienced Walter, within the setting of the bimonthly NRDDB meetings. The analyses of the next chapter largely focus on and around the performance of Walter and demonstrate how he came to develop an intercultural style as chairman which went some way to achieving his desire to combine a role as a speaker from the floor with a confidence and skill in controlling and adapting the flow of information and activity from the chair. In Chapter 6 I focus on the interplay of field, tenor and mode in creating alternative voices and the scope for collaboration between these voices.

5 Taking Control

CEWs, please be brief in your reporting. We know that you attended NRDDB last meeting and thi:s and tha::. Also what you would say, we know about it. What we want to know is, like, what new things have been taking place in communities that <u>we</u> are not aware of.

(Walter, NRDDB Meeting, Yakarinta, 19/1/2002)

In the last chapter I suggested that there might be different types of symbolic capital at play within any field of discourse and that, while these different capitals might be employed strategically and competitively at any given point in the discourse, this does not mean that they will not ultimately be employed collaboratively towards a common goal. Quantitative data was used to compare the use of key linguistic features by Andrew, Uncle Henry and Gordon as indices of the authority and expertise each speaker assumed with regard to local development and so to determine the particular type of symbolic capital each appropriated to themselves, within the contrived context of my interviews at least. The analytical categories used in compiling the quantitative data were developed to capture as far as possible the dynamics of real-time utterances in that they were based on the various speech act functions of the modals and mental projections rather than on their uncontextualised grammatical meaning. However, quantitative analyses of this type are always open to the criticism that they rely on "policies of simply counting the number of questions, or coding the type of question asked [. . . while . . .] not being sensitive enough to the more basic sense of context . . . the local . . . sequential context of talk in which utterances are produced" (Hutchby and Wooffitt 1998:164; cf. Widdowson's criticisms in Chapter 1, this volume). So, to build on the quantitative analyses of Chapter 4 and the general categories of symbolic capital they suggested, in this chapter I will analyse in detail five texts from NRDDB events spanning the 18-month period from July 2000 to January 2002, each of which demonstrates in its own way the linguistic means by which members of the NRDDB were able to exercise strategic control over "the sequential context of talk" in terms of the participation of other speakers and the nature of the content that was produced. In particular the following texts show how Walter managed to develop a style of authoritative discourse that combined his role as chair of the board with his traditional status within the community. The texts are presented in chronological order to give some idea of the continuity of these developments, but the analyses are not directly comparable as there are different strategies employed and different linguistic features highlighted within each text and so each is analysed in its own terms.

158 *Hybrid Voices and Collaborative Change*

Each text is presented as a relatively detailed transcription. As with Text 3.1 this is followed by a gloss of salient features of the text which is, in turn, followed by an interpretation of the discourse in terms of control over participation and meaning, drawing on the theoretical apparatus and the historical background of earlier chapters. In the concluding section I bring these analyses together to discuss in general terms the shifts in control and relations of power they illustrate and how they contrast with Text 3.1.

CHRONOLOGICAL ANALYSIS OF NRDDB DISCOURSE

Text 5.1 was recorded a couple of months after Text 3.1, this time at an NRDDB meeting in the Bina Hill Institute, an impressive structure purpose-built by the community as a centre for NRDDB business. As stated in Chapter 2, NRDDB meetings stretch over two days and bring together representatives from all 13 communities of the North Rupununi, from Iwokrama and other development organisations, and from the government. Meetings are normally attended by between 30 to 40 people. Present at the meeting from which the following text was taken were the Minister for Amerindian Affairs and representatives of the United Nations Development Programme (UNDP). This analysis shows Walter (W in the transcript) as a confident speaker from the floor and demonstrates how, in this capacity, he is already using some of the same rhetorical techniques as the then-chairman Sam (S in the transcript), who at the time was by far the more experienced in dealing with national and international bodies. The following analysis focuses on the strategies employed by Walter and Sam in making indirect yet extremely forceful requests. Immediately prior to the extract Walter had been talking about the complications that the road from Brazil would cause.

In the two stretches of text from Walter (1–6&7–16) there is a movement in the ideational content from stating an existing problem to proposing a possible solution. The first stretch leads from the threat of the new road (1–2) to the possibility of drafting new legislation that would provide Amerindian communities with the means to police their own territories (2–6); the second moves from the limitations of a committee established to discuss these issues (7–11) to the preferred option of recognising extended Amerindian lands within the region (11–16). In both cases the solution is presented: (i) as hypothetical, through "probably" (2, 3&12), "could" (3, twice), and a conditional clause (12); and (ii) as contingent on outside help, expressed through prepositional phrases with the relevant processes nominalised in "with the assistance of the programme manager for the UNDP" (2–3) and "with the approval of the Minster" (12–13). The first request is rounded off with a reassurance that there is a solution to the problem, expressed through a projection with high-certainty KNOW (5) and "no obstacle" CAN (6), while the second, conversely, emphasises the

Taking Control 159

Text 5.1   NRDDB Meeting, Bina Hill Institute, 7/7/00

1   **W:** . . . and time and again you hear the Chairman saying, like, "If we don't use the road, the
2   road will use us." So, probably, with the assistance of the programme manager for the
3   UNDP probably we could put something paper and I could send it, I don't know how the
4   Minister would erm look into this, the Amerindian Act is so vague, and there isn't anything
5   that we could be . . . rely upon in the Amerindian Act, but I know that there is some
6   provision where we can make, subsidiary legislation, but . . .

((Walter tells an anecdote about the difficulties of removing a birdtrapper from the road and suggests setting up a committee to protect Amerindian rights.))

7   **W:** So my kind of proposition is that we sit down and draft a proposal as to how the committee
8   can function. I know that erm . . . Dr Ivor Hives had proposed some brilliant ideas, and I like
9   the idea about M- also, if we could have more of those erm activities within the area,
10   where we can work in partnership with these NGOs, it would be quite erm much more
11   safer. But Ivor was saying that have traditional fishing and hunting areas been declared,
12   although it would be out of community boundaries, and . . . probably, with the approval of
13   the Minister, if we can do that, just have the traditional erm hunting and fishing areas, also
14   logging areas, to be declared as Amerindian uhm fishing, hunting areas, just for that
15   purpose, in case these uhm outsiders would come in and exploit everything and leave us
16   bare. Thank you.

((Sam responds, winding up his contribution as follows))

17 **S:**   . . . So we need to think about these things and I'm quite certain Minister is
18   going to. .not sleep on it, but think of it, and, probably, with some more ideas coming—
19   feed it back to Minister, I'm quite certain he would be happy to have like erm suggestions
20   coming from all of us. You can never tell what will come of all this. So we need to look
21   at it. And that is what . . . that is what we need to look at in the fight against
22   poverty—and not against poverty alone, but against other things. Probably that might be the
23   next erm project UNDP could help us with. Fight against intruders.

---

consequences of inaction (15–16) through the strongly predictive WOULD rather than the more hypothetical MIGHT or COULD (15).

Sam's contribution from the chair contains many of the same linguistic features as Walter's. He twice uses high-certainty "I'm quite certain" (17&19) to project the Minister's collaboration, and he reinforces this with a double use of NEED expressing "essential element" (20&21). Sam's contribution is also hedged, though the use of PROBABLY (18&22) and modalised clauses expressing conditionality (19), uncertainty (20) and hypotheticality (22). And like Walter, Sam provides an extremely negative evaluation of any alternative action in, in this case through the attitudinal lexis of "I'm quite certain the Minister is going to . . . not sleep on it" (17–18).

Interpretation of Text 5.1

In this extract we see how, rather than formally request help, Walter as good as *presupposes* the contribution of influential participants at the meeting, the Minister for Amerindian Affairs and UNDP representatives. This is

160   *Hybrid Voices and Collaborative Change*

achieved by two different linguistic strategies: nominalisation and projection. In lines 2 and 12 Walter nominalises the sought-after processes of assisting and approving as complements within prepositional groups. This is a strategy that makes the processes less negotiable, less deniable, than if they had been realised as finite verbs, and the element of contingency is similarly obscured through the use of WITH as compared with IF. Walter thus construes the assistance and approval as more concrete, as closer to givens, than if he had used the alternative phrasing "if the manager for the UNDP assists us" or "if the Minister approves". A level of presupposition is also achieved by Walter's words "I don't know how the Minister would erm look into this" (3–4), a projection of how rather than if this help will be forthcoming (WOULD is used in Guyanese English to refer to future plans and not just to hypothetical events). As both the Minister and representatives of the UNDP were present at the meeting and would have to respond to Walter's contribution, these strategies *set them up* in a position which is appropriate to their symbolic capital and which they must in some way fill or be seen to avoid. As a result the onus is very much on them to explain any discrepancies between their own proposed course of action and Walter's presuppositions. Given this level of imposition, Walter's use of hedges serves to tone down his statements in deference to the status of his intended interlocutors. PROBABLY, for example, is used three times (2, 3&12) to frame the implicit demands, a strategy reinforced through the use of "I don't know" (3) and modality expressing hypotheticality through COULD (3 twice, 9), the lack of obstacle through CAN (10), or conditionality (10&12). However, Walter subverts the impact of the hedges in both stretches of talk. In the first case, he ensures that the pressure is still on the Minister to provide through his high-certainty projection of what is possible "but I know that there is some er provision that we can make" (5–6). In the second case he makes a strong prediction of the disastrous effects of failing to extend territorial rights: "outsiders would come in and exploit everything and leave us bare" (15–16). Walter thus sets himself up in a position of authority while coercing the Minister to use his own authority to meet the community's expectations or appear to be failing in his duties.

The strategies used by Walter from the floor are almost exactly mirrored by Sam from the chair, who produces two strong presuppositions of assistance through "I'm quite certain" (17&19) and also uses modality to disallow inaction in "we need to look at it" (20&21). Sam's contribution, like Walter's, is respectfully hedged, while the concessive force of his hedges, as with Walter's, is quite undermined by an extremely negative evaluation of any alternative action: "I'm quite certain the Minister is going to . . . not sleep on it" (17–18).

In these extracts we see both Walter and Sam using modality and other linguistic devices to set up positions for themselves and for others, drawing on their symbolic capital as community elders, displayed *in idealis* by Uncle Henry in Text 4.2, to state the community's needs and aspirations

Taking Control   161

strategically *in realis* before a demanding *linguistic marketplace*. In both cases Walter and Sam play on the paternalistic and advocating tendencies of outside agents, putting pressure on them to take particular courses of action through presuppositions of help and bald statements of the consequences of inaction. These presumptive strategies are attempts to force the hand of the Minister and the UNDP representatives later in the discourse, as not to deal explicitly with the topics proposed would at best need explanation and at worst be construed as "sleeping on it" (18) or allowing outsiders to "come in and exploit everything and leave us bare"(15–16). In this way both Walter and Sam exploit the symbolic capital that they hold within the community in general and in the NRDDB in particular (and note that Walter refers to Sam in his institutional role as the "Chairman" in line 1) to co-opt the efforts of those who hold power at a higher level, while acknowledging this external power through the extreme hedging of these assumptions. In this regard, the invisible institutional structures that disempowered Walter at the Iwokrama-led Management Planning Workshop, as illustrated in Text 3.1, would seem to have their empowering counterparts within the institutional structures of the NRDDB, reinforced here through the symbolic example of Sam as an accomplished office-holder and the physical setting of the Bina Hill Institute, purpose-built by the community for just such meetings, as a 'space' that "becomes [a] 'place', a particular space on which senses of belonging, property rights and authority can be projected" (Blommaert 2005:222).

In Text 5.2 we see how Walter, now chairman of the NRDDB, and Sam, speaking from the floor, draw on the symbolic capital of their *institutional position* within the NRDDB to co-negotiate a position that is contrary to that of Sara as Iwokrama speaker. The discourse up to this point has dealt with a document jointly prepared by representatives of the NRDDB and Iwokrama which was due to be discussed by the entire Board. However, as not all those present have read it and there are considerable doubts as to the level of understanding from community representatives, the participants are discussing the best way to proceed with the discussion. SUAs are Sustainable Utilisation Areas, parts of the Iwokrama Forest where non-timber products will be exploited for commercial use. (**W** is Walter; **AvD** is André van Dijk, a UNDP representative; **UH** is Uncle Henry.)

We join the discussion as Sara, having questioned the level of understanding of the document and its purpose (1–4), explicitly ("it's up to you" in lines 4&6) and emphatically ("clearly" in line 4) cedes authority to the board to decide how the discussion should proceed. However, Walter (7–17) does not follow up this course of action, but chooses instead to justify his earlier report on the meeting in which the document was produced. His report was not "in detail" as he assumed the document would be discussed at the present meeting (9). As a result, Walter is not sure how to remedy the situation (16) and leaves the issue hanging, as signalled with his unfinished conditional clause and rising intonation (17). At this point Sara makes an

162   *Hybrid Voices and Collaborative Change*

Text 5.2   NRDDB Meeting, 4/11/2000, Bina Hill Institute

 1 **Ssts:** This document is given to the representatives to ask you if we are
 2   understanding you correctly. Our purpose in this meeting is to ask the NRDDB
 3   if you agree to us meeting with those representatives in between the SUA
 4   meetings. So it is clearly up to you, the NRDDB, to decide for (xx), to decide
 5   what (xxxxxxxx). We don't have to stick with it, (the idea is complex, it's
 6   xxx). So it's up to you to decide what time you want to give.
 7 **W:**   Uhm, what I was doing in my report . . . earlier, I . . . did you notice I just gave you
 8   the main points? And that is more or less what is on the agenda . . . I did not go
 9   into detail because I thought you would pick it up, this here. So that is why I
10   didn't go into what is goal number one, what is goal number two, three, four,
11   five and so on, what are the key environmental aims and what is the key
12   (element) of the environmental aims. I didn't go into that, thinking that it
13   would have been, erm, would be picked up in this piece of document. That is
14   why I kind of changed my reporting . . . that is not the way I planned to report,
15   but I did it so . . . so that we could go into this through this piece of document
16   here. I don't know wh. .what. .what course we would take now, if we could
17   (reverse our xx scheme)?
18 **Sara:** If I may make a suggestion, maybe it would (fall into our xx), maybe what I
19   could do, if you would agree to it, is . . . is go through this, we wrote this, so we
20   know what we're talking about, and it's . . . if the language is not appropriate, so
21   maybe if I were to go through the points quickly, maybe in a more basic way, if
22   you still want to use the document as a basis, and then we say what was
23   meant . . . what we interpret what's meant (xxx) instead of us reading (?aloud)
24   the whole document. Would that work?
25 **W:**   You see, the idea of where we wanted to discuss this is so that the kind of
26   information that we would need from this thing (that was here) and the thing
27   that was . . . that I am referring to, this is what we want to disseminate this
28   information, the management planning team, so that you could go out back to
29   your communities and at least have an idea of what . . . we're talking about, one,
30   one i, and one, two i, and so forth. You would be able to explain to the
31   community that this is what we are saying and so forth. (It's not very clear).
32   Yes, I would be happy if Sara would go through it, if you agree.
33 **Sam:**   So, I don't want to continue with=it sounds terrible but. .I, my thought was
34   (xxxxxx) and by now, if we had gone through this thing page by page, saying
35   that this is the general idea of what took place, "Our participation was so forth,
36   this is what we did and so forth", and erm the stories were (confirmed) your
37   contribution, I thought it would have set the floor for participation, you know,
38   for you now to "Oh, now I understand", because I realise that some persons
39   have not read this document as yet, since yesterday afternoon till now. So, er,
40   that is . . . how (I've been looking at) this thing. It, it's a beginning for us, at the
41   first we took some time before we took office and we had like people in the
42   know and that is something new. So, it's something new here for us, so all,
43   probably, (if there's any yet to say) "Yes, well, the people should go out there
44   more and give us, er, regular feedback in whatever form, because then you
45   would know well, How? Why? How do I begin, why should I support . . . ?"
46   And that is what I was just asking about from the beginning. I realise that to
47   get the (x) of what's reporting . . . erm . . . in some cases it was (xx) repetition, so
48   you have this sort of °(xx), happen (xxx).°
49 **AvD:**   I don't know what your agenda is but . . . maybe . . . it give time to read it
50   and discuss it later on in the day, 'cause it doesn't make sense, I think, to

(continued)

51		discuss a complex document like this, and people don't, haven't read it, you
52		know? I don't know if you have time in the afternoon, if you give people an
53		hour during the day between lunch, to quickly go through it, split into groups
54		and everybody, you know, erm, discuss one point rather than discussing all the
55		points together, maybe one group will specialise on one point, something like
56		that—how many points here? Seven? So if you split into seven groups and
57		each group takes one point, rather than focusing on the whole document, we let
58		them go for an hour, come back to report, or at least ask questions, I don't
59		know.
60	Sam:	I think everybody needs to know what this whole thing is about, if you pick
61		up like maybe individual things, you still would be at a loss because, "What is
62		it really talking about?" (Everybody's like they leave something) at home, you
63		know. So I was, if you get the general picture, "That is actually a picture,
64		okay", well after that mm ↑you could . . .
65	W:	All right, erm, as I said, I gave this out since yesterday and (you had till) nine
66		o'clock this morning (so could you not) take a couple of minutes at breakfast
67		and if you were really serious about it, I think you should have gone through it,
68		maybe this morning, and pick it up and start to read it through. (Maybe) some
69		of it was, I didn't know that this, like I said earlier, was that this was just our
70		contribution and not the entire report of yesterday evening meeting. So . . . you
71		know, I have a system of if people don't read . . . read it . . . at home, well then
72		we read it together. I would . . . if you want we to do that . . . so that though we
73		wouldn't read it here, I don't think it would when you return, that you would
74		read it either. So, if this is erm on the agenda for discussion we should go
75		ahead discussing and reading it and probably find (such) find you have
76		explanation and would say . . . if you are willing to say, "Well, Chairman, I don't
77		understand what is written", and perhaps ((Iwokrama representative)) could
78		break it down in detail. Then how does that . . .
79	UH:	Mister Chairman, I would like to make some comments.

attempt to direct the process in a contribution laced with hedges (18–24). She begins her contribution with an extremely polite request expressed as a modalised conditional, "if I may" (17), and continues with a sequence of MAYBEs (18, twice, & 21, twice), three conditional clauses (19, 21&21–22), which are further downplayed through the use of WOULD (19) and the subjunctive "if I were to" (21), and ending with a conditional interrogative (24) to make it clear that the final decision is the board's. Two of her conditional clauses are also explicit concessions to the will of the board: "if you would agree" (19) and "if you still want" (21–22). In contrast with these hedges, however, is the bald "we wrote this, so we know what we're talking about" (19–20).

Walter continues to mull over the problem, reiterating the intentions behind his proposed discussion (25–31), eventually stating that he is "happy" to allow Sara to resolve the problem, if the board agrees (32). At this point Sam intervenes. After apologising in advance for changing the tack of the discussion again (33), he puts forward his own proposal that the document is discussed "page by page" (34), in direct contrast

164   *Hybrid Voices and Collaborative Change*

with Sara's suggestion not to discuss the "whole document" (23–24) but to "go through points quickly" and in a "more basic way" (21). While Sam formally diminishes the strength of his suggestion as just thoughts (33&37) and by couching them in hypothetical language with "if we had gone through this thing page by page . . . it would have set the floor for participation" (34–37), he twice switches to the direct speech of imaginary community members, first to bring to life the contents of his proposed discussion (35–36), with responsibility for confirming the CEWs' reports ceded to Iwokrama (36–37), and secondly to suggest that such an approach would have led to better understanding (38). Sam then makes excuses for the time-consuming approach he has suggested on the grounds that local leaders are relatively inexperienced in holding office (40–41) and are simply responding to community demands, which he presents once again through imaginary direct speech (43–45).

The contribution from André, a UNDP representative (49–59), is an attempt at a compromise, suggesting that the participants discuss different sections of the document in groups and come together afterwards. Sam counters this suggestion on the grounds that everyone needs to know the whole document (60), with his contribution again mitigated as a thought (60) but framed in the imaginary direct speech of local participants (61–62&63–64). Walter then speaks from the chair to give his verdict on the situation (65–78), signalling with his opening "all right" (65) and the repetition of the summative "so" (66, 70, 72&74) that his decision has been made after considering the options. Walter summarises the situation in terms that echo Sam in implicitly criticising community representatives (67–68), while continuing to justify his own approach of earlier (71–74), and he ultimately decides on the course of action proposed by Sam (74–77), also requesting that Iwokrama could help in interpreting matters (77–78).

Interpretation of Text 5.2

In this extract we see a slight tussle between the different symbolic capitals of Iwokrama's imported knowledge and the moral authority of the community elders, enhanced here through their institutional status as chair and ex-chair of the NRDDB—a further form of symbolic capital, embodying a different order of indexicality, to those discussed in Chapter 4. A striking example of this comes with Sara's bald assertion that "we wrote this, so we know what we're talking about" (19–20). This claim to authority-through-knowledge from Sara is an explicit reference to the particular form of symbolic capital Iwokrama holds in relation to the local communities and suggests that the extensive facework (18–24) framing the proposed change in format was purely in deference to interpersonal conventions of politeness that acknowledge the symbolic capital held by Walter as chairman.

Sam reciprocates Sara's deference in presenting his counter-argument to Iwokrama's proposal as just thoughts (33&37), but he then draws on his own symbolic capital as a spokesperson for the community to counter Sara's knowledge-based capital through the use of imagined community voices that vindicate his approach (61–62&62–63). Here his use of concrete illustrations (35–36) is in direct opposition to Iwokrama's suggestion that they "interpret" events (23) and seems designed to appeal to the community's preference for practice over theory, discussed above. This show of solidarity with the community serves as a buffer to the following critical comments in which Sam explicitly points out that some of the participants have not read the document yet (38–39), while maintaining common ground with the community in being faced with "something new here for us" (42). As an outsider, Sara has to display extreme courtesy towards her hosts, while Sam, as a community elder, is in a position to criticise and to lay blame. Sam's second contribution repeats this general strategy, with his contribution once more framed as merely a thought (60), but with the repercussions of alternatives expressed through imaginary direct speech (63–64), again emphasising Sam's solidarity with the community through his ability to put their thoughts into words.

Walter's summing up also contains overt criticisms of local participants (67–68), and the force of his final judgment, introduced with the claim to personal authority "I have a system" (71) and set out with an unmitigated 'if not x, then y' formula (71–72), is also dependent on his standing as a community elder and NRDDB chair. Similarly to Sam, Walter draws on imagined community voices to justify his authority (76–78), but makes a concession to Iwokrama's alternative symbolic capital, as represented by their knowledge, in asking them to break down and sum up the document (77–78). Text 5.2 thus shows that Walter is coming to terms with juggling the various manifestations of power within NRDDB–Iwokrama discourse. Whereas tensions between the two forms of authority go some way towards explaining his self-confessed difficulty in simultaneously playing facilitator and community elder in the earlier Workshop, by the time of Texts 5.1 and 5.2 we see a more comfortable Walter, buoyed up by the experience and skills of Sam and able to draw on his locally based moral authority while leading what is essentially an imported institutional format. The analyses of Texts 5.3 to 5.5, from over a year later, will further demonstrate Walter's growth into this role.

As well as demonstrating the aforementioned variations of *tenor* in the negotiating strategies of the various participants, the topic of Text 5.2 is also relevant to a consideration of voice as it concerns the *mode* of presenting information in the meeting and, in particular, the role of written text and its appropriateness to community practice (see Bartlett [2006] for a fuller discussion of these issues). The opposition here is not between written and oral exposition, but between written-to-be-read and written-as-a-prompt-for-orality, a difference made explicit when Walter says of his reporting style that "I did it so that we *could go into it through* this piece of document here" (15–16; my emphasis) and Sam says "if we had gone

166 *Hybrid Voices and Collaborative Change*

through this thing page by page . . . it would have set the floor for participation" (34–37). Similarly, in closing his (admittedly fluctuating) argument against Sara's suggestion that the Iwokrama representatives merely gloss over the document because "we wrote this, so we know what we're talking about" (19–20), Walter says "we should go ahead discussing and reading it" (74–75). Here Sara shares the concern with Walter to "use the original as a basis" (22), but she sees the question as one of comprehension and time and so does not see the need to read through it together. However, the distinction between written-to-be-read and written-as-a-prompt-for-orality, as made by Heath (1983:230–235), is not simply a question of different abilities in literacy or technical comprehension, but rather one of participation. For example, when André (52–56) suggests that things would be made easier by discussing different sections of the text in groups and reporting back, this idea is knocked back by Sam, who emphasises the need for the community as a whole "to get the general picture" (63). The idea of group participation is relevant in two ways. Firstly, the switch to written-as-prompt mode brings NRDDB discourse closer to community modes of socialisation, as Walter described it (above) in his comparison of indigenous and centralised schooling:

> *The Makushi culture is not something that you learn, you know, on a book or something, it's something that is be passed on, yeah, from your parent, parent['s] parent, that's why, the thing that I would know, the sum of the thing that I know, what my father taught me, is what his father taught him, what his father taught him, going back, all the way back.*

However, viewing the move as no more than a concession to textual tradition would be to miss how a change in the mode of discourse, as an aspect of voice particularly salient within different orders of indexicality, can have important repercussions on the balance of symbolic capital between local and professional groups and the positions each is able to adopt. In the development context, written text *qua* written is iconic of the power of professional and governmental groups, establishing a particular set of power relations even before content is considered—an idea captured in Sara's "we wrote this, so we know what we're talking about". The switch to written-as-prompt mode to some extent neutralises the authority of the written text and transfers it to the text's interpreter. Thus the community gets a boost both through the 'official' recognition of their discourse system and through the individual semiotic performances of those who interpret the text. As a more dynamic mode, however, there is wiggle room for the negotiation of authority, and Walter's calling on Sara to "explain to the community that this is what we are saying and so forth" (30–31), as with similar recognition of Iwokrama's role (77–78), shows that he now feels in a position to bring Iwokrama's authority into play when he sees fit. Heath (1983:234–235) reaches the following conclusions on the use of written text in her celebrated case study of literate traditions in Roadville and Trackton:

> In Roadville, the absoluteness of ways of talking about what is written fits church ways of talking about what is written. Behind the word is an authority, and the text is a message which can only be taken apart insofar as its analysis does not extend too far beyond the text and commonly agreed upon experiences. New syntheses and multiple interpretations create alternatives which challenge fixed roles, rules, and 'rightness'. In Trackton, the written word is for negotiation and manipulation—both serious and playful. Changing and changeable, words are the tools performers use to create images of themselves and the world they see. For Roadville, the written word limits alternatives of expression; in Trackton, it opens alternatives.

In the NRDDB context, the switch to written-as-prompt is an example of the opening up of the professional and community discourse systems to mutual appropriation and the creation of new genres in which there are new balances and interplays of ideology, a point to be taken up below and in the following chapter.

Text 5.3 comes from an NRDDB meeting 14 months after Text 5.2 and 18 months after Text 5.1. In order to increase participation from community members not formally connected to the NRDDB, it had been decided to rotate meetings between the 13 communities of the North Rupununi whenever possible. The meeting from which Text 5.3 is taken took place in the village of Yakarinta, a five-mile jeep ride, a river crossing and a mile's trek on foot beyond the Bina Hill Institute. Text 5.3 is from the first day of the two-day meeting, a day usually given over to local issues with Iwokrama only participating peripherally. However, as Dr. Trudy Hunt, who has been the Director General of Iwokrama for six months, has undertaken the difficult journey from Georgetown to attend her first meeting, she is invited to address the community. Walter, who is now chair of the NRDDB, introduces her with the following words:

In this brief extract Walter lays great stress on Trudy's status: through the general sign of respect "none other than"[1] (1–2); twice through reference to her institutional status as Director General (2&3); and lastly

---

Text 5.3   NRDDB Meeting, Yakarinta, 18/1/02

1 **W:** Anyway, once again, as I mentioned to you earlier, that we have here with us none other
2   than the Director General herself, who we'll be seeing attending more
3   meetings more regularly since she has taken up the position of Director General for Iwokrama
4   International Centre, who is no other than Mr ((sic)) Trudy Hunt, Dr Trudy Hunt.

168 *Hybrid Voices and Collaborative Change*

through the use of her academic title of doctor (4). However, between the two references to her role as Director General Walter inserts the qualifying comment "who we'll be seeing attending more meetings more regularly" (2–3), a high-force modalisation that hovers between an epistemic and deontic use and gains something of the character of an injunction through Walter's current institutional authority as chair of the NRDDB. There is a thinly veiled criticism here in the juxtaposition of Trudy's responsibilities as Director General with a reference to her attending "more meetings more regularly" (2–3), as more in the future might be taken to imply not enough in the past. In this way, even before she speaks, Walter has set Trudy up in an ambivalent position as holding a prestigious position within Iwokrama, but a position which, at least here and now, is *subsumed* within the institutional framework of the NRDDB. Trudy's position is thus in many ways the mirror image of the position set up for Walter in Text 3.1, where his prestige as a local elder was subsumed within the Iwokrama-led framework of the Management Planning Workshop. The ambiguity of her position is not lost on Trudy, and she proves to be equally as insecure as Walter was in Text 3.1 when she is called on to speak some minutes later:

5 **W:** We'll now want to have some brief presentations made by . . . to be <u>made</u> by the
6 various persons I mentioned just now. And we start off with the new Director General.
7 **T:** Thank you very much. ((3s)) I did go to the Board meeting in June, when I was almost
8 literally just arrived, and, erm, since then, I'm afraid that I've said "Yes, I'll come to each
9 one", your timing and my timing didn't work, but you know, I'm er really pleased that I
10 was able to come to this one, and particularly it gave me the chance to come to another
11 village, because I did say when I arrived, and I did mean it, that I wanted to come to every
12 community and see where you lived and the types and . . . situations you were facing and the
13 problems and so on. And erm although I've been down to the Rupununi and to the Field
14 Station several times over the six months that now I've been in office erm, I haven't got to
15 erm many villages I'm afraid, as I expected. Erm . . . but I have er spent a little bit more time
16 here than just coming in and coming to these meetings and saying these few words and
17 whizzing off again, because I was able to come down over the New Year and I stayed over
18 in River Valley, erm, and sampled a little bit of er how it felt to be in the Savannah in that I
19 helped them round up their cattle, 'cause I'm a horse rider. So, I'm starting to get a feel er
20 of a little bit of what it's like to live on the Savannah, and erm certainly erm I have been to
21 a few of the villages and you don't know I've been, 'cause I've gone through, when you've
22 all been busy. ((2.5s)) Erm, what I'm hoping, if I can, is that the representatives of the
23 board . . .
24 ((Trudy continues))

Trudy begins by contradicting the gist of Walter's implicit criticism, using the full mood form "did go" (7) to counterbalance Walter's negative interpretation while stressing that her actions went beyond reasonable expectations (7–8). She immediately follows this approach with an apology introduced by "I'm afraid" (8), followed by a justification of her failure (9) and an expression of willingness to rectify things (9–11). Trudy again uses

Taking Control   169

contrastive polarity (11) both to stress that her original plan was to come to the Rupununi (11–13) and in her expression of sincerity, "I did mean it" (11). Lines 13–16 include a concessive clause (13) as she continues to justify her absence, and another apologetic "I'm afraid" (15), before she introduces a counter-concession through BUT (15), a justification introduced by BECAUSE (17–19), and a conclusion introduced by SO (19–23) that seems to be intended as a direct rebuttal to the implied criticism with which Walter introduced her.

Interpretation of Text 5.3

At the beginning of this extract Walter introduces Trudy as Director General of Iwokrama, a strategy that on the surface accords her the respect she is due within the institutional context of the NRDDB, but which also serves as the basis for an implicit criticism that she has been failing in her responsibilities in not having attended any NRDDB meetings to this point. Walter thus pits the institutional authority of the NRDDB against Trudy's personal authority as Director General, a tactic that has Trudy falling over herself apologising for not having been to the board before and promising to come in the future, with her turn having the following extremely elaborate argument structure:

[contradiction^amplification^apology^justification^positive evaluation^justification^
expression of sincerity^concession^counter-concession^justification^conclusion].

Walter is able to do this as the NRDDB has by this time been fashioned into a forum with its own agenda and an established framework of institutional roles and discourse conventions: that is to say, its own voice and order of indexicality. This is a very different context from the Management Planning Workshop of Text 3.1, with the balance of power having shifted away from Iwokrama domination towards a more complex distribution of authority, with Walter's institutional authority enhanced at this point as Iwokrama holds no official sway over the first day of meetings. The redistribution of power within NRDDB meetings is very likely both the result of enhanced performances from key participants such as Walter and Sam and the cause of these, as was suggested in the way that Walter was able to reproduce the same strategies employed by Sam in Texts 5.1 and 5.2. Text 5.3 represents an opportunity for Walter to accelerate this ongoing shift towards local control as Trudy, still new to her position as Director General of Iwokrama, is operating in unknown territory and struggles to assert herself. And through the convoluted apology and justification for her previous absence Trudy ultimately adopts the position within the institutional authority of the NRDDB that Walter had set up for her. Text 5.3 can thus be seen as a further example of the importance of *ownership* of discursive spaces, and in particular the relative disadvantage of newcomers to these spaces. Trudy is at a double

170   *Hybrid Voices and Collaborative Change*

disadvantage here as this is her first visit to the NRDDB and she is having to make her maiden speech not on "Iwokrama day", but on the first day of the meeting, over which local participants are institutionally in control. Added to this, she is a foreigner, who might feel at home in the corridors of power in Georgetown, but who is operating literally as well as metaphorically in unfamiliar territory here. In contrast, William, as chair of the NRDDB operating on home territory, has the confidence to exploit his advantage to full effect, subsuming Trudy's authority within Iwokrama under the institutional authority of the NRDDB. The following texts from the same meeting illustrate that Walter is perfectly capable of using the authority of the chair to rein in the old Iwokrama hands as well as the new, displaying a level of control that was entirely missing in his role as facilitator at the Management Planning Workshop, a role set up for him by Sara as an Iwokrama representative, and that he achieved only with support in Texts 5.1 and 5.2.

Text 5.4 comes from the second day of the January NRDDB Meeting in Yakarinta. This is "Iwokrama Day" and Iwokrama representatives are therefore in positions of greater authority than on the previous day. At this point in the meeting Nicholas is speaking about the CEW programme and Sam is waiting to respond when Hilda, a long-serving Iwokrama representative with a Euro-Guyanese background who is involved in many community-based projects nationally, interrupts from the back of the floor. (H is Hilda; W is Walter; S is Sam):

The text begins with an unsolicited and unprefaced interjection from Hilda (1). Walter, however, steps in and refuses to allow Hilda to speak at will (4), prefacing her first name with "Miss" and referring to Sam with the even more formal "Mr. Bramley" (4). Sam responds humorously with the excessively subordinate "Thank you, sir!" (6), before speaking uninterrupted for over two minutes, after which Walter uses his role as chair to select Hilda as next speaker, addressing her by first name only. Hilda takes

---

Text 5.4 NRDDB Meeting, Yakarinta, 19/1/02

```
 1  H:  Erm, is there a (xx) in the SUA=
 2  W:  =I would like=
 3  H:  =I mean this=
 4  W:  ((quietly)) Miss Hilda, can we have, erm, Mr Bramley . . . first?
 5      (2s)
 6  S:  Yes, thank-you, sir!
 7      ((Sam speaks for 2m 10s))
 8      That is what I would like to see happening here. (xx). Thank-you.
 9      (2s)
10  W:  Going to say something, Hilda?
11  H:  Yes, Chairman, just to respond to er Mr Nicholas's comment . . .
```

Taking Control   171

up the offer to speak, addressing Walter with his official title of "Chairman" and referring to Nicholas as "Mr, Nicholas"(11).

Interpretation of Text 5.4

This extract begins with Hilda interrupting proceedings, as all Iwokrama representatives are prone to do, drawing on informal interpersonal styles that serve to de-emphasise differences in symbolic capital between professionals and local groups. Walter, however, responds by asserting his authority over Hilda, despite her position as an important member of Iwokrama, addressing her gently with the semi-formal "Miss Hilda" (4) and politely requesting that Sam, who he refers to as "Mr. Bramley" (4), be allowed to speak next. This use of formal titles to refer to people who are both close friends of Walter's not only accords Hilda the respect she is due as a prominent member of Iwokrama, so softening the blow of Walter interrupting her , but also serves as a contextualisation cue that it is the institutional relations of the NRDDB that are in play here, not the more familiar relations that might be appropriate in other contexts. This strategic use of formal titles can also be seen in Text 5.2 (79) and in Text 6.2, in the following chapter, where Uncle Henry refers to his son Sam as "Mr. Chairman". After Walter's intervention, Sam, who is renowned for mixing business with laughter, apparently recognises the face-threatening dynamics at play and is able to make light of the situation by severely downplaying his own authority, related as it is to Walter's and in opposition to Hilda's at this point (6). When Sam has finished, Walter recognises Hilda's right to speak and reaffirms his solidarity and friendship by using her first name only (10). When Hilda responds by referring to Walter by his official title and to Nicholas as "Mr. Nicholas" (11), she would appear not to be shunning this peace token, but acknowledging her position as under the authority of the NRDDB as an institution at this point and hence implicitly accepting blame for her initial interruption. While both parties come out of this simple exchange well, it is most noteworthy as an example of Walter's growing ease in the chair and his control of the authority that this position confers upon him, with his alternating reference to Hilda in formal and informal terms a sign that he has come to terms with his previous difficulty in reconciling the formality of his role in chairing the Management Planning Workshop with the community-based prestige he was able to deploy from the floor. It is instances such as this that over time gave me the impression that the NRDDB was growing in autonomy and losing its reliance on the symbolic capital of Iwokrama—though, as the following chapter will suggest, this is still a crucial element in the mix. This new-found ability is very clear in the following text, recorded earlier on the same day.

At the beginning of Text 5.5 Walter is setting the agenda for the day, writing it up on the blackboard as he does so, but there is some confusion as to

172 *Hybrid Voices and Collaborative Change*

who is ready to speak and whether the appropriate representatives are present to hear different reports. (**W** is Walter; **G** is Gordon; **H** is Hilda):

Text 5.5 starts with Walter calling on Gordon, who he refers to semi-formally as "Dr. Gordon" (1), to take the floor. Gordon responds by making an alternative suggestion that Robert, who he refers to by first name only, presents his report first (2). This begins a series of challenges to Walter's proposed timetabling for the meeting, in the form of interruptions and overlaps from two senior Iwokrama figures, Gordon (2–4, 6, 8&10) and Hilda (12, 15–16, 19–20&22). Walter signals his acceptance of the

---

Text 5.5   NRDDB, Yakarinta, 19/1/02

1	**W:**	So we call on Dr Gordon to come up.
2	**G:**	Just. .quick . . . just ask Robert to give his report? (Xxx) doing most of the
3		surveys and managing most of the surveys so . . . so, I would suggest that they
4		[xx].
5	**W:**	[I thought] you would have erm =
6	**G:**	=Just rub it out=
7	**W:**	=walked with² the WP/SUA thing.
8	**G:**	That's separate from fisheries. .report=
9	**W:**	=That's why I call you for the [(xxx)]
10	**G:**	[The Audubon] not (xx).
11		(3s)
12	**H:**	We have CEW reports first or Gordon first?
13	**W:**	No, CEW reports we're taking after lunch.
14		(4s)
15	**H:**	I was just saying that Sam wanted Minister's representative to be here for the
16		Touchaus' report and so on . . . If you wanted to erm, anyway, I think that's okay=
17	**W:**	=So you're saying we would would—we could take the Touchau report
18		[after lunch?]
19	**H:**	[The CEW] reports. .while the Minister (xxxx) here, maybe the CEWs could
20		report and finish with that (xx). The (MRU's getting) ready.
21	**W:**	Ah (4s) yeah but CEWs . . . maybe we could ah take the CEWs' [report . . .]
22	**H:**	[We finish] with that.
23		(7s)
24	**W:**	Okay, Dr Gordon, you could er get more prepared. We will take the CEWs on
25		the floor. (2.5s) CEWs, please be brief in your reporting. We know that you
26		attended NRDDB last meeting and thi:s and tha::. Also what you would say, we
27		know about it. What we want to know is, like, what new things have been taking
28		place in communities that <u>we</u> are not aware of. So, we don't want to know
29		that . . . we don't want you to come up here, "CEW report, erm, year 2001, period of
30		so, so, so. We attended NRDDB meeting, we this, we this, we went"; no, we
31		want to know after you attended the NRDDB meeting you went into community
32		meetings, what was the response of the people, did you. .er .how successful you
33		were at these meetings, and what new agenda you have all taken on board. And
34		that shouldn't be a whole paper that is put out. Those reporting format is more or
35		less to, kinda, say that you were working for Iwokrama. (2s). Okay?
36		((Walter continues.))

changes with "okay" (24), once again addressing Gordon semi-formally as "Dr. Gordon" (24), a level of formality that extends through his directive to Gordon, couched as a suggestion, that he "could get prepared" (24). Walter then uses an imperative, prefaced with "please", to instruct the CEWs, who are members of the local community, to "please be brief in your reporting" (25). In his following instructions to the CEWs (25–35) Walter adopts a more familiar tone, marked phonetically through the long vowels and dropped /t/ of "thi:s and tha::" (26), lexically through "like" (27) and "kinda" (35), and pragmatically through the use of imaginary reported speech (29–30) and the reformulation of complex ideas in simpler terms (32–33).

Interpretation of Text 5.5

This extract shows Walter coping with complications to his proposed time-tabling and his successful management of Gordon and Hilda's interruptions in rearranging the timetable as a joint effort. While this time Walter eventually goes along with their suggestion (24), what is of interest is the way in which he is able not only to take this alteration to plans in his stride, but also to draw it into his own way of doing things in a stretch of talk (24–35) that mixes formal, semi-formal and informal features in a hybrid voice that combines his institutional role as chairman with his status as community elder. The casual and extended vowels of "thi:s and tha::" (26) at the beginning of this turn not only mark a change in formality, but are iconic of the excessive length of some of the CEWs' reporting styles, an aspect that Walter is about to criticise. Walter further mimics the formulaic reporting style of many CEWs with his "We attended NRDDB meeting, we this, we this, we went" (30), but the familiarity of the closing lines and the hedging of "kinda" (34–35) reassert the solidarity Walter is expressing with the CEWs through the use of his community voice.

What is particularly striking about Walter's contribution here is that he is able to use his role as chair in what is essentially an imported institutional format to subvert the format itself, recalibrating the field, tenor and mode of the discourse simultaneously. The interpersonal switches between institutional and community voice, discussed above, are fairly explicit and generally serve to facilitate Walter's control over participation, as was the case in Text 5.4. However, Walter's instructions to the CEWs also contain an implicit challenge to Iwokrama's authority and the place of Iwokrama-imposed styles of reporting within the order of indexicality operating within the NRDDB as an institution. As described in Chapter 2, the CEWs have a role as go-betweens for community custom and imported science, and control over their activities is a moot point between NRDDB and Iwokrama. Walter's redirection of their reporting style, in terms of both the mode of their delivery (29–30&34–35) and the content of their reports (25–28&31–33), can thus be seen as a move to impose the authority of the

174   *Hybrid Voices and Collaborative Change*

NRDDB, a point he almost makes explicit, but not quite, in his dismissal of the existing reporting format as "more or less to, kinda, say that you were working for Iwokrama" (34–35).

In summary, this extract shows Walter successfully blending his role as chair of the NRDDB as an institution with his role as a member of the North Rupununi as a community, a synthesis which, by his own admission, he failed to achieve as facilitator within the institutional setting of the Management Planning Workshop. As a result, while the change in timetabling was proposed by the Iwokrama representatives, the *nihil obstat* for adopting the change comes from Walter as NRDDB chair and he is clearly in control of both the turn-taking nature of the event and the content that is to be allowed.

PERTURBATION POTENTIAL

In this chapter I have analysed five texts that clearly demonstrate local control over discourse, chiefly from Walter, and contrasted this with Text 3.1, in which Walter was demonstrably ill at ease in his role as facilitator and formal control passed from him to Sara, as the Iwokrama representative who had organised the Management Planning Workshop, though Walter remained an active presence and continued to participate from the floor. As stated above, Walter later explained to me that he had difficulty combining his local position and accustomed means of running meetings with the institutional role he had been allocated, and throughout the analyses in this chapter I have highlighted occasions where Walter seemed to have reconciled these positions. With the title of this book I have suggested that such a change was a diachronic process, the result of the growing confidence of those in the NRDDB and the strategies they adopted to *perturb the context* towards a *local autonomy* model of empowerment that squared with the vision set out in the NRDDB Constitution rather than that of the Amerindian Act and early development discourse. It could, of course, be argued that the differences between Text 3.1 and the texts analysed in this chapter are purely synchronic, brought about by differences in context[3], or equally that the differences reflect only a growing confidence in Walter. Ultimately, it makes little odds, as the contrasts between the texts still hold as examples of Iwokrama-controlled discourse and locally-led discourse respectively and the analyses point to factors that are responsible for these differences, either contextual or strategic. It does not seem unreasonable to conclude, however, that there is a diachronic shift at play. Firstly, and most obviously, Text 3.1 is the earliest of the texts, from 19 March 2000, with the texts in this chapter spanning a period from 7 July 2000 to 19 January 2002. Secondly, factors such as the creation of the Bina Hill Institute, the appointment of a new Director General of Iwokrama, and the support Walter received as chair from Sam's skill and experience all represent

Taking Control 175

diachronic factors that led in their own ways to increased potential for community members to participate more actively in proceedings and to take greater control over them. Throughout my time in Guyana the impression I got was certainly that the NRDDB was maturing as an institution, gradually becoming less of a part of Iwokrama's outreach programme and more of an independent body, and in the last meeting I attended before leaving Guyana, Walter referred to the NRDDB as "the Daddy of the whole home" (NRDDB Meeting, Bina Hill Institute, 2/11/01). This was not down to the efforts of the local participants alone, however, but relied also on a particular conjunction of features in the wider social context, most notably Iwokrama's shared concern for sustainable social development and their willingness to act as collaborators rather than as instigators or primary actors. All of these factors contributed to the potential for change, and in this section I will discuss some of the recurring features across Texts 5.1 to 5.5 in terms of the wider social context, drawing on the theoretical concepts of voice, symbolic capital and the Positioning Star of David and on the collaborative model of power as developed in previous chapters.

In Chapter 4 I suggested that the Positioning Star of David could be read in two ways, as representing either contextual constraints on action or the means of perturbing the context through strategic action, and in this section I will focus on this *perturbation potential* (Bartlett, forthcoming): the different configurations of structural features and individual histories that allow for the immanent recalibration of the field, tenor and mode of the discourse context—changes that over time will potentially alter the structural conditions within the NRDDB and beyond to the context of local development in Guyana in general (cf. Canagarajah [1993] on the effects of an emancipatory approach to second-language teaching on wider social relations). This calls for a brief re-examination of what is meant by *context*, a term that is notoriously difficult to pin down and that is used in different ways by different theorists. In line with the general approach I have implicitly adopted thus far, I shall treat context at three distinct yet interacting levels. The most immediate and variable of these is the *semiotic context*. This is the SFL concept of context and it comprises the field, tenor and mode of discourse: the activities that are being carried out through the discourse itself; the interpersonal relationships brought into play by the discourse; the function of the text—as a sermon, a lesson or a casual conversation, for example; and the channel through which it is realised—as written or spoken, for example. As a *linguistic* theory, SFL is interested in the functions that language can perform and, though it seeks to describe these in ways that can be applied to wider social concerns, it limits itself to those aspects of context that are established linguistically. It is important to note here that while all these features can be read off from the text, given an adequate understanding of the voices in play, they are not in themselves linguistic features, even when they are illusory, as in the field of fairy tales or the adoption of an egalitarian tenor between speakers

176 *Hybrid Voices and Collaborative Change*

of different status. However, while the SFL notion of context is limited to those features that are *illuminated* (Hasan 1995:219) by variables within the three domains of field, tenor and mode, these can combine in myriad ways to respond to the requirements of specific situations, which represent a second level of context and which I shall refer to as the *environment*. In the SFL literature this is usually referred to as the *Material Situational Setting* and it is theorised as constraining the possible semiotic contexts that can be created[4]. I shall not use this term as it obscures the crucial point that many relevant aspects of the environment are not material but the understandings, expectations and attitudes that individual participants bring with them to any discourse (van Dijk 2008). The *environment* thus comprises such diverse features as the physical setting of the discourse, the cultural background and personal and professional status of the different participants; the history of previous interactions as these inform the participants' understanding of the current discourse; and even such seemingly obscure features as the time of day and season of the year (Scollon 2005) and the participants' hair colour (see Bartlett, forthcoming). Which leads us to the third level of context, which I shall refer to as the *macrocontext*, for it is impossible to understand the meaning and the relevance of the various features of the environment without a broader understanding of factors such as the politics, institutions and ethnic relations that characterise the culture, or cultures, within which the participants are operating. This is the reason why I provided a relatively detailed, though ultimately limited, description of international development and the context of local development in Guyana in Chapters 2 and 3, something that is all too frequently missing from discourse analyses that proceed as if the discourse can be understood in terms of the texts alone. The macrocontext is, of course, made up of many disparate though interrelated histories and social groupings: The Makushi culture of the North Rupununi is vastly different from the coastal culture of Guyana while the institutional culture of Iwokrama is unique in itself. Moreover, none of these 'cultures' is uniform in itself, though each contains overarching tendencies, shared conventions and expectations that create social cohesion and allow for the successful performance of everyday life. These conventions take on linguistic life through the notion of *voice*, the discursive realisation of communal activities, interpersonal relations and rhetorical traditions. Voice is thus the link between the semiotic context, the environment and the macrocontext, and one way to perturb the environment is to draw on voices that *profile* the cultural conventions and expectations of different social groups within the macrocontext. This can be achieved in two different ways: either through the use of an existing voice that has been previously marginalised or through the creation of a new voice that captures the distinctive features of a new environment, in this case that of NRDDB meetings. Both these approaches are evident in Texts 5.1 to 5.5 and I will use the model of the Positioning Star of David to describe each in turn.

Taking Control 177

First I shall look at the use of previously marginalised voices. As described above, a particular voice is realised by variables of the field, tenor and mode of discourse as they relate to the social life and conventions of a specific cultural group. Altering any of these linguistically construed variables will thus represent a change in voice, a change that allows for different relations of symbolic capital to be brought into play. In Text 4.1, for example, we saw how Andrew focused on the subfield of farming within the wider context of local development and how this enabled him to speak authoritatively, drawing on his capital as a farmer well acquainted with local conditions. In Text 5.1 we see something very similar, where Walter relates the issue of land demarcation to the specific subfield of "traditional fishing and hunting" (11), a move which raises his existing but historically marginalised local capital and puts him in a position to make the face-threatening act of presupposing help from the Iwokrama programme manager and the Minister for Amerindian affairs—an act that carries all the more force for being made from the chair.

Turning to tenor, there are several examples in Texts 5.1 to 5.5 where community-based interpersonal relations are evoked through the use of local voice. One means of achieving this is *ventriloquism*, whereby both Walter and Sam animate their contributions with the imaginary speech of local participants. We see this in Text 5.2, where Walter (76–77) and Sam (34–38&61–64) use direct speech to suggest how community members might participate in the oral discussion of Iwokrama's written text, and in Text 5.5 where Walter mimics the overly long contributions from the CEWs (29–30). Both these instances occur at points where Iwokrama's control is being challenged, in the first case with regard to the method of reading the prepared text and in the second with regard to the role of CEWs, and in ventriloquising local voices in this way Walter and Sam are able to display solidarity with the community participants in ways which are not open to the Iwokrama representatives and so steal a march on them. However, this is a very marked form of solidarity, in that on both occasions there is also an element of criticism directed towards the community members: for not having already read the written document in Text 5.2 and for their manner of reporting in Text 5.5. Walter and Sam's contributions thus display both solidarity and control, a combination marking the traditional authority of local elders. This combination is also evident in the strategic use of another tenor variable, the markedly informal speech (25–35) that characterises Walter's instructions to the CEWs in Text 5.5.

In terms of mode, we saw in Text 5.2 a protracted battle over how the prepared document was to be read, either privately as a written text, as proposed by the Iwokrama representatives, or communally as a prompt for orality, as proposed by Walter and Sam. As suggested in the analysis of this text, use of the latter mode, which was ultimately adopted, diminishes the inherent authority of the document as a written artefact and replaces this with the authority of the interpreters, in this case the local community

178 Hybrid Voices and Collaborative Change

themselves, but primarily Walter and Sam as elders. A similar struggle over the mode of discourse, this time in terms of the rhetorical style employed rather than the channel, took place in Text 5.5 when Walter challenged the manner of the CEWs' presentations to the Board. However, in this case it would not appear to be so much a traditional mode of delivery that Walter is seeking to impose as a specifically NRDDB style, which he explicitly contrasts with the Iwokrama-oriented style of previous presentations (34–35).

This leads us onto the other means of perturbing the context, through the creation of a new voice, an outcome that is primarily achieved in the preceding texts through the introduction of novel tenor variables that relate neither to local community custom nor standard Iwokrama practice. Specific examples in Texts 5.1 to 5.5 are the different means of address that are employed in establishing control over participation. In Text 5.1 Walter refers to his friend Sam as "the Chairman" (1), a strategy mirrored by Uncle Henry at the close of Text 5.2, where he addresses his son Sam as "Mr. Chairman" (79). Likewise, in Text 5.5, Walter twice (1&24) calls on Gordon to participate through a mix of his academic title and first name, "Dr. Gordon". This semi-formal usage, evoking both solidarity and respect, is in marked contrast to Hilda's use of Gordon and Sam's first names only at the beginning of the same text (12&15)—the strategy also used by Sara throughout Text 3.1. As was mentioned earlier, this informal usage is typical of Iwokrama's dealings with local communities and reflects common NGO practice in attempting to (artificially) minimise status differentials, an approach rejected by Walter and Sam in favour of establishing formal roles that are defined by participants' status within the NRDDB, with institutional and semi-formal terms of address serving as *contextualisation cues* (Gumperz 1982) that institutional relations are in force. This is not to say that there is no room for a little code-switching where necessary, and in Text 5.4 we saw how effectively Walter was able to move between institutional and familiar forms of address to maintain over the proceedings— with a little help from both Sam's use of humour (6) and Hilda's readiness to accept his interpersonal framing of the event (11).

The growth in stature of the NRDDB as an independent institution demonstrates a further way in which the context can be perturbed in terms of the extent to which it comes to represent a novel marketplace, a physical and symbolic space that prompts new expectations from participants and so opens up and legitimates new positions and new distributions of symbolic capital. This is evident in the contrast between Text 3.1 and all the texts analysed in this chapter. In Texts 5.1 and 5.2 ownership of the physical setting of the Bina Hill Institute was suggested as an important factor in creating a new marketplace, but nowhere are the effects more striking, and almost comical, than in Text 5.3. Here Trudy finds herself entirely wrong-footed in this new context and, far from enjoying the prestige she would enjoy in the more familiar institutional marketplaces of Iwokrama meetings, she is forced into an elaborate apology and justification for her

Taking Control   179

absence from previous NRDDB meetings—a situation that is enhanced through Walter's references to her institutional and academic titles rather than in spite of them. Here, as throughout this chapter, we can see how

Table 5.1   Summary of Salient Lexicogrammatical Features as Analysed in Texts 3.1 and 5.1 to 5.5

	Text 3.1	*Texts 5.1 to 5.5*
Lead Speakers and Institutional Context:	*authority primarily external:* S *as ultimate facilitator and evaluator at Iwokrama-led workshop;* W *as temporary facilitator and trainee*	*authority primarily internal:* **Walter** *and* **Sam** *as chair at NRDDB Meetings; Iwokrama representatives speaking from floor*
Field	External approach to management planning drawing on local knowledge; conflict between practical and theoretical matters.	Subfields of territorial rights and hunting and fishing (5.1); mode of information transfer in NRDDB meetings (5.2); excuse for non-attendance (5.3); turn-taking rights (5.4); reporting at meetings, particularly form of CEW reports (5.5).
Tenor	Use of first names throughout; direct commands; overlaps and interruptions turning to elicitations from S once in control; W largely fails to elicit responses from floor and eventually contributes from floor as S assumes control; S speaks for W; institutional authority of Iwokrama.	Use of names and titles as contextualisation cues for different control-solidarity axes; overlaps at beginning of negotiations with W assuming control; extreme hedging of presuppositions, bold requests and strongly negative comments from both sides; indirect requests through presuppositions; use of imaginary community voice to criticise, mock and show solidarity; mix of institutional authorities of NRDDB and Iwokrama.
Mode	Context-focused Actions and Commentaries from S and Commentaries from N; Context-external Recounts and Generalisations from W; spoken, with flipcharts.	Generally spoken; Context-focused Commentaries (5.2, 5.4, 5.5); Community-focused Reflections (5.1); personal Recount (5.4); use of written text as prompt for orality (5.2); redirection of mode of CEW reporting (5.5).

180 *Hybrid Voices and Collaborative Change*

Walter has grown into his institutional role within the NRDDB, encouraged no doubt by the participation of old hands such as Sam, and how, in contrast to his performance in Text 3.1 and Trudy's gaucheness in Text 5.4, he has become comfortable within the new marketplace this represents, displaying an acute *intercultural competence* as he switches between his role within the NRDDB and his community status as local elder as the situation demands.

Table 5.1 summarises some of the key contrasts between the linguistic features that maintained Iwokrama control over proceedings in Text 3.1 and those which served to perturb the context towards the traditional discourse patterns of local community life or the novel institutional marketplace of the NRDDB as an institution.

CONCLUSION

In this chapter I have drawn on the theoretical apparatus set up in previous chapters, related to the description of the social background in Chapters 2 and 3, to illustrate the various means by which prestigious community members were able to gain control over both participation within the NRDDB (Texts 5.2 and 5.4) and the content of the discourse (Texts 5.1, 5.3 and 5.5). However, as has been mentioned earlier, this did not come about without the willingness of the Iwokrama representatives, nor would it have been successful without their input, as repeatedly called for by Walter in particular. These texts can therefore be seen as examples of effective collaboration between the two groups and the different knowledge and authority they possess. Nonetheless, Texts 5.1 to 5.5 show that the knowledge and authority of the Iwokrama representatives is *subsumed* within the institutional authority of the NRDDB and that the *nihil obstat* over proceedings ultimately belongs to the local communities, specifically through the person of the Chair of the Board, a role which combines the community-based capital of the local elder with the institutional capital of the NRDDB. In the following chapter I will analyse lengthy texts from Sara and Uncle Henry to explore further how a hybrid voice has been created that embeds the external prestige and expertise of Iwokrama within the knowledge and authority of the local community.

6 Interdiscursivity, Capital and Empathy

> *Anyway, thanks to Mr. Henry, and these are the kind of resource person that Iwokrama should be looking in future to contact to do kind of workshops, conduct workshops on these . . . on whatever they would want to, what it's, what it is to do with communities. Because, like, Sara said it over and over, and we ain't understand what is said. And old Henry come and . . . about half an hour, I believe most of us understand what she had talk about since the zoning workshop and other meetings we've had, and you've got an idea of what it is.*
>
> (Walter, NRDDB Meeting, Bina Hill Institute, 4/11/2000)

In Chapters 3 and 5 I analysed a number of texts from NRDDB–Iwokrama discourse to illustrate the various strategies employed by prominent members of the NRDDB in maintaining control over both the speaking rights of the different participants and the content and form of their discourse. Focusing on Walter's performances over this 22–month period, I suggested that he had developed a style of discourse that successfully blended his capital as a local elder with his capital as chair of the NRDDB through the adoption of different voices at different moments in the discourse. As a result, while the different groups within the meetings all contributed to the discourse according to their own status, Walter by and large ensured that the contributions of outside experts and officials were directed towards the goals of the NRDDB and that the symbolic capital of the different speakers was subsumed within the institutional authority of the Board. The texts analysed in Chapters 3 and 5 were largely *dialogic* and demonstrated how this mingling of symbolic capitals was achieved across the participation of several speakers. In this chapter I will analyse two lengthy contributions, from Sara and Uncle Henry, to demonstrate how Uncle Henry is able to create a hybrid symbolic capital within a single *monologic* contribution, but also how the effect of Uncle Henry's discourse was in some ways dependent on Sara's previous contribution, subsuming her capital as an outside expert within his own complex positioning as his discourse followed *in the slipstream* of what she had said. The effect of Uncle Henry's contribution was not only to enhance his own authority within the NRDDB, however; it also served, according to Walter in the preceding extract, to improve local participants' understanding of some of the issues being debated through his reformulation of the abstract and novel ideas contained in Sara's contribution in ways that resonated with community experience: that is, through

182   *Hybrid Voices and Collaborative Change*

the use of local *voice* at key point in his contribution. The analysis and discussion in this chapter therefore adds to the concept of power developed above as control over participation and the content of discourse the equally important notion of *audience uptake*, without which control over meaning is a futile exercise. Before moving on to these analyses I will expand a little on the relationship between context and voice in order to clarify the strategies by which a skilled speaker such as Uncle Henry, with his unique status within the community and NRDDB, is able to draw on multiple voices simultaneously to achieve his goals.

CONTEXTS, VOICES AND INTERDISCURSIVITY

In the previous chapter I introduced the SFL notion of the *semiotic context* of discourse, that is, the context, real or imaginary, that is construed through the discourse itself. This context is not linguistic in itself but the activities, interpersonal relations and rhetorical purpose of the talk that are *brought into play through* language. However, as this is a linguistically construed context it can be described entirely according to the functional capacities of language as a meaning-making device. The resources of language function to create experiential, interpersonal and textual meanings, and consistent patternings within these three areas construe the field, tenor and mode that between them construe the semiotic context. The semiotic context therefore refers to the non-linguistic features that are brought into play through discourse, while the array of linguistic features that are drawn upon to create the experiential, interpersonal and textual structure of the text are referred to as the *register* of that discourse. Thus, for example, a text that has as its subject matter medical conditions, that is dialogic, but with one participant controlling the dialogue, and that moves from an account of the less powerful participant's current well-being to a prescribed course of action from the more powerful participant, would represent a specific register, one that is the norm within the context of a medical consultation in a doctor's surgery in Britain. A text with similar subject matter but that is monologic in providing expert information from a position of authority and was built on generalisations leading to predictions would represent an altogether different register, one that would be the norm in the context of medical journals but totally out of place in the consultation room. Of course, this is a very broad-strokes characterisation, but it serves to demonstrate how the register of a discourse, as the configuration of experiential, interpersonal and textual meanings, varies according to the purpose of the text, and how the semiotic context created is dependent upon the wider social context in which it is produced. Registers can therefore be said to realise different voices, in the first case the voices of a British family doctor and a typical patient in a British surgery, and in the second case the voice of an expert contributor to a medical journal. In Chapters 3

Interdiscursivity, Capital and Empathy   183

and 5 I was primarily concerned with how the register of the different texts, or specific variables of register, represented the voice of the local communities, Iwokrama workers or representatives of the NRDDB board, inasmuch as the field, tenor and mode of discourse could be said to reflect the social organisation of these different groups. However, as was also noted in the analysis of these texts, it is possible that within a single discourse the register, and hence the voice it represents, might vary as the text progresses. As well as the notion of a text as a single coherent stretch of discourse (Halliday and Hasan 1976, 1985), therefore, we also need to consider the different *phases* (Gregory 1988) of such texts, stretches of a discourse that are individually consistent in register but which vary in a motivated way across the text as a whole. In the following analyses, an examination of such phases and the ways in which they are related will allow us to see how changes in register represent shifts between community, Iwokrama and NRDDB voice and how these three distinct voices are combined in a single discourse to produce something new. This mixing of registers, or voices, is what Fairclough (2003:218, drawing on Bakhtin 1981) refers to as *interdiscursivity*:

> Analysis of the interdiscursivity of a text is analysis of the particular mix of genres, of discourses, and of styles upon which it draws, and of how different genres, discourses or styles are articulated (or 'worked') together in a text. This level of analysis mediates between linguistic analysis of a text and various forms of social analysis of social events and practices.

The potential for such interdiscursivity is, as demonstrated in Chapters 3 and 5, constrained by the contextual *environment* of the discourse: that is, the material situational setting, the latent capital of the participants and the understandings and expectations that these participants bring to the event. And these environmental features are, in turn, a function of the social background of the two groups and the discourse history between them. In this way we can see how the multiple variables of the macrocontext shape the environment, which in turn constrains the potential for creating semiotic contexts through the three variables of field, tenor and mode.

In Chapters 3 and 5 my focus was on the different symbolic capitals that were cued through the use of different voices, a notion that I will also develop here in conjunction with an exploration of how the use of different voices can affect the *understanding* of the intended audience. This requires a division of the term *understanding* into its two component ideas of *comprehension* (as in "I can understand French") and *empathy* (as in "I understand what you're going through"). The point I will make in analysing these two texts is that a sufficient understanding of complex concepts does not depend on comprehension of the language alone but also depends on the audience being able to relate to the concepts, that is, to empathise

184   *Hybrid Voices and Collaborative Change*

with them. In the analysis that follows I will suggest that such empathy is enhanced when the register of the speaker's discourse is a manifestation of community voice; in other words, when the semiotic context construed is consistent with the social context of the local community (or, in Bourdieu's [1990b] terminology, when the *field of action* is aligned with the audience's *field of experience*).

Fairclough (2003:18) draws a distinction between such interdiscursivity and *intertextuality*, which he describes as "the presence within [a text] of other texts . . . which may be related to (dialogued with, assumed, rejected, etc.) in various ways". As an example of intertextuality, Uncle Henry (below) echoes aspects of Sara's preceding contribution, which was based entirely on her knowledge and authority as an Iwokrama worker, and integrates these into his own discourse. But his contribution goes beyond this, drawing on a mix of registers to create a hybrid voice that enables him to explain Iwokrama's ideas in terms that resonate with community life, and so enhance local understanding of the concept, while stamping his authority of the proceedings, and any consequent action, through a mixture of local authority, local knowledge and externally derived expertise. Hymes (1996:51) states that "the central problem [to intercultural communication] is not that some people have one [coding orientation] and others do not . . . The central problem is the management of the relation between the two." In the following section I will use a phasal analysis to demonstrate how Uncle Henry employs both intertextuality and interdiscursivity to achieve his goals and to suggest that, taken together, his contribution and Sara's represent an example of *collaborative interdiscursivity*.

INTERDISCURSIVITY IN ACTION

The texts analysed in this chapter both come from the NRDDB meeting of 4/11/2000 at the Bina Hill Institute (the same day as Text 5.2) and are explanations to the local participants of Iwokrama's zoning programme. This is the process by which the Iwokrama Forest is to be divided into Sustainable Utilisation Areas (SUAs), where the sustainable commercial exploitation of non-timber products is encouraged as a means of conserving the biodiversity of the area, and Wilderness Preserves, where no such activity will be allowed. Attempts had been made to explain SUAs on several previous occasions and a special zoning workshop had been held, so it was hoped that at the present meeting Iwokrama would be able to take an understanding of the concept as read. However, it had become clear that these previous attempts at explanation had been unsuccessful and in Text 6.1 Sara attempts to explain the process once again. Despite her attempts, Walter, as chairman of the NRDDB, suggested after her contribution that she had not been understood and he and several other participants then attempted to provide further explanation. These attempts were also unsuccessful and

Interdiscursivity, Capital and Empathy   185

it was not until Uncle Henry's contribution in Text 6.2 that the process was considered by Walter and others to have been adequately explained, as Walter states in what I have used as the epigram for this chapter:

> *Anyway, thanks to Mr. Henry, and these are the kind of resource person that Iwokrama should be looking in future to contact to do kind of workshops, conduct workshops on these . . . on whatever they would want to, what it's, what it is to do with communities. Because, like, Sara said it over and over, and we ain't understand what is said. And old Henry come and . . . about half an hour, I believe most of us understand what she had talk about since the zoning workshop and other meetings we've had, and you've got an idea of what it is.*

In the following sections I analyse the texts from various angles to identify why Uncle Henry's contribution was better understood than previous explanations, an analysis that also demonstrates how Uncle Henry imposes acceptance of the need for SUAs through discourse strategies that foreground his symbolic capital as both local elder and knowledgeable associate of Iwokrama. The analyses relate to the combinations of field, tenor and mode that define Uncle Henry's discourse and their relation to the different voices of the local community, Iwokrama and the NRDDB.[1]

I shall look first at mode, though this is the hardest to conceptualise of the three variables of register and I have treated it largely in passing thus far. In basic terms, if *field* refers to the activity realised through a discourse and *tenor* to the interpersonal relationships construed, then *mode* refers to the role of the text itself as the platform for this discourse. One feature of mode is the *channel* of communication, and in Text 5.2 we saw the importance to the local community leaders of whether the Iwokrama-prepared document was to be dealt with as a written text or as a prompt for orality. As Texts 6.1 and 6.2 are both unprepared spoken texts channel will not be discussed further here. A second feature of mode is the *rhetorical function* of the text, and this operates at two levels. Individual stretches of text, referred to as Rhetorical Units (RUs), can be functionally defined as Commentaries, Recounts or Generalisations, for example, in terms of the degree to which they are embedded in the here and now of the immediate context or summon up some previous, timeless or hypothetical event. RUs thus "construe . . . the role of language in the social process, conceptualised as a continuum at one end of which language is ancillary to the task in hand and at the other, language constitutes the activity" (Cloran 2000:174, 176; see also Cloran 2010). RUs are labelled according to their place on this continuum. For example, stretches of discourse demanding goods and services, whether directly or indirectly, are labelled Action RUs, and stretches of discourse describing contemporaneous events within the immediate setting are labelled Commentaries. With these two RUs discourse is considered highly contextualised, or even as ancillary to the activity in hand, where text and

186 *Hybrid Voices and Collaborative Change*

action combine to realise the action. RUs such as Conjectures or Generalisations, in contrast, come closer to constituting self-contained events, largely divorced from the non-verbal activity of context, while Reflections on participants' routines come somewhere between the two in that they refer to events that are relevant to immediate participants but which are removed in time from the setting (see Appendix 1 for a complete table of Cloran's [2000:175] categories and her continuum of contextualisation). At a higher level, the *rhetorical function* of a complete text refers to its overall purpose as a sermon, an inaugural address, a science lesson or gossip, for example. This function is largely defined by the patterning of lower-level RUs within the text and shows considerable variation between different social groups (Hasan 2009; Blommaert 2005:84). An analysis of the patterning of RUs within Texts 6.1 and 6.2, therefore, can be used to contrast the different ways in which Sara and Uncle Henry construct their explanations of the concept of SUAs through the combination of RUs and the extent to which these are either contextualised or decontextualised with respect to their audience and their daily lives. According to Celce-Murcia and Olshtain (2000:168), contextualised discourse is easier to interpret generally. In terms of the overall register of different phases of the speakers' discourse, a combination of contextualised language with familiar topics and community-based tenor relations (discussed below) can be expected to increase the audience's empathy with the speaker.

Texts 6.1 and 6.2 are marked up for RU type in the left-hand margin and also show the semantic relationship between the RUs. RUs can be *embedded* within each other, when a topic is maintained but approached from a different angle within a new RU, or they can serve as *expansions* of previous RUs, when a new topic is introduced but its relation to the old topic is signalled (see Cloran [2010] for a fuller explanation of the linguistic means by which these relations are created). In both cases there is a continuation of the text as a semantic unit, though this continuity is more immediate in the case of embedded information. Thus in Text 6.1 Sara's Plan in clauses 11 to 16 is seen as contributing towards the Account that comprises clauses 3 to 26, a relationship Sara overtly signals through the placement at the beginning of clause 11 of the cohesive "what they thought they could do". This level of cohesion is represented graphically by the boxing of clauses 11 to 16 within the stretch of discourse from clauses 3 to 26. It is also possible for embedded RUs to contain further embeddings as speakers progressively develop their ideas from different angles, and the level of embedding of RUs is graphically shown as boxes nested within boxes. The number of decimal points before the RU labels also represents the level of embedding. A dotted line signals that the following RU is an expansion.

In terms of the field of discourse, the analysis focuses on the semantic development and interrelations of the participants and concepts in Uncle Henry and Sara's construals of the zoning process. For the representation of semantic development I have drawn on Martin's (1992:chap. 5)

Interdiscursivity, Capital and Empathy 187

approach of plotting *taxonomic chains* that trace reference to (aspects of) the same entity throughout a text and that label the sense relations of each reference to the last.[2] As this section considers the text from the point of view of the finished product, I develop Martin's process-based representation of taxonomic chains into the two-dimensional product-based semantic maps of Figures 6.2 and 6.3. As with the degree of contextualisation of the texts, the familiarity of the audience with the topics of discourse can be considered a factor in strengthening their empathy towards the discourse.

In terms of the tenor of discourse, I will analyse how the use of personal pronouns serves to unite or divide local and outside participants; the way in which statements, questions and commands are used to engage with the audience; and the way in which modality is used to construe relations of expertise and control. The analysis of Texts 6.1 and 6.2 also demonstrates how the tenor and field of discourse combine to manifest different modes of authority. Moral authority, for example, can be realised through a combination of [+control] modality, varying [+solidarity] and [-solidarity] pronominal use and a [+solidarity] field of discourse that covers topics closely related to community life. This concept is explored further below.

Turning to a consideration of the text as process, relevant features of field, tenor and mode will then be brought together to represent the generic structure of each text as a progression of *phases*, those stretches of discourse in which there is "a significant measure of consistency and congruity" in register (Gregory 1988:318). In these terms a significant shift in any of the three variables of register leads a text into a different phase with a different function. In Tables 6.1 and 6.2, I will set out the structure of the texts in terms of the progression from one phase to the next and the functions of each phase. The grammatical features and overall structures of Texts 6.1 and 6.2 can then be compared in terms of: (i) their employment of different experiential, interpersonal and textual features; (ii) the relationship between these features and the voices of the different participants in NRDDB–Iwokrama discourse in terms of the symbolic capitals employed and the degree of empathy that is engendered; and (iii) the interdiscursive means by which the two texts contribute to collaborative dialogue. Given the nature of the following analyses, the numbering in Texts 6.1 and 6.2 refers to clauses rather than lines of text.

TEXTS 6.1 AND 6.2

Text 6.1 represents an explanation of the zoning process by Sara, as Iwokrama representative, to the NRDDB meeting of 4/11/00 and, as has been said earlier, it is an attempt to clarify previous explanations as it has been suggested that a large number of participants on the floor do not fully understand the process. As such the contribution is totally unprepared.

188 *Hybrid Voices and Collaborative Change*

Text 6.1 Sara's Explanation of the SUA, NRDDB Meeting, Institute, 4/11/2000

Commentary

1 Sam just asked me if I could tell you a little more about the SUA process, how it's working.

2 I'm not with—in Iwokrama the person in the department who's managing the whole SUA.

Account

3 The process is (xxxx xxxxxx),

4 and they have come up with a system where they meet...

5 they have created a team,

6 and on that team you have the four NRDDB representatives,

7 and there are two representatives from the gov-, from the Guyana Forestry Commission,

8 which is a government agency,

9 Guyana Environmental Protection Agency has representatives there

10 and it's all listed in there.

.1 Conjecture

11 So, the idea was, what they thought they could do was bring together communities, these government representatives, Iwokrama, to sit down and think about what would be the best way to plan the area, to plan the businesses that they would develop in the area, the management of the land in terms of SUA.

12 The thinking behind it is that these people would meet quarterly,

13 that's (xxxx) the couple of months in between,

14 and what they would do is sit down and talk about how the process is going

15 and they could share what are their concerns and what they think should happen.

16 So from the community perspective the idea was that the NRDDB representatives would be able to bring to the meeting what they think are important for their villages.

---

17 Because, remember, the SUA is really Iwokrama developing businesses in the preserve.

18 And those businesses are going to operating, it's—

19 one possible business is logging;

20 a second is ecotourism;

21 a third is harvesting things like nibbi and cassava, for selling,

22 they call it non-timber forest products.

.2 Conjecture

23 And so the idea was: How could this affect the communities?

24 How could the communities become involved,

25 the community can benefit, from what was being preserved?

---

26 What we have discussed so far at Iwokrama is whether it will be possible to, for, in between those meetings, when the NRDDB reps meet that there's a smaller meeting just with the communities.

Plan

27 Now you know Janette runs the community programme,

28 so the idea was,

Interdiscursivity, Capital and Empathy   189

.1 Reflection

29	even though NRDDB would be meeting,
30	it was big meetings,
31	a lot of issues come up,
32	and it's four days,
33	and you never finish the discussions,
34	so a lot of things leave hanging,

35	and if we could have a meeting in between, just with the communities
36	so we are clear about what it is you expect,
37	and we are clear,
38	there's a clear sense of what the communities want Iwokrama to do, and a clear sense from Iwokrama of what we are capable of doing.
39	So it's…it's…the idea is to see how we can meet in between the general SUA Meetings to think through—manage expectations more clearly,
40	and for us to be sure that…

.2 Reflection

41	you know that Walter described when you're having a discussion on economics,
42	only some people could be involved in that discussion, because of the level and the kinds of language that was being used…

43	So the idea of an in-between meeting is to be able to break that stuff down:
44	we are sure we are hearing what Iwokrama is saying—what the communities are saying to Iwokrama,
45	and that we are sharing with you
46	in a way that you are also clear about what it is that we're doing up here.
47	And the idea is that now the NRDDB would think—
48	we would try to meet this afternoon and think about what would be the best way to—how to have outreach, in the villages,
49	so that people know what's going on in the villages as well with regard to the SUA.

Recount

50	We talked about this at Iwokrama
51	(after we/when you) had left with the representatives of the forest

.1 Plan

52	and the newsletter that came, that came from Danny Hagan— the thing with a picture on it, just one page?— the idea was this newsletter would go to the village councils to share with the communities.

1.1 Commentary

53	But the details, the details of the discussions, are things that are in this document.

54	So one of the first things that we would like NRDDB to think about is whether you are interested
55	and you think it would be useful for the community reps to meet in between of the bigger SUA (making plans).

190 *Hybrid Voices and Collaborative Change*

Text 6.1 (continued)

1.2 Commentary
56 I'm not sure I'm using the right language
57 to (grip) all of you.
58 So that—so NRDDB select the four people for the SUA meetings.

---

59 The SUA meetings will happen quarterly.
60 What we're proposing, and asking if the NRDDB is interested, to meet—for the reps to meet with us also in between (those meeting times)
61 so we can hammer out some of the issues
62 and be sure we understand what's going on.
63 So, that's kind of the proposal that will go out
64 for you to think about
65 and decide.
66 And if you do,
67 we can start at this particular meeting—not, not today but, necessarily, but this time
68 when we're all in the same place
69 (could we have) a meeting with four reps and Tommy, who's from Fair View, and myself,
70 and sit down and meet—
71 that'll be the first time?
72 And then we could have a chance tomorrow to tell you a little more of what happens.
73 The idea is,
74 if we could discuss at the big group some of the points raised,
75 and then in the afternoon or maybe tomorrow if we could meet as a small group to hammer out what are priorities in terms of what is expected of us,
76 we are clear on the list,
77 and then we can show that back to the big group
78 and see if you agree
79 and then take that back with us, to Iwokrama.

.1.3 Commentary
80 Matt, is that clear?

.1.4 Action
81 So, that's for you to decide

After Sara's contribution Walter and several other participants attempted to gloss the contribution. However, the attempted clarifications from these other participants were unsuccessful until Uncle Henry rose to make his intervention, given in part in Text 6.2.

Interdiscursivity, Capital and Empathy 191

Text 6.2 Uncle Henry's Explanation of the SUA, NRDDB Meeting, Institute, 4/11/2000

Commentary

1	Mister Chairman, I would now like to ask a question and then make some comments,
2	because it seems that (xxxx xxxxx).
3	Now, I would want to ask the question:
4	How many of you here understand the interpretation of SU—Sustainable Utilisation..Area?
5	How do you interpret it?
6	What do you think it really means?
7	Because that the core of what we are discussing.
8	D'you all understand it?
9	Many of you don't understand,
10	it mean that you wouldn't grasp readily what this meeting is all about.

Recount

11	Now the meeting that...the meeting we attended with this group of all the representatives from various organisations:
12	We sat down there to discuss (relatively commonplace) intuitions,
13	but we discussed the Sustainable Utilisation Area in depth.

.1 Account

14	The Wilderness Preserve is another area,
15	that is where the zoning is important.
16	And to mark that place, zone, to identify the Sustainable Utilisation Area, here is where your knowledge—all of us knowledge comes into play.

.1.1 Reflection

17	Because we are the people who are familiar with that forest,
18	we are people closest to the forest more than anybody else who live outside,
19	because it's, we have a way of life that's part of it,
20	and we are the ones to give an advice.

.1.1.1 Action

21	And we should take it in that vein.

22	Because whenever you're down,
23	whoever comes (from there) will return,
24	we remain here.
25	And whatever is built or constructed, whatever it is,
26	we will remain.
27	Of course some of it is (not).
28	But then we're working to defend it,
29	because all of us, you know, worry.

30	Now, the Sustainable Utilisation Area mean the area which you can use natural resources there in a sustainable way.
31	You keep it...not going down,
32	But if possible you keep it increasing
33	so that those things, whatever it may be, whether it be vine, medicinal plants, frogs, centipedes, snakes, fishes, baboon, or what-you-call-it,

.1.2 Action

34	it must remain there
35	and you must not be de-, de-, depleted.

36	So that our generation that (xxxx) to keep it.
37	You take out,

192 *Hybrid Voices and Collaborative Change*

Text 6.2 (continued)

.1.3 Action

38 but then you must help to have that recycling going on
39 so that the reproduction of the resources going on.
40 Whatever you do for reforestation,
41 planting seedlings should grow up.

.1.3.1 Conjecture

42 If you find a special medicinal plant.
43 Because
44 if you find—
45 obviously if you find a very valuable medicinal plant,
which can cure some diseases,
you'll have it in that.
46 Which means if you go and take out that natural resource you have there,
47 you're going to be depleting (established connexion).

48 So you have (TAPE TURNS)...
49 ...(slender) lines,
50 so that you can observe...changes.
51 How things changes?
52 How do they form?
53 What happen within a year after, within a year, five year, a ten-year,
a 15-year period?

.1.4 Prediction

54 So, you would get to understand the forest better
55 and those things would be left in their normal state.

.1.5 Reflection

56 Because there are other important issues which we,
57 because we live among them,
58 we live inside,
59 it's a way of life,
we take it for granted.
60 We are not (x),
61 many of us do not have sense of value,
62 don't know how valuable those things are to us,
63 and we just discard it, like many of us who pushing fire in the savannah–
64 you know how many innocent birds' lives you destroying
65 (probably, even though xx xxx)?
66 If a snake (xxxxxxx xxxxxx) inside your house?

.1.5.1 Action

67 So, don't blame the snakes
68 where you can't put fire in the savannah,

.1.5.1.1 Reflection

69 it's not good,
70 it's a very bad habit, like poisoning,
71 all these things are detrimental.
72 But because we never study it in depth,
73 we don't know how disastrous it is.

.1.6 Commentary

74 So these are things which we are now asked to participate in our
knowledge (about it), to find certain things.
75 And when we come to sustainability of the forest,
76 it does not confine that to Iwokrama alone,
77 we have to look on the other communities way outside.

Interdiscursivity, Capital and Empathy 193

.1.6.1 Conjecture
78 Because you might not find
79 (when it—
80 when the plant come,) to assess it:
81 "What do we have?
82 Okay, this piece of thing, yeah yeah,
83 we'll try this for sustainable utilisation."
84 What is there that we can use sustainably?

85 One of the things you have to do is research.

.1.7 Recount
86 A lot has been done with animals, reptiles, birds, and all those things.
87 Bit of a botanical collection was done,
88 there's a lot more to be done.
89 The greenhearts of Iwokrama, that was one of
    the key elements they (classified).

.1.7.1 Account
90 They want to do (away with them) now.
91 Because no sense putting up all the Wilderness Preserve
92 and then there's no greenheart in there.

.1.7.1.1 Prediction
93 And we leave that for commercial harvesting, sustainable...
94 in a short while it will disappear.

95 So they have to pinpoint those areas.

.1.8 Commentary
96 Now they have a good idea,
97 but I'm still a bit sceptical about certain areas I notice that are for sustainable—
98 I look at the map,

.1.8.1 Account
99 "Oh oh of course it just ends there",
100 and to have a wilderness preserve,
101 and you have a sustainable portion (xxxxxxx)—

.1.8.1.1 Prediction
102 to my mind it will backfire after you get (x) population,
103 because this wildlife (is our stuff).
104 as soon as applications start here,
105 (we're started...xx).
106 And once they adapt,
107 there are migration uhm migratory routes which they will take
108 and they will find themselves right up in Pakaraimas for the next year.

109 So these are things still to be discussed
110 because there is not—

111 I don't think that that is already confirmed where (x),
112 those are just tentative demarcation (x).

.1.9 Reflection
113 However, our part to play is what we can do to help, (xx sustainability).

.1.9.1 Commentary
114 Okay, we are looking at the moment at non-timber products,
115 we are not talking about extraction of timber on a (mineral) basis.
116 Non-timber products.

194   *Hybrid Voices and Collaborative Change*

Text 6.2 (continued)

| | 117 | We are looking at things like general handicrafts, nuts that we can harvest, native (xxxx), dyes. |
| 118 | And other things that you can use from the forest that can bring cash. |

.1.9.1.1 Generalisation.
119	Because
120	if you are going to be sustainable, you have to make money.
121	You can't go begging on (xxx).
122	Nothing is free.
123	After we've done our bit of regeneration,
124	it isn't free,
125	somebody has to pay for it (to be free).
126	So, nothing is free,

.1.9.1.1.1 Action
| 127 | don't worry the things you hear people say that it is free, |

128	It's not free.
129	And this where we are sitting, sitting here now, that is sustainable out the forest (xxxx).
130	So, the forest (is free).

| 131 | Then, doing that, one of the recommendations that I made was |

.2 Plan
132	in a small way the community should participate
133	and can give their support in doing some identification of things that you can use, things that you traditionally use.
134	Collect small samples
135	and hand it in
136	so that it (xx) analysis, how good it is, and if there is a market for it.

.2.1 Generalisation
137	Because there's no sense going and collecting a whole set of things
138	(xx) expensive research on it,
139	and then you find there is no market.

.2.1.1 Conjecture
140	Or if you find a small, like I said before, something very limited,
141	but it has a very good market,
142	but then we do not have the quantity to supply the market,
143	that (contractor xxxxx will say) "They have it but they can't supply it,"
144	so they forget you
145	and they find somewhere else for it.

| 146 | That is bad business. |

.2.2 Account
147	So these are the things we are looking for in Sustainable Utilisation,
148	and that's the whole essence of Sustainable Utilisation Areas.
149	It's this:

.2.2.1 Action
150	look at the places,
151	what is there,
152	how you can use it,
153	if there's a market for it
154	and you guarantee to produce it,
155	whether it be handicraft
156	or it have to be refined, in a more sophisticated manner and (use other things).

Interdiscursivity, Capital and Empathy   195

Commentary
    157   So I know // you understand what is Sustainable Utilisation now

.1 Plan
    158   so that everyone can participate.

    ((Uncle Henry continues))

MODE AND THE CONTEXTUALISATION OF DISCOURSE

At a certain level, the two contributions in Texts 6.1 and 6.2 are very similar in their use and sequencing of RUs.[3] If we temporarily ignore embedding and expansion relations between RUs we can see that the main rhetorical drift of both speakers is as follows, where the caret symbol ^ represents the sequencing of elements[4]:

Sara: Commentary(1–2)^Account(3–27)^Plan(28–79)^Commentary+Action(80–81)

UH: Commentary(1–10) ^Account (14–130)^Plan(132–156)^Commentary+Action(157–158)

Such superficial similarities are not surprising given that the two texts share the same communicative goal and operate within the same institutional constraints: They are both expert contributions to the NRRDB explaining the SUA process to the participants in general. Where the texts differ, however, is in how they combine RUs in more complex relations to achieve different subgoals. In this respect it could be said that Uncle Henry *appropriates* Sara's formal structure for his own ends, following it at a superficial level while repeatedly employing embedded RUs to project community values through this surface structure. The complex structure of Uncle Henry's central Account of the SUA process (11–130) provides a good illustration. This stretch of text in fact begins with a Recount of a meeting Uncle Henry attended along with "this group of all the representatives of various organisations", but this Recount framework serves only to project[5] the Account, which has embedded within it three Reflections (17–29, 56–73, 113–130) on the bond between the community and the forest; an extended Action that specifies the steps necessary for sustainability in terms of immediate community practice (38–47); two Commentaries that contribute to personalising the text as an interaction (74–84, 96–112); and a Recount of the classification process (86–94). There are also two minor embeddings (34–35, 54–55) as well as embeddings within embeddings. In such ways Uncle Henry's contribution becomes progressively more contextualised, more immediately relevant to the local participants, while remaining close, on the surface level, to the rhetorical structure of Sara's contribution. The result of this strategy is that the SUA process is described not as simply an abstraction but as having immediate relevance to the lives of the local community and as such a topic on which they can pass comment.

196 *Hybrid Voices and Collaborative Change*

```
Recount
     Account
          Reflection
               Commentary
                    Generalisation
                         Action
```

Figure 6.1   RU structure of Text 6.2, lines 113–130.

Uncle Henry's most complex use of embedding occurs between lines 113 and 130, superficially the Account of the SUA process (projected by the Recount), but with the structure in Figure 6.1 (where each indentation represents a further level of embedding).

Sara, in contrast, employs very few embeddings and those she does employ generally serve to describe the SUA process in progressively more abstract terms through the use of largely decontextualised Plans, Recounts and Conjectures. As in Uncle Henry's contribution, however, Sara uses embedded Reflections (29–34, 41–42) to illustrate her Account with examples from shared experience and Commentaries (53, 56–58) to relate with the audience, but such examples are far more limited in scope than Uncle Henry's.

A further point of interest with regard to the two speakers' deployment of RUs is the way these are used, directly or indirectly, to provide information[6] to regulate behaviour or to establish interpersonal relations, what Bernstein refers to as socialisation contexts (see Cloran 1999). Notably, both speakers begin and end on an interpersonal note, but there are similarities and differences in the strategies used over their two contributions. For the main work of her contribution, Sara employs the straightforward strategy of setting out the background of the SUA in an informative context (4–53), interspersed with a couple of short regulatory sections (29–34&41–42), before moving on to a regulatory context in order to organise further meetings (54–79), softened by a short interpersonal preface (56–57). Again, Uncle Henry's contribution appears to mirror this movement from instruction to regulation, and again this is all surface form as Uncle Henry repeatedly and at length embeds one socialisation context within another. Of particular interest is Uncle Henry's creation of a regulatory context (30–47) through what is overtly an informative description of life close to the forest but which in effect construes the obligations and duties of the local community as part of the very fabric of the natural history of the area. To take this point further, lines 17–29 are regulatory in function, though they are presented as part of his description of a previous meeting and they are realised rhetorically as a Reflection. In other words, Uncle Henry is talking about what must be done (regulatory context) in the immediate language of real-life experience (Reflection) as a means of instructing his audience on the history of the SUA process (informative context). This mixing of functions, while complex, highlights Uncle Henry's consistent strategy of explaining development not in terms of scientific facts but through the needs and activities of everyday life. Uncle Henry's use of RUs and socialisation contexts could thus be said to come closer to the ideal of praxis, the combination of theory and practice that is valued by community members and that Walter clearly sought to achieve in the Management Planning Workshop in Text 3.1.

Uncle Henry's constant changing and embedding of RUs and socialisation contexts means that the social purpose of his message is often *invisible* in that it must be inferred by his hearers (Cloran 1999:60, after Bernstein 1975). The section of Text 6.2 from line 30 to line 47, for example, is largely put across through an Account and a Conjecture, RUs that at face value provide information, yet the underlying message here is clearly regulatory. Sara, on the other hand, creates a very visible informational context through an Account and a Conjecture (4–26) before moving on to an equally visible regulatory context (27–81) realised as a Plan. According to Bernstein (1975), invisible strategies prove a handicap to understanding for social groups who find themselves in unaccustomed contexts; yet according to the feedback both during and after the meeting, Uncle Henry's approach proves to be the more effective means of communication. This would suggest that if discourse is sufficiently contextualised, especially if the field of discourse is relevant to community life and presented by speakers with appropriate local capital, then highly visible strategies are not needed. Conversely, such visibility is ineffective where discourse is overly decontextualised, the topic unfamiliar, and the speaker lacking in appropriate local capital. To put it another way, Uncle Henry's rhetorical strategies have brought the alien field of action of NGO-style institutional meetings closer to the field of experience of the local communities.

FIELD AND THE REPRESENTATION OF REALITY[7]

If we look at the two texts from the point of view of the semantic development of the concept 'Sustainable Utilisation Area' we find marked differences between the two speakers. As described above, the semantic development of the concept SUA through each text was tracked following Martin's dynamic approach, and Figures 6.2 and 6.3 are synoptic representations of the semantic relationships identified in this process. These figures demonstrate the very different *semantic mappings* employed by the two speakers in developing their explanations of the SUAs. In brief, Sara begins by subcategorising the SUA into "system" (5) and "team" (6), which elements are then further subcategorised (7–9). From this point on, Sara's explanation of the SUA process is overwhelmingly framed in terms of meetings and discussions. Though there are occasional sidelong glances at resources and businesses (19–22), the effect of the programme on local communities

198   *Hybrid Voices and Collaborative Change*

(23–25) and issues of communications (41–43, 47–49, 52&56–57), there is a constant emphasis on the *workings* of the SUA programme as a theoretical process while the relevance of the SUAs to the communities seems to relate more to the community role in outreach (47–49) than to the basis of the programme in daily life and its effect upon it. Where Sara does relate the process to community life, this relationship is seen as a result rather than a cause of the process (23–25), while the relationship between land and business, central to Uncle Henry's definition below, is subordinate to her explanation of the workings of the SUAs (11–22) as an Iwokrama-dominated process, as explicitly stated as in lines 17–25&73–79. This emphasis on process over content mirrors Sara's concerns in Text 3.1.

In contrast to Sara's explanation, Uncle Henry defines the SUA programme in familiar terms from the outset. After briefly problematising local understanding of the concept (1–10), he refers to the zoning process that identified the SUAs (14–16), a process that needed the local knowledge of the people as the inhabitants of the zone, now redefined as the "forest" (17) and later expanded to the "area which you can use natural resources there" (30). In this way Uncle Henry develops his principal representation of the SUA as a combination of people (16–29) and resources (30–50) that is dependent upon understanding (16). This relationship is not straightforward, however, and Uncle Henry introduces the key concept that familiarity can breed either contempt or understanding (51–74). The key to understanding is research (78–112) that combines local familiarity with outside techniques (113–158), so overcoming the limitations of the purely local (78–96) or the purely external (97–112). And the result of this collaboration is sustainable economic development for the community (118–130&140–156). From the beginning to the end of his contribution Uncle Henry presents the SUA process in terms that have immediate local relevance: The initial development of the concept SUA is as the land

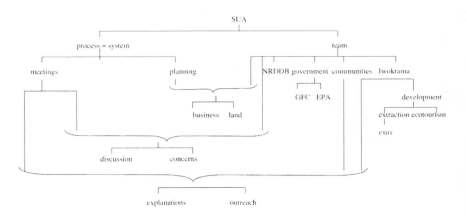

Figure 6.2   Sara's construal of SUAs.

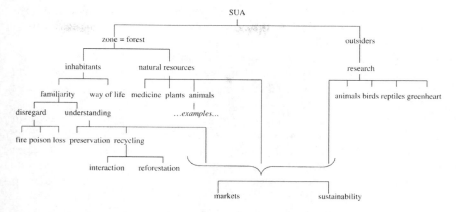

Figure 6.3 Uncle Henry's construal of SUAs.

and the relation of the communities to it, while the final picture is of the SUA programme as the source of economic development for the community through the sustainability of markets. The component parts of the term *SUA* are thus the *Area* as the forest and the community that knows it and their *Utilisation* of it for community livelihoods which are *Sustainable* through local knowledge in combination with outside expertise. This reliance on a locally relevant field of discourse resonates with the high level of contextualisation of Uncle Henry's discourse.[8]

TENOR AND THE CONSTRUAL OF FACE RELATIONS

The tenor of a discourse relates to the following:

1. The control each speaker exercises over the flow of discourse, especially through the *mood* of their utterances (as declaratives, interrogatives or imperatives). This is not covered in depth here as, apart from one or two rhetorical questions and imperatives from Uncle Henry as he engages with his audience, both texts are essentially monologues made up almost entirely of declarative clauses.
2. The force each speaker feels able to give to their speech acts in terms of the truth value or the level of obligation they convey, especially through the use of *modals* such as MUST, MIGHT and SHOULD.
3. The identification of the speaker with various sectors of the audience and the wider community, especially through the use of inclusive or exclusive *personal pronouns* and *naming procedures*.

These features in combination can be analysed to reveal the relationships between various participants in terms of *solidarity* and relative *authority*.

200 Hybrid Voices and Collaborative Change

As described above, authority can derive from either a speaker's social position or their knowledge. Authority and solidarity can be combined in different ways and, especially when the relative familiarity or technicality of the field of discourse is also taken into consideration, it is possible to identify complex categories of symbolic capital such as *local knowledge, external knowledge* and what I have labelled *moral authority*, that is, the positional authority of the local elder.

Uncle Henry's opening lines immediately throw up points of interest in terms of both authority and solidarity. With respect to authority, Uncle Henry's *Mister Chairman, I would like now to ask a question and then make some comments* is noteworthy in that Uncle Henry not only stands to speak unbidden, in contrast to Sara, who is asked to speak, but also in that he *prebooks* his further comments (1) and continues to speak uninterrupted for the eight minutes and 55 seconds transcribed here and beyond. In this time Uncle Henry, whose qualifications are largely gained from experience, not only expounds upon matters scientific and economic, but does so in the wake of failures, at this meeting and in previous workshops, from 'expert' voices within the power-broking community. That Uncle Henry is able to speak uninterrupted for so long at this juncture and on these issues reflects not only the esteem with which he is held by his fellow community members, but also his authority as a *legitimate speaker* (Bourdieu 1977, in Norton 2000:69) in negotiations with Iwokrama. In claiming and exploiting this authority for himself, he is redressing the power imbalance between 'local' and 'expert' voices in general, reducing the *interpersonal awe* that such distance creates and opening up space for the legitimation of other local voices.

In terms of solidarity, Uncle Henry's opening is again interesting in his use, commented on already, of *Mister Chairman* to his eldest son, Sam. Through the low solidarity of this address, Uncle Henry signals that his contribution is to be interpreted in terms of the formal institutional structures of the NRDDB rather than in the solidary terms of the North Rupununi as a community (cf. Text 5.2). In contrast, Sara refers to Sam by his first name, possibly as an attempt to diminish the distance created by Iwokrama's prestige as an international organisation. Uncle Henry's confident presumption of the right to speak, claimed through the use of formal titles, thus seems to be a function of the complex notion of the NRDDB as a space owned by the community while still very much an institutional space.

Solidarity relations are also construed through the use of pronouns to the extent to which they signal inclusivity (WE, including the addressee); exclusivity (I/WE as opposed to YOU); or distance (HE, SHE, IT and THEY). Influential speakers can use these forms to draw on different sources of authority. Of particular interest in the NRDDB setting are: (i) relationships of high solidarity based on common cause; (ii) the moral authority of the community elder who is set apart from the rest of the community yet whose status is dependent on shared values, history and experience; (iii)

Interdiscursivity, Capital and Empathy 201

the practical skills of the local expert, with uncommon ability in common matters; and (iv) the technical knowledge of the certificated expert who is separated from their audience by both the level of their expertise and the rarity of their knowledge.

Analysing Text 6.1 from this point of view, Sara seems at first to distance herself from the decision-makers in Iwokrama, referring to them in the third person (5–6, 11, 12, 14&22), perhaps in an attempt to show some solidarity with the local representatives by implying that both are being controlled within the SUA process rather than controlling it. However, by line 26 Iwokrama is again WE for Sara, contrasting strongly with the oppositional YOU in lines 26 to 38 as the WE of Iwokrama is depicted as having to reorganise meetings that the YOU of the local communities have failed to carry out effectively. The relationship of high solidarity aimed for in the opening lines has turned into a contrastive (though not necessarily oppositional) power relation at this point. Sara reverts to what seems to be an inclusive WE (39) to refer to the two groups as equal participants in future meetings, but WE is soon used once again to refer to Iwokrama, who take on the powerful positions of evaluators (40&44); providers of knowledge (45); and elevated participants, "up here" (46). From this point to the end reference switches between WE as Iwokrama (50, 54, 60&79) in contrast to YOU the communities (51, 54, 55, 64, 66, 78, 81), on the one hand, and the inclusive WE of Iwokrama and the communities meeting together (48, 61, 67, 68, 69, 72, 74, 76, 77), on the other. In this last section, however, when Sara creates a social distance between the two groups, she uses negative politeness strategies (Brown and Levinson 1987) to enhance the power of the local communities, as evidenced by the extreme deference of the request for them to participate at the in-between meetings that brings the contribution to a close. Here the use of "we would like NRDDB to think about . . ." (54), the expression of requests indirectly through conditional clauses (60&66), and the politeness of distal COULD (69, 72, 74&75) all serve to recall that ultimately the local communities have a power of veto over any proposed activity. The flurry of modal forms here serves to highlight their virtual absence elsewhere, an absence which can possibly be explained by the contrast between Iwokrama's power base in superior objective knowledge and the subjective moral overtones the use of modality often carries. The relationship construed by Sara in Text 6.1 is thus one of Iwokrama and the local communities as co-workers, but with each side possessing latent powers: Iwokrama's control over technical knowledge and the potential for non-cooperation of the local communities.

In Text 6.2, Uncle Henry begins his contribution by underlining his personal authority, through his use of the first person I (1&3) and through his assumed right not only to speak at will (1&2), but also to question publicly, if rhetorically, the level of imported knowledge of other members of the community, referred to as YOU (4, 5, 6&8). The authority to do this stems from the combination of Uncle Henry's high solidarity with his

202 *Hybrid Voices and Collaborative Change*

community and his connections with external power, as epitomised in this instance by Iwokrama. The immediately following section emphasises both these aspects. The WE of 11–13 is non-inclusive, referring to the group of local participants who attended the previous SUA meeting and thus stressing their acquaintance with external knowledge systems; however, lines 17–29 seem to turn this on its head as the oppositional YOU referring to the community in general is incorporated into a wider "all of us" (16) and the importance of shared community knowledge and values is stressed as Uncle Henry launches into a litany of WEs that not only expresses his high solidarity with the community, but also suggests that there is some level of moral duty on the communities as the true experts on the forest to assert their knowledge over Iwokrama in terms of local issues and forest life. This is made explicit through the use of SHOULD in "we are the ones to give advice. And we should take it in that vein" (21).

Uncle Henry constructs an authoritative role for himself in order to regulate community behaviour, just as Sara did. However, while Iwokrama's authority was based solely on differences in external knowledge, Uncle Henry constructs a position of moral authority over the behaviour of the community through a combination of symbolic capital based on distance and symbolic capital rooted in solidarity. His personal authority is constructed through the subjective expression of obligation MUST (35&38), and through the use of direct imperatives (67, 127, 134, 135&151) within behavioural directives directed at the community as YOU (31–50, 64–68, 120–156). Exhortations to the community to maintain its shared life experiences and traditions (17–29&56–60) are addressed to a solidary WE and explicitly opposed to 'the other' through the contrast between "anybody else who live outside" (18) and "whoever comes from there [and] will return" (23). This difference is clearly seen in lines 59 to 63 where the WE of community life carries on into a series of directives before it is adjusted to the YOU (64) that would be expected in such regulatory contexts.

Such a combination of authority and solidarity reflects Uncle Henry's community-based *moral authority* as opposed to the knowledge-based authority of Iwokrama. However, Uncle Henry's authority is also based on knowledge, though in his case this relates to both community practice and to external technology. While his opening lines emphasise that he is more acquainted with external knowledge systems than the majority of the community, when there is a choice to be made between the two types of power, as when collaborating with Iwokrama in research and training (75–118), Uncle Henry places himself firmly on the side of solidarity: Iwokrama are THEY (89, 90&95), while the community is very much WE (77, 81, 83, 84, 93, 105, 113–117). And where Uncle Henry most exerts his personal knowledge–based authority, it is to oppose his own highly regarded community-based knowledge to the external knowledge of the experts (96–108), a move which seems to construct solidarity with the community and a level of knowledge-based authority over it simultaneously. Another feature combining face relations is Uncle Henry's frequent use of CAN (45, 50,

Interdiscursivity, Capital and Empathy   203

68, 113, 121, 133 twice, 134&152) to define what is possible, a usage that mixes aspects of the moral authority of permission and a scientific evaluation of the viable—what I labelled his *nihil obstat* in Chapter 4. Overall, then, Uncle Henry has constructed a complex position for himself, with his power based to some extent on both external and local forms of knowledge but chiefly on his moral authority within the community, a power which relies on a continuing relationship of local solidarity.

PHASAL ANALYSIS OF TEXTS 6.1 AND 6.2

Following Gregory's (1988) notion of phase, whereby significant changes within any one metafunction count as a shift in phase, the different phases in each speaker's contribution are set out in Tables 6.1 and 6.2.[9] Functions for each phase within the contribution as a whole are suggested, and the progression of these makes up the rhetorical structure of each text. The registerial variables that constitute each phase and which were identified in the previous sections are included to support the analysis.

From Tables 6.1 and 6.2 it would appear that the contributions of the two speakers were produced to serve quite different purposes, and these differences can be related to the model of language and symbolic capital built up in Chapters 3 and 4 in terms of the different roles the two speakers construct for themselves and the meaning of these roles within the different social contexts in which the two speakers chiefly operate. In Text 6.1, for example, Sara's overall goal would appear to be to explain the workings of the SUA process as a *system* and to allocate roles and responsibilities for the various groups as they work together, culminating in an indirect but fairly clear request for cooperation in the last phase before the conclusion (54–79). This ethos of collaboration certainly runs counter to the government's ideology of paternalism, as construed through the Amerindian Act; however, Sara's consistent construction of Iwokrama's authority through knowledge, the rapid outpouring of new information, and the emphasis on the SUA process as a structure combine to suggest that Iwokrama is ultimately in control of this structure and that the local communities are to collaborate according to the place allocated to them. In these terms Text 6.1 could potentially be characterised as co-optive. Similarly, despite appeals for collaboration, Sara's attempts to explain external ideas in their own self-contained terms remain to some extent fixed within a banking method of instruction which reflects and reproduces the more centralised knowledge-based relations within the local context. This aspect of her contribution also relates to wider structures in that it allows the exchange of information to be quantified, 'evaluated' and compared at a distance by the transnational groups that fund Iwokrama and for whom the presentation of information often counts as a goal achieved and a box ticked, irrespective of the level of understanding achieved (cf. Chambers 1997:65), a tendency noted by Walter when I interviewed him a few days after the NRDDB meeting from which the texts are taken (Toka, 8/11/00):

204 Hybrid Voices and Collaborative Change

Table 6.1 Rhetorical Features of Sara's Contributions in Text 6.1

Phase:	Function:	Mode:	Field:	Tenor:
1–2	**Justify intervention and establish credentials.**	Commentary. Interpersonal context.	SUA as process.	I as knower, YOU as receivers
3–22	**Explain thinking of Iwokrama underlying SUA.**	Account of SUA as system; embedded Conjectures on proposed meetings (11–16). Informative context.	SUA as system and team; make-up and duties of team.	Iwokrama = THEY controlling speaker and communities creates [+solidarity] with community participants.
23–26	**Metacommentary to present issues.**	Conjecture (embedded in Account) about community involvement and benefits. Informative context.	Involvement of communities and affect on them.	Third-person *communities*. Theoretical possibilities.
27–46	**Contrast with past and existing communication problems.**	Plan for future meetings, embedding Reflections (29–34; 41–42–51) on past difficulties. Informative context with regulatory embedding (29–34).	Scheduling and make-up of different levels of meetings. Content of general SUA meetings. Iwokrama as collaborator.	Iwokrama = WE Community = YOU [+knowledge] for Iwokrama Iwokrama as WE enabling and evaluating communities as YOU. CAN and BE ABLE. Very strong [+knowledge] for Iwokrama. WE up there as knowers. [+power/knowledge] for Iwokrama.
47–49	**Move from theory to action.**	Plan for immediate action. Informative context.	Possible outreach.	WE as NRDDB + Iwokrama meeting together.
50–53	**Justification of action.**	Recount with embedding Plan (ll.87–88). Informative context.	Sharing of information between Iwokrama and communities.	WE as Iwokrama YOU as NRDDB members at meeting. Information from Iwokrama out. [+Power/Knowledge] for Iwokrama.
54–79	**Request for goods and services: participation.**	Plan. Regulatory context.	Setting up and content of in-between meetings, feedback to bigger meeting.	WE mixes Iwokrama alone and both together. YOU = NRDDB. Indirect requests with interest as qualifying factor. CAN, COULD, WILL. [-power] and [+solidarity] between Iwokrama and NRDDB.
80–81	**Wrap up.**	Commentary. Interpersonal context.	Metadiscourse.	Question, first name. [+solidarity] with community.

Interdiscursivity, Capital and Empathy 205

Table 6.2 Rhetorical Features of Uncle Henry's Contribution in Text 6.2

Phase:	Function:	Mode:	Field:	Tenor:
1-10	Introduction, setting up knowledge and authority differences, establishing credentials.	Commentary. Interpersonal context.	Meaning of SUA.	Establishes right to speak. Emphasises institutional context through title of Chairman. UF as I has knowledge, uses authority to question knowledge of communities as YOU through rhetorical questions. [+power/knowledge] for UF.
11-29	Justify attendance at meeting on SUA in terms of traditions and sustainability of community life and importance of local knowledge input.	Recount of meeting introducing embedded Account. Multiple embeddings increasing familiarity. Informative context with regulatory embedding.	Conservation as Wilderness Preserve and Sustainable Utilisation Area; importance of local familiarity with and permanence in area.	WE =invitees THEY = Iwokrama, leading into to YOU = community at large as knowers, leading into WE = community. SHOULD for duty of communities. [+solidarity] UF with communities. +[power/knowledge] for communities over Iwokrama.
30-47	**Explain relevance of recycling etc to life, SUA as duty as well as process.**	Account of SUA projecting Reflection. Multiple embeddings. Informative context projecting regulatory context.	Sustainability, recycling, depletion of natural resources.	(Generic) YOU as being regulated through instruction. Subjective MUST for moral obligations. [+Moral Authority] of UF.
48-55	**Importance of observation of changes as transition to call for collaborative research.**	Plan. Regulatory context.	Observation of changes leading to better understanding.	Maintains this with rhetorical questions.
56-73	**Problematises local familiarity with respect to sustainability**	Multiple embeddings contextualising complex ideas. Informative context projecting regulatory context.	Abuses of forest resources resulting from familiarity.	WE as community, but becoming YOU for worst errors. Bare imperative. [+moral authority] through distance within solidarity.

(continued)

206 Hybrid Voices and Collaborative Change

Table 6.2 (continued)

74-95	Relates benefits of outside knowledge to above.	Commentary on participation. Conjecture on possible problems. Recount of important but incomplete outside research and potential problems. Regulatory context with informative embeddings.	Complementary means of research carried out on various natural resources of the forest. Limitations of both in isolation.	WE as grassroots research for community benefit; THEY as Iwokrama doing more theoretical research. [+solidarity] and [-knowledge/power] between UF and communities, [+power/knowledge] Iwokrama over communities.
96-112	UF's knowledge used to question imported knowledge.	Commentary embedding Prediction. Regulatory context projecting interpersonal and informative contexts.	Potential failings of imported knowledge and mapping.	I as sceptic [+power/knowledge] of communities over Iwokrama and of UF within community.
113	Introduces idea of complementarity of knowledges and efforts.	Reflection.	Collaboration.	WE as community involved in grassroots research. Declaration of responsibilities.
114-130	Relates local input to economic benefits and hence sustainability in a general way.	Reflection projecting Commentary projecting Generalisation on need to work.	Community research on various non-timber products.	WE as community involved in grassroots research. Uncle Henry mixing moral and knowledge power through CAN x3 Generic YOU for work ethic ending up as WE as community. Imperative. [+moral authority] of UF
131-146	More specific recommendations and exemplification of mutual benefits of collaboration.	Recount of recommendations, projecting Plan embedding Generalisation projecting Conjecture. Regulatory context.	Uncle Henry's recommendations for community input into Iwokrama research on traditional activities leading to identification of sustainable markets.	I as advising on interaction between generic YOU of community and and THEY as Iwokrama. CANx4. +[knowledge/power] of UF over communities.
147-156	Summary.	Account of SUA projecting Action. Regulatory context prefaced by instructional.	Activities necessary for Sustainable Utilisation.	YOU = audience, imperatives to answer earlier rhetorical questions. [+power/knowledge] for UF over communities.
157-158	Job done as set out in intro re transfer of knowledge.	Metadiscursive Commentary leading to Prediction/Plan. Interpersonal context.	Community knowledge of and participation in Sustainable Utilisation.	I know YOU understand. [+power/knowledge] for UF over communities.

I would say that in the inception of the workshop they [the community participants] hadn't understand exactly what it was all about . . . so, like Sara and the other speaker were just building up from that, you know, keep building up. So if you don't understand anything at the bottom, you wouldn't be able to get what is going on at the top.

In contrast, Uncle Henry does not explain sustainable utilisation either as a self-contained process or through the provision of new information. Instead he seeks to explain what is essentially an alien concept in relation to the existing knowledge and practice of the communities he represents and in terms of its relevance to daily community life, an approach corresponding to the community preference for practice over theory referred to several times above. This approach emphasises the importance of community tradition as a force that has maintained sustainability until now but which is in danger of becoming the contempt born of familiarity. Uncle Henry therefore emphasises that Iwokrama's imported knowledge can be drawn upon to revitalise community practice and, as Sara had before, he stresses the need for cooperation between the two knowledge systems. However, where Sara emphasised the importance of external systems and community participation within a wider Iwokrama-dominated process, Uncle Henry represents Iwokrama's knowledge as being assimilated into the wider practice of the community in order to reform it. In these terms collaboration with Iwokrama represents a major shift in community life and practice so that Uncle Henry must draw not only upon his moral authority as community elder in order to sanction such disruption, but also upon the knowledge he possesses within each system in order to justify it. Uncle Henry's contribution therefore emphasises the solidarity through common experience on which his moral authority is based, yet distances him with respect to the regulatory power he commands within the local realm and his knowledge in both local and imported terms.

Considering Texts 6.1 and 6.2 together, however, it could be claimed that Sara's contribution is just as important as Uncle Henry's in that Uncle Henry not only builds on what Sara has said, but, more significantly, he is able to *subsume* the symbolic capital she displays as an outside expert into his own complex position as expert, arbiter and gatekeeper in areas of intercultural assimilation. In this way Uncle Henry's contribution is not in opposition to Sara's failed explanation, but rather draws on it and *recontextualises* it in locally effective terms through the content of his discourse, that is, the field, and through the interpersonal tenor and the rhetorical mode that define the style of this discourse. Some months after the NRDDB meeting from which these texts were taken, I asked Uncle Henry what he thought were the main differences between his own contribution and Sara's (Surama Rest House, 22/6/02):

Well, it's just a matter of difference of culture, you see. You see, the people who from Iwokrama, whoever comes, whichever resource

208 *Hybrid Voices and Collaborative Change*

person, (xxx) or consultant that comes to give a talk, they come at a professional level . . . which is far above the local people. Now, there are times you would listen to the presentation and you look at the audience, and you know they ain't get raas [i.e. understand bugger all], *you see, what really being thrown out. So this is where I at times interject and ask to say something, and I try to break it down in a simpler Creolese form so that they can understand, and I normally would call some instances in everyday life, so they get a better idea of what really's being said, so they could understand.*

Interestingly, while Uncle Henry undoubtedly breaks his contribution down in terms of clause structure (as analysed in Bartlett 2003), there is no evidence in Text 6.2 that he uses vernacular Creolese English to any significant degree while his use of technical terms is in fact higher than Sara's (also in Bartlett 2003). What the analyses of the two texts in this chapter suggest is that Uncle Henry's adoption of a "simpler Creolese form" in practice relates to his adoption of a locally appropriate voice through the registerial variables of experiential, interpersonal and textual meaning that define the field, tenor and mode of his discourse and which make his explanation effective through the level of empathy he is able to achieve and the symbolic capital with which he legitimates his position. While an adequate level of comprehension is of course a prerequisite for genuine community participation within the discourse of development, in the terms of voice, choice and space, discussed in Chapter 3, discourse such as Uncle Henry's goes beyond facilitating the comprehension of the local community in NRDDB meetings to *indigenise* the meetings and so open them up to other community voices as local participants increasingly relate to the NRDDB as an institution and develop a sense of ownership over it. As a result, it would not seem unreasonable to suggest that the interdiscursive expertise that Uncle Henry displays here was a contributing factor in the growing confidence exhibited by Walter through the texts analysed in Chapter 5. In my concluding chapter I will develop this idea in relation to the model of language, symbolic capital and collaboration developed throughout the book and suggest how these concepts can contribute to the theory and practice of Positive Discourse Analysis.

7 Positive Discourse Analysis
Spaces of Collaboration and Resistance

To begin this concluding chapter I return to the theme with which Walter's words opened the book, this time in a lengthy comment from Nicholas (Toka, 10/11/00) as he talks about the prejudices experienced by the Amerindian communities of Guyana and the need for them to reclaim their heritage, to "buck the system" a I have called it: to challenge the view of Amerindians as backward communities, as passive recipients of first-world beneficence, a characterisation that underlies much of the Discourse of Development in general and that is encapsulated in the Guyana Amerindian Act in particular. In this extract Nicholas eloquently captures a number of key ideas from the perspective of his own lived experience, ideas which, in a mirror image of Uncle Henry's "indigenising" of Iwokrama's language in Chapter 6, I will then attempt to recontextualise in more abstract (if far less eloquent) terms.

> So when you look at that, what I'm saying is that, you're going to still have schools, you're going to still have a lot of things, er, you would still have people that would speak Makushi, and that should be encouraged, right, because what I find today, one of the big problems with Amerindians, I think it's very important, one of the big things I'm finding out, is why we can't go forward? Why we are ashamed? Ashamed of our culture, and we know we get this nametag that they put on us as 'buck' in Guyana, but we are always ashamed when people call us 'buck' and these kind of thing, and they always look down on us because "You are no good; you're a non-entity; you're the one that knows nothing", right? And they can tell us that because we don't know what we know. We don't know where our roots are, right? And if you go back to the East Indians, they could always look back to India, they don't look to Georgetown, what makes them proud is India. And even the Africans are proud because of Africa.[1] [. . .] But with the Amerindians, especially like the Makushis and the Wapishanas, those in Guyana, the Caribs, Waraus, whatever it might be in Guyana, nine tribes, they don't have nothing to look to, but perhaps a few mountains, a few thatch-roof houses, right? Some naked savages

210   *Hybrid Voices and Collaborative Change*

in the fifteenth, in 1492, right? So that's all we've got to look to, look at, right? And then, as our tribes we don't have any heritage, we don't have anything to look back, history to show that we have any civilisation, so when people tell you, like, it's real to you, right? But then that's if we look at ourselves as Makushi and Wapishana; if we look at ourselves as the Amerindian people that escaped, that came over across the Bering Strait and came travelling down this way, if that would be the right thing, right, if we look at that, then we could go back to the Incas, the Mayans, the Aztecs, and when we look at that we see great civilisation, then we have something to be proud of, and until Amerindian people . . . now if you notice, the African people have a similar problem, where you find that Martin Luther [King] and all of these different men, Bob Marley, they came back and they started singing to like establish Africa, and now they go back and they start to use things like 'The Cradle of Civilisation is Africa'. That put something into them. Now if the Amerindians could actually see we actually had links with the Aztecs, we actually had links with the Incas, we actually had links with the Mayans, our empires were great, we are a great people [. . .] So you see these things could be taught to the children in school at a early age; when they coming back you wouldn't be able to go and tell . . . you could imagine you go outside and I use this in one of my, erm, presentations, you go out there and . . . I used to go to school in Lethem, and these boys are coming, you know I used to smoke then, and they would come and say, erm, I would say "Gimme a ciggy, nah?" and they would turn and say, "(xxxxx), buck people have no got cigarettes." And you know the first people that actually smoked was Amerindians, you know? Then, you didn't know that, right, so you feel so bad, you know, like, you really didn't, you didn't <u>know</u> about smoking, then it should have been in the reverse: I should have been telling them "Yeah, yeah, this is buck people thing, you know." If these things are taught to the people you finds that there's a cultural, I don't know how to put it, I guess there might be some anthropological term [. . .] something like, they could look back at those things and it makes them (xx) heritage. They have a heritage . . .

THE NRDDB AS A "THIRD SPACE": CONTRADICTION OR RESISTANCE?

In the preceding six chapters I have described and analysed discourse within the context of the NRDDB as an intermediary space between the indigenous communities of the North Rupununi, Iwokrama and the Government of Guyana. In order to understand the dynamics of possibility behind these emergent discourses I situated the analyses within a discussion of international development as it has evolved as a concept in the post-war period and in terms of the attitude of the Government of Guyana towards the Amerindian population, specifically as this is enshrined in the Amerindian Act. These descriptions revealed a degree of *tension* between the paternalistic attitude of the government, on the one hand, and the increasingly progressive attempts within international development organisations to integrate local communities into their decision-making processes, on the other. As a third perspective I discussed the attitudes of the local communities themselves to intercultural discourse. As well as interview data and documents such as the *Report on Region 9's Poverty Reduction Strategy Consultations*, I analysed the NRDDB Constitution and demonstrated how this document codified the communities' desire for greater autonomy in determining their future that was evident in the other data. Taken together, these analyses suggest that a forum such as the NRDDB is potentially a conflictive space, with the different histories and assumptions of the various groups involved constraining the dynamic possibilities for truly collaborative discourse.

From the perspective of the local communities, with their desire for material development without sacrificing their cultural identity, participation in such spaces is an exercise fraught with tension given the paternalistic attitude of the government and many of those involved in international development and the environment of prejudice in Guyana generally, as captured in Nicholas's comments above. Sánchez Gómez (1998:50–53; all translations mine), a Tseltal Indian from Chiapas, Mexico, describes the tension inherent in such spaces as a conflict between "resistance" and "contradiction". In relation to his native Oxchujk' (Oxchuc), he describes a *space of resistance* to European influence, a "final refuge . . . the nucleus of indigenous governance", a space which is "jealously cared for by the indigenous leaders". Around this nucleus is the *space of survival and contradiction*, where, "for reasons of survival, the existence of institutions from outside the community is permitted" so as to "protect the nucleus from the onslaughts of national society". This is a dangerous and ambiguous zone, inhabited by "government agencies, the priest, the doctor, the bilingual teacher, the community development programme officer":

> Now when the school and the bilingual teacher are divorced from the space of resistance, that is, when the teacher stands apart, becomes acculturated and favours national society, the community itself places them in the space of contradictions; therefore, by definition, they are apart from the indigenous community, even though they are indigenous by origin, and come to be seen as an agent of the state. But when the bilingual teacher aligns himself more with the indigenous community, then the school and the teacher are situated within the space of resistance. (Sánchez Gómez 1998:51–52)

Bhabha (1994) makes a related, though distinct, point when he talks about the creation of a *third space* in which local cultural forms come

212   Hybrid Voices and Collaborative Change

together with dominant practices from outside, not merely to insulate the nucleus from outside influence, but to forge something new from the encounter. In Bhabha's terms continued adherence to traditional practices within the post-colonial context would bring with it "the dangers of the fixity and fetishism of identities within the calcification of colonial cultures" and the idea "that 'roots' be struck in the celebratory romance of the past" (1994:9). As a counter to this danger, Bhabha suggests the need to foster a space that:

> demands an encounter with 'newness' that is not part of the continuum of past and present. It creates a sense of the new as an insurgent act of cultural translation. Such an act does not merely recall the past as social cause or aesthetic precedent; it renews the past, refiguring it as a contingent 'in-between' space, that innovates and interrupts the performance of the present. The "past-present" becomes part of the necessity, not the nostalgia of living. (7)

For this to take place, Bhabha (1994:34; emphases in original) goes on to argue, there is a need for subjugated communities to become conscious of, and to forcefully declare, their cultural *difference*, "as knowledge*able*, authoritative, [and] adequate to the construction of systems of cultural identification", a position that echoes both Sánchez Gómez's concept of a *space of resistance* and Nicholas's call for a reassertion of Amerindian heritage. In contrasting the civilisations of the Incas, Aztecs and Mayas with the materially impoverished conditions of the Makushi and Wapishana, Nicholas does not intend to denigrate the Amerindian communities of present-day Guyana but, on the contrary, he is stressing the need for local communities to be aware of their heritage and to assert themselves on the basis of a justifiable pride of who they are and where they come from. Conscious of the failure of the Guyanese government and international development organisations, with their explicit or implicit assumption that "[a]ncient philosophies have to be scrapped; old social institutions have to disintegrate; bonds of cast, creed and race have to burst; and large numbers of persons who cannot keep up with progress have to have their expectations of a comfortable life frustrated" (UN Department of Social and Economic Affairs in 1951, in Escobar 1995:4), Nicholas is claiming that in order to "go forward" it is these very aspects of Amerindian life that must be maintained. This idea that local communities must simultaneously recognise existing community practice while striving to "go forward" was also explicitly stated at the Iwokrama Workshop on Critical Issues in the Guiana Shield (Pegasus Hotel, Georgetown, 6/12/00) by the Touchau of Touchaus for Region 8, Tony James, when he spoke of the need for Amerindian peoples to "reconcile to the modern world" but went on to claim that before this was possible it was first necessary for the indigenous population to regain respect for their own culture. In Bhabha's terms, it is necessary,

Positive Discourse Analysis 213

before confronting *the other*, to undergo a critical discourse with the self, to go beyond the impression of a culture that is monolithic in itself and discrete from all others. Once the multiform and dynamic nature of one's own culture is recognised, it becomes possible to understand in greater depth the significant similarities with and differences from other cultures and ultimately "to conceive of the articulation of antagonistic or contradictory elements . . . the *negotiation* of contradictory and antagonistic instances that open up hybrid sites and objectives of struggle" (Bhabha 1994:25). According to Fishman (1989:85), such "syncretism is a far greater principle of nonideological daily life than either intellectuals or elites care to recognise", in which case Bhabha's critical approach is merely a conscious attempt to speed up and control the natural processes of cultural syncretism and development and "[u]ltimately the issue becomes not *whether* but *what* or *how much* to admit into the inside" (Fishman 1989:85).

In previous chapters I have argued that one means for declaring cultural *difference* while negotiating alternative perspectives is to recontextualise these external perspectives in terms of the community-based knowledge, interpersonal relations and methods of cultural transmission that comprise the field, tenor and mode of local voices. This is what I suggested in Chapter 6 was the true meaning of "Creolisation" of the discourse of development: neither a retreat into traditional custom nor merely the alteration of surface features of outside discourses, but the adoption of new ideas within a local voice, a way of discoursing that interprets outside ideas according to local practice and that has the authority to pronounce the final *nihil obstat* as to what can be done in the local context—what is at once viable and permissible. Such a process requires local communities to approach change with a full knowledge and esteem for their existing social practices and, because rather than in spite of this, not to fear change.

Gordon (Iwokrama, Georgetown, 24/4/01) provides an example of how the *nihil obstat* of local elders, rather than representing a return to the "dead-end of conventional authority" (cf. Cooke 1994:30), can combine with new knowledge in a way that brings material benefits to the local communities. Whereas traditionally local elders, as the sources of both local knowledge and authority, would frighten community members off fishing in understocked pools through the use of myths such as the kanaima or mermaids, as described in Chapter 2, such prohibition, while still the prerogative of the elders, is now the result of dispersed knowledge and discussion:

> *We actually have more arapaima now than we did last year. So the management's happening, but it's not happening becau- in the same way that you have management plan, and everybody follows the management plan, it's actually happening because people, individuals are making decisions at different levels and some are—the more and more individuals are making decisions to do, to go this way rather than to go that way [. . .] and it happens through communication, and it's*

214 Hybrid Voices and Collaborative Change

not, it's not the old way of managing where the touchau would decide. But that's starting to come back too. The authority figures are starting to appear in the communities and they are making decisions. And they're being respected. [. . .] If the powerhouses make decisions, it does affect a number of their constituents. So, yeah it is making a difference, and yes, things are being managed, but it's not, it's not like the management plan says "Do this, do this, do this, do this, do that." It's a very diffuse thing, and it's very loose, and it's not something that you could really grab hold of.

Andrew (Rupertee, 28/2/01) similarly points to the benefits of combining community authority in drafting plans with outside assistance:

what I notice now, people, in Annai of itself, generally, there is a lot of mixing up going on. Right. And if you go to NRDDB you see how many people mix up. Right, and the mixing bring up what? Togetherness. Unity. And because why? At that level they understand what to relate on, how important is relationship. Without CIDA[2] we could not have got money. That's one good thing relating with CIDA. Right? We could not have got the expertise to draft out the plan if we had not been mixing. So that mixing up brings about what we hold today in our community.

In Habermas's (1984) terms (Chouliaraki and Fairclough 1999:83–89; Cooke 1994), the traditional fiat of community elders represents *communicative action*, an ordering of society through unreflexive reliance on existing social hierarchies and practice, what Habermas calls the *lifeworld* of the local communities. This contrasts with what Habermas sees as the modern practice of *communicative rationality*, the negotiation of positions through reflection and the creation of expert management systems. The juxtaposition, or "mixing up", of the traditional and the modern, as is the case in the North Rupununi, creates tensions between the authority of local tradition as lifeworld and the expert systems of the dominant society. These tensions can be resolved either through the *colonisation* of the lifeworld by the system and the acculturation of the former within the dominant pattern, as demonstrated for the processes of paternalism, advocacy and co-optation, or through the *appropriation* by minority groups of valuable structures from the dominant system and their incorporation into their own cultural dynamic—an idea Sam captures with respect to the challenges presented by the imminent road from Brazil: "Use the road, or the road will use us". 'Using the road' represents a broadening of the local cultural system through the appropriation and adaptation of external influences in a practice of dynamic expansion, of communicative rationality as "the increasing capacity of people to use communicative action to reflect back on and redeem itself" (Chouliaraki and Fairclough 1999:85), and of

Positive Discourse Analysis 215

the formation of "'post-conventional' identities, people who are not [rigidly] positioned within traditions but able to creatively remake themselves through creative reworking of inherited social resources" (Chouliaraki and Fairclough 1999:84). Such a rationalisation of the lifeworld introduces the mechanisms and routines necessary to "reduce the burden upon communicative action" as local practice "vastly expands in scope and scale at a potentially crippling cost" (Chouliaraki and Fairclough 1999:85). However, while Habermas views such communicative rationality as a universal goal, I would suggest that, rather than relying on a single, objective mode of discourse, a more effective approach in the context of the North Rupununi is to embrace and understand difference, that is, to comprehend and empathise with difference and so transcend it (a concept similar to Bakhtin's notion of *polyphony*). In contexts such as the North Rupununi this *discourse across difference* entails the integration of modern systems of management within the dynamics of local practice, and the aim of this book is to demonstrate how the NRDDB has developed as a collaborative space that is nonetheless a *space of resistance* rather than a *space of contradiction*. In the following sections I will first briefly revisit my discussion of critical approaches to discourse analysis from the opening chapter and then bring together the various methods and concepts that I have developed piecemeal throughout the book and suggest these as a framework for enhancing *PDA* as a critical approach to discourse analysis that focuses on solutions rather than problems but which, rather than celebrating resistance *as resistance*, demonstrates how competing discourses can be effectively combined. In the final section I will consider some of the limitations of this analysis and suggest areas for future work.

CRITICAL APPROACHES TO DISCOURSE ANALYSIS: FROM CONFRONTATION TO COLLABORATION—VIA CELEBRATION

In the opening chapter of this book I took issue with both CDA and PDA practice: with CDA for predominantly focusing on the ways in which discourse is either manipulated by dominant groups or conceals a hegemonic and socially damaging ideology that has been naturalised, taken for granted, as a result of this process; and with its offshoot PDA for celebrating counter-discourses without adequately addressing how these might be capable of challenging the naturalised common-sense position of such hegemonic discourses. In other words, for failing to take forward its proclaimed agenda to understand "how change happens, for the better, across a range of sites—how feminists re-make gender relations in our world, how indigenous people overcome their colonial heritage, how migrants renovate their new environs and so on" (Martin 2004:9)—a failing which, in Martin's own words, "hampers design". In this section, as seems appropriate

216   *Hybrid Voices and Collaborative Change*

given my emphasis on collaboration and discourse across difference, I suggest how elements from each approach may be combined within a general analytical framework that also focuses increased attention on *voice* as the contextually contingent relationship between the features of different speakers' discourse, the diverse social groups in which they participate, and their roles and status within and across these different groups.

Chouliaraki and Fairclough (1999:117) make a significant move in this direction in proposing that, rather than focusing on disembodied discourses as if these carried a life of their own, analysis should move to the way that these specific discourses are transmitted in local contexts by socially situated agents and the potentially unstable relationship between text and producer:

> In an analysis of a specific discursive practice . . . we should separate the question of what orders of discourse are brought together from the question of what voices are brought together. Such a procedure allows CDA to explore relations and tensions between the discursive practices in place within a particular conjuncture and the specific discursive endowments of agents operative within them—a potentially powerful and explosive mix.

While this formulation seems to tally with my approach in the preceding chapters, there are, however, two important differences. Firstly, although Chouliaraki and Fairclough here invoke the concept of voice as a means of shifting attention from macrostructural forces to interaction between individual speakers and the emergent properties of real-time discourse, their approach does not include a detailed examination of the relationship between individual voices and the different social contexts that have formed these and in which they operate. Theirs is therefore a valuable though somewhat diminished notion of voice as the orientation of individual speakers to a specific discourse at a given time, an idea that is included in, but does not define, the concept of voice as I have used it in this book. Secondly, while introducing the important concept of *tensions* between speakers' individual positions and the discourses with which they are, at least nominally, aligned, Chouliaraki and Fairclough, as is common in CDA writing, tend to view power as homogeneous and so identify the tensions they refer to as potential weak points in an oppositional and zero-sum struggle over legitimacy, to be exploited by those armed with true ideology. As a result, there is a focus on antagonism over collaboration, a point I will return to shortly.

From the perspective of PDA, Martin (2004:31) sees a similar need to shift attention from the reproduction of hegemonic discourses to the ways in which these might be challenged, but for him the most pressing concern is to focus on the power of renovatory discourses themselves rather than on tensions within the dominant bloc:

Positive Discourse Analysis 217

to move beyond a preoccupation with demonology, beyond a singular focus on semiosis in the service of abusive power—and reconsider power communally as well, as it circulates through communities, as they realign around values, and renovate discourses that enact a better world.

As I have suggested above, however, this is an area in which PDA has as yet failed to reach its potential through its tendency to focus on the textual and underanalyse the historical and social conditions that constrain such renovation, an aspect that has, in contrast, underwritten much work in CDA. Moreover, while Martin's suggested approach moves beyond the "demonology" of much CDA, it is still antagonistic in that it views the renovatory discourses it seeks to promote as essentially in direct opposition to the hegemonic discourses currently circulating. The view I am putting forward, combining both these approaches and going beyond them, is that it is possible to view the tensions in dominant discourse not as weak points to be attacked but as potential areas of commonality with the more progressive discourses that Martin seeks to explore in isolation. The goal, therefore, is to seek out those areas of *productive tension* that break down the *insulation* (Bernstein 2000) between hegemonic and renovatory discourses and allow for the development of localised hybrid discourses in which seemingly antagonistic participants can collaborate as a first step in wider-reaching change: *polyphony* as opposed to a single true ideology; evolution as opposed to revolution. In identifying discourses that speak across difference in this way, framing analysis within the specific historical and sociocultural conditions of context, it might be possible to uncover and stimulate voices, in isolation or in combination, that are empathetic, comprehensible and legitimate within both social groups simultaneously. In other words, whereas CDA and PDA view power as a unitary and oppositional phenomenon, each focusing on different poles of this opposition, the view taken here is that the workings of power as a diverse and multifaceted phenomenon reveal tensions that can be productive in providing the wiggle room within which a collaborative practice can be mapped out as *spaces of resistance* open up within the dominant order, *third spaces* where dominant and dominated come together.

I have argued in this book that the NRDDB represents just such a space and focused on the circulation of power within the NRDDB in terms of the politically and culturally conditioned workings of *symbolic capital* in socially diffuse and realisationally distinct forms. Through the analyses in previous chapters I have suggested that the interplay of symbolic capitals within and between ideologically opposed groups such as the NRDDB, the government and Iwokrama is a more complex affair than the shifting of the balance of power from one side to the other; it rather involves the *collaborative mixing* of the symbolic capital that circulates within each group and which is realised through discourse features appropriate to each

218 *Hybrid Voices and Collaborative Change*

participant's position in the specific context, a relationship that is captured through the concept of *voice* and only uncovered through an ethnographic account of the sociocultural contexts in which discourses circulate. By placing current discourse practice within its historical context and demonstrating how voices that correspond to the various interactants are mixed to create hybrid discourse patterns I intended to show how *tensions* become evident in the dominant discourses of development while *commonalities* between Iwokrama's progressive approach to development and traditional practice were instrumental in creating a collaborative discourse around the common cause of sustainable local development.

In the spirit of all that has been said so far, however, it would be inappropriate to provide a global model, an *immutable movable* in Chambers's (1997) words, for the hybridisation of discourse in these terms; rather:

> instead of searching for grand alternative models or strategies, what is needed is the investigation of alternative representations and practices in concrete local settings, particularly as they exist in contexts of hybridisation, collective action, and political mobilisation. (Escobar 1995:19)

From the point of view of sustainable discourse, this formulation contains three key elements which might provide suitably mutable universals:

- an investigation of alternative representations
- an investigation of alternative local discourse practices in concrete local settings
- an investigation of hybridisation as it relates to collective action and political mobilisation

This basic three-stage method can be superimposed upon Chouliaraki and Fairclough's (1999:60) methodological framework for CDA, below, in order to create a compatible approach, though one which is more suitable to the collaborative perspective I have outlined above. Chouliaraki and Fairclough's analytical schema involves identifying the following features in turn:

1. A problem.
2. Obstacles to it being tackled:
    a. analysis of the [historical] conjuncture [that created the obstacle];
    b. analysis of the [current] practice re its discourse moment [i.e. relating current practice to the social conditions that sustain it and that it reproduces];
    c. analysis of the discourse.
3. Function of the problem in the practice.
4. Possible ways past the obstacle.
5. Reflection on the analysis.

Positive Discourse Analysis   219

However, where Chouliaraki and Fairclough's approach, embedded as it is in the critical approach to CDA, tends to focus on removing obstacles, my modified approach is aimed at identifying the sheep tracks that already pass around them through an analysis, in turn, of:

1. A problematic issue.
2. For 'opposing' discourses:
   a. analysis of the historical conjuncture that created the obstacle;
   b. analysis of current practices re their discourse moments;
   c. analysis of the discourses as representative of different *voices*.
3. Function of each discourse within current practice.
4. Tensions and areas of commonality as revealed by the analyses.
5. Conditions of possibility for the assimilation of local discourse practice to be legitimised within an accommodating dominant practice.
6. Reflection on the analysis with participants.

I suggest this approach as a broad, flexible, global framework that can be adopted and changed to suit local conditions, with lessons learned from local experience feeding into the wider global body of knowledge, to be localised, if and as appropriate, elsewhere. Unlike the traditional approach to international development, one size most definitely does not fit all. The particular route I took along this path is set out in detail below.

OVERVIEW OF THE ANALYTICAL APPROACH DEVELOPED

I began Chapter 1 by suggesting that on the North Rupununi Savannahs of Guyana the indigenous Makushi communities had succeeded in "bucking the system" in that they had been able to adapt the discourse of dominant institutions to their own ends. Drawing on the theoretical work of Bhatt (2010) and Bhabha (1994), I suggested that, in contexts such as the North Rupununi, this corresponded to the formation of "post-colonial identities", not through an "abrogation" of dominant, largely colonial voices, but through "a new semiotic process and ideology of plurality and hybridity, through which people imagine their identities as being dialogically construed through resistance and appropriation" (Bhatt 2010:526–527). Bhabha (1994) refers to such a process as the creation of a *third space* where the discourses of local and dominant groups, together with the knowledge and authority they represent, are brought together and *hybridised*. As a theoretical concept in analysing this process I introduced the concept of *voice*, moving from Blommaert's (2005:255) definition as "the capacity to make oneself understood" to my own definition as "the means of behaving appropriately through language". Voice was presented as the key concept underlying the analyses in this book as it represents the linguistic means by which different speakers are able to orientate ongoing

220　*Hybrid Voices and Collaborative Change*

discussions to their own experience and aspirations and to relate these to other discourses. This is achieved, at least in part, through the *field*, *tenor* and *mode* of discourse by which the speakers construe activities, play out interpersonal relations and organise and present information respectively. Related to voice is Blommaert's concept of *orders of indexicality*, which includes the idea that the prestige afforded to different voices is hierarchically ordered but that these hierarchies are context dependent, a key element of later analyses. In Text 1.1 I introduced some of the main protagonists in NRDDB discourse on local development within the North Rupununi, Walter, Nicholas, Gordon and Sara, and showed how they manipulated these three variables of discourse in a discussion on the limits of local autonomy, a major theme of this book.

In Chapter 2 I drew a picture of life on the Rupununi Savannahs in order to provide the necessary background in discussing the NRDDB as an *intercultural* institution and in analysing discourse as representative of different voices. I began with a description of the material culture of the Makushi, the interpersonal relations that maintain their social system and the ways in which this culture is passed from generation to generation. I focused on these three categories as they relate to the field, tenor and mode of discourse that can be said to characterise local voice within the discourse of development. I described how the encroachment of the national state and other outside influences had disrupted the Makushi way of life in such a way that neither traditional organisation nor these new influences were entirely effective in fostering sustainable local development, with the result that the local communities remained socially marginalised and economically underdeveloped. In particular I emphasised how traditional subsistence farming was unable to meet the demands of the money-based economy and the opening up of the Rupununi to the coast and beyond; how local authority was being undermined by the increased presence of external regulatory systems as well as by increased knowledge and the subsequent decrease in mythology; and how highly contextualised means of passing on knowledge were being replaced by formalised schooling, the content of which was inappropriate to local needs. In response to this new situation, I drew on local discourses and documents produced by the Regional Council to suggest that while the local communities were keen to embrace change, they wished to do so in a manner that preserved their distinctive Makushi identity. In order to achieve such a transition successfully and without loss of identity I suggested that *local autonomy* over the development process was necessary, and contrasted this with the *paternalism* of the national government, as captured in the Amerindian Act, and the tendency towards *co-optation* and *advocacy* that characterised early dealings with Iwokrama. I also suggested, however, that the progressive attitude of Iwokrama and their willingness to promote local culture was a key condition in promoting a degree of local autonomy within discourse between the two groups, while the local communities themselves, in the NRDDB Constitution, recognised

Positive Discourse Analysis 221

the need for *collaboration* with outside groups and formalised a role for such groups in the development process and the proliferation of organisational structures and the specialisation of knowledge necessary in managing the move to modernity. In this way the former social organisation of the Makushi communities, reliant on absolute control based on the knowledge and authority of local elders, could be replaced by *hybrid* structures in which both local and external expertise and authority had their roles to play. I suggested that such collaboration represented a *discourse across difference*, characterised by the mixing of local and modern voices.

This led into a history of discourse relations between local communities and development organisations, and I began Chapter 3 with a discussion of international development as a concept in order to suggest the extent to which such discourse across difference was possible. Following Escobar (1995) I described how the concept of *international development* was promulgated in the post-war period as a means of modernising 'backward' communities and transforming their societies along the same trajectory as the already industrialised countries. I suggested that such attempts were misguided for two related reasons: firstly, in that they ignored the fact that such 'modernisation' would have to take place within a very different international context from that in which the 'developed' countries were able to transform themselves; and, secondly, in that this approach failed to take into account the specifics of each situation and that in rejecting the existing social organisation of the communities involved, preferring instead to scrap such "ancient philosophies", international development efforts were unable to *assimilate* existing knowledge and authority into a viable framework. I then compared this enclosed and unaccommodating approach to development with more recent trends that sought to develop *space* for local groups to make informed *choices* and to develop a local *voice*, but suggested that such approaches still viewed community voice as a quantitative commodity rather than the qualitatively different phenomenon outlined in Chapter 1. As a result, development was still a largely top-down affair, though demonstrating a shift from the paternalism of early development discourse and the Amerindian Act, towards co-optation and advocacy, with undue prestige attributed to professional development workers over community participants as a result of the history of development and the discourses that surround it. I introduced the concepts of *cultural capital* and the *symbolic capital* this translates into when the communities *misrecognise* the origins of external authority, and showed how these concepts could help to explain the shift in control from Walter, as a community elder, to Sara, as an international development worker, in Text 3.1, an example of early community–Iwokrama discourse. I also suggested that imbalances in communication could be explained in terms of relative familiarity with the institutional context and the associated ways of speaking. I finished the chapter by introducing the *Positioning Triangle* as a means of relating a speaker's discourse to an ongoing historical storyline, as internalised in

222 *Hybrid Voices and Collaborative Change*

the audience's *mental models* of the context, and suggested that different storylines could potentially lie latent in a particular situation and that these could be *foregrounded* unexpectedly as the result of speakers' words that realised ambiguous positions within the ongoing discourse.

In Chapter 4 I developed and modified Bourdieu's concept of *symbolic capital* to suggest that both the sources and manifestations of such capital were far more varied than in Bourdieu's analysis and that as a result there were many distinct types of capital *in play* within any specific discourse situation, each related to different *orders of indexicality*. Specifically, I modified Bourdieu's framework to suggest: (i) that domination over discourse is a matter not only of controlling speaking rights, but also of controlling meaning; (ii) that the balance of speakers' symbolic capital in any given discourse is not simply a function of "the size of their respective capitals of authority", but is also dependent on the *linguistic marketplace* in terms of the relationship between the *type* of symbolic power different speakers embody and the perceptions and expectations of their audience within a multiple hierarchical ordering of society; and (iii) that the relationship between a speaker's social capital and the linguistic features that realise this capital in discourse are not arbitrary, but related through the concept of voice to the different social backgrounds of the audience. In light of this further analysis, I expanded on the Positioning Triangle, introduced in Chapter 3, to produce a *Positioning Star of David* that incorporated the additional factors of symbolic capital and the mastery of *code* necessary to realise this capital within a specific linguistic marketplace. I described how these additional features could be seen as either *constraining* the positions open to different speakers or of *recalibrating* existing contexts. Recalibration of the context could be accidental and result in the *disruption* of the ongoing discourse (as demonstrated in Text 3.1) or a *strategic manipulation* of the context, primarily through alterations of the field, tenor and mode of discourse and hence the voices in play and the different symbolic capitals that are associated with these. In order to illustrate the different types of capital that are liable to be in play within the context of the NRDDB, and as a prelude to later analyses, I examined interviews with three differently situated participants within NRDDB discourse in which we discussed issues of local development. In analysing these interviews I compared the speakers' use of modality and mental projections as indices of the *knowledge* and *authority* that they displayed within this field of discourse, and hence the symbolic capital they implicitly assumed for themselves. Relating these features to the social position of the different speakers I proposed three categories of symbolic capital that were likely to be influential in NRDDB discourse: the *moral authority* of the local elder, the *local knowledge* of local farmers and fishermen, and the *external knowledge* of professional development workers. However, I also suggested that these categories need not be discrete, as illustrated though Uncle Henry's combined capital in all three categories, a position that afforded him particular authority in sanctioning any changes to community life. To finish the chapter, I sketched a model of discourse relations in which these different forms of capital could be used in *collaboration*, though ultimately under the authority of the local community, as represented by Uncle Henry's *nihil obstat*, rather than in the zero-sum competition for control suggested by Bourdieu. I introduced the caveat that the interviews allowed the different speakers to realise their distinctive capitals *in idealis* and contrasted this with their potential use *in realis* within the more challenging context of NRDDB meetings. As such the categories of symbolic capital identified in this chapter would serve as potential interpretative devices in the analysis of such situated discourse.

This was the aim of Chapter 5, in which I returned to analysis of NRDDB discourse and contrasted the performance of local representatives over time with Walter's performance as facilitator in the contrived context of the Management Planning Workshop analysed in Text 3.1. In particular I demonstrated how the variables of field, tenor and mode could be strategically manipulated in order to *perturb the context* in ways which favoured the symbolic capital of local members of the NRDDB and their control over participation both in discourse and the content. In terms of field, one way in which this was achieved was through focusing on specific *subfields* in which community members held expertise, with Walter's focus on local farming and fishing practices in Text 5.1, mirroring Andrew's discourse in Text 4.1, allowing him to speak with authority to the Minister of Amerindian Affairs. Another example of the manipulation of field was Walter's redirecting of the content of CEW reports in Text 5.5. In terms of tenor, hedges were used as signs of respect for the different participants and the symbolic capital they commanded, while strategies such as the switching of titles and the use of informal language and imagined community voices served as contextualising cues as to the relations of symbolic capital ultimately in force, in particular the moral authority of the local elder and the *institutional authority* of the NRDDB, identified as a type of symbolic capital in addition to those categories suggested in Chapter 4. And in terms of mode, I discussed the use of written texts as prompts-for-orality in Text 5.2 and Walter's redirection of the form of CEW reporting in Text 5.5, strategies that *profiled* the authority of the local elders and the NRDDB as an institution.

I also discussed the importance of *ownership* of space, emphasising the importance of the *physical space* of the Bina Hill Institute and the *symbolic space* of the first day of NRDDB meetings, on which Iwokrama and government representatives were more 'invited guests' than organisers. This was most clearly demonstrated in Trudy's faltering response to Walter's veiled criticisms in Text 5.3 as she struggled to adapt her institutional authority as Director General of Iwokrama to the local setting and its own institutional structures. This text also illustrated the ways in which prestigious figures in the NRDDB were able to *set up* outsiders in terms of the latter's symbolic capital and the obligations this imposed on them, and to *subsume*

224   *Hybrid Voices and Collaborative Change*

this institutional capital within that of the NRDDB—as was also evident Sam and Walter's manipulation of the Minister for Amerindian Affairs in Text 5.1 and, to a lesser extent, in Walter's use of titles in Text 5.4. Taken together, these texts demonstrated the extent to which community members held the *nihil obstat* over proceedings, as was further evidenced in Walter's confident handling of conflicting proposals in Texts 5.2 and 5.5. And if Text 3.1 showed Walter struggling to combine his community role as elder with his contrived institutional role of facilitator in the Management Planning Workshop, the texts in Chapter 5, in which Walter is the main participant, showed how he had, over time, developed an effective *intercultural competence* that enabled him to switch between these two roles as the occasion demanded.

I finished Chapter 5 with a further discussion of the notion of *context* and described how the *semiotic context* that is created through the field, tenor and mode of discourse in texts such as those in Chapter 5 is dependent on the *environment* in which these discourses take place, which is, in turn, dependent on the *macrocontext*, the social background and discourse histories that were described in Chapters 2 and 3. Returning to a point made in those chapters, Walter's mix of discourse features that create the semiotic context can be seen as changing the environment through the juggling of voices that correspond to different aspects of the macrocontext in terms of the social structures of the different groups involved in NRDDB meetings. Conversely, the extent to which these features can be juggled, that is, the *perturbation potential* of the environment, can only be evaluated with reference to the features of the macrocontext, a relationship captured in the *Positioning Star of David* as a heuristic model.

In Chapter 4 I suggested that in the specific context of the North Rupununi the symbolic capitals of the different protagonists could be combined collaboratively and produced a model for such collaboration. My analyses in Chapter 5 demonstrated this model in practice, through the production of *hybrid* discourse patterns as these were constructed *dialogically*. In Chapter 6 I analysed two texts in depth, one from Sara and the other from Uncle Henry, to illustrate both how Uncle Henry was able to combine shows of solidarity with various types of authority within a single *monologue* and how the effectiveness of his discourse was to some extent reliant on Sara's preceding contribution. The analysis involved dividing each contribution into distinct *phases*, stretches of text that varied in *register*, the combination of linguistic features realising field, tenor and mode, with each phase drawing on different voices to perform specific functions as part of the wider goal of explaining SUAs to the local community. In discussing the combined effect of these two contributions, I drew on the concepts of *interdiscursivity*, in which distinct voices are brought together to create something new, and *intertextuality*, in which parts of one discourse are reproduced within another. Comparing the contributions of the two speakers in this way I showed how Uncle Henry,

Positive Discourse Analysis 225

while superficially mirroring the *rhetorical structure* of Sara's contribution, was able to *appropriate* this institutional format while *recontextualising* the abstract and unfamiliar language of Sara's contribution in terms that were familiar to the local audience and which were related to their everyday experience. In this way Uncle Henry's contribution allowed the community to understand the thinking behind SUAs not only in terms of *comprehension*, but also of *empathy*, at the same time as he *subsumed* Sara's knowledge-based capital within his moral authority as a local elder, the crucial element in providing his *nihil obstat*. I further argued that in *indigenising* the discourse of the NRDDB in this way Uncle Henry was opening up spaces for other community members to contribute, and, in particular, that Walter's enhanced performances in Chapter 5 could potentially be seen as a result of this process.

In the first section of this chapter, Chapter 7, I discussed the tensions apparent within community–Iwokrama discourse, tensions that affect both traditionally powerful groupings, such as the government and international development organisations, and the local communities themselves. These tensions are apparent within the dominant groups in the disparity between the Amerindian Act and traditional paternalistic approaches to development, on the one hand, and on the other more progressive approaches to development and local autonomy, as demonstrated in the local context by Iwokrama's collaborative approach. Within the local community, these tensions are the result of a desire to maintain a Makushi identity while adapting to change. In Sánchez-Gómez's terms, echoing Bhatt's (2010:526–527) description of post-colonial identities founded on "resistance and appropriation", the NRDDB is potentially either a *space of contradictions*, where local elders are co-opted into a process in which the dominant *system* is said to *colonise* the *lifeworld* of the local communities, or a *space of resistance*, where the system is *appropriated* towards local ends. Drawing on Bhabha's notion of a *third space*, I suggested that for fora such as the NRDDB to represent a space of resistance it was necessary for local communities to be *knowledgeable* of the value of their existing practice and to reproduce this as local voice within intercultural discourse, ideas captured in Nicholas's discussion of Amerindian culture in the epigram to this chapter. I then produced testimonies from local participants to suggest, along with the textual analyses in Chapters 5 and 6, that in the context of the North Rupununi the communities had been successful in shaping the NRDDB as a space of resistance in which outside assistance had been subsumed within local practice in ways which had allowed local communities to adapt traditional activities and interpersonal relations while maintaining their identity and enhancing their local knowledge. I described this as a process whereby the *communicative action* of traditional community practice was able to develop into a *discourse across difference*, a situation that incorporated a greater degree of traditional practice than Habermas's concept of *communicative rationality*.

226 *Hybrid Voices and Collaborative Change*

I stated above that many CDA practitioners had gone as far as to say that they do not expect to contribute to change and that their role does not go beyond that of bringing to light what they see as injustices within existing discourse practices. This statement to me seems to neglect the fact that bringing injustices to light is the first step towards their resolution, an attitude explicitly adopted in an approach to discourse analysis labelled *Critical Language Awareness* (Fairclough 1992). However, I think the statement contains an important element of truth in that, ultimately, it is not the responsibility of the linguist to determine changes that would lead to an improvement of the situation. This is equally true of the more 'positive' approach to discourse analysis I am advocating here. For while applied linguists (in the broad sense) can contribute to local participants' understanding of their situation and provide new angles for interpretation, this is the limit of their expertise and to overstep these limits would be potentially to fall into the trap of paternalism or co-optation. As Roberts and Sarangi (1999:366) say with regard to similar applied work in the field of medical discourse:

> At most—and it is a considerable 'most'—what applied linguists can do . . . is to attempt joint problematisation and suggest complementary analytical frameworks that, through processes of mediation, may achieve some utility . . . in the end, it is for the practitioners . . . to acknowledge and decide what matters and what is applicable.

REFLECTIONS AND LIMITATIONS OF THE PRESENT STUDY

Throughout this book I have attempted to suggest and illustrate ways in which work in CDA and PDA might overcome the *textual bias* indentified by Blommaert and others, focusing on the need to understand individual discourse events within broader sociopolitical context and in terms of the ways of speaking within each community as these relate to their internal social structure. In the previous section I summarised the variety of approaches I have taken in the individual chapters of the book and suggested how these have contributed to my general theoretical framework. In developing and illustrating this framework I have attempted to describe community–Iwokrama discourse in some detail and from a variety of angles in order to provide a more holistic and multifaceted account than is usually found in CDA and PDA, pushing these approaches towards a more ethnographic perspective. In this concluding section I shall take a more personal approach to discuss the limitations of my work, particularly in terms of the variety of contextual data I gathered during the period of my fieldwork and of how my personal investment in interpreting these data in the intervening years may have affected my analysis. In discussing these limitations I shall also suggest specific areas where further work is necessary.

Ethnography or Fieldwork?

As stated at the beginning of the book, I am not a trained ethnographer and this has affected my work at several levels, most significantly in the preparation I undertook before my fieldwork and in the amount and type of data I collected: Were I to start again I would do it differently. And, strange as it now seems to me, without reference to my original PhD proposal I cannot accurately remember what it was my intention to achieve when I began my fieldwork, though I do know it had something to do with increasing the 'anthropological detail' in bilingual dictionaries and in making these more user-friendly for indigenous communities. This idea had developed from my years as a lexicographer in Britain and from work I had undertaken in Mexico on a series of dictionaries in Spanish, Zoque and the various Mayan languages of Chiapas. I had originally intended to return to Chiapas to carry out my fieldwork, but when my wife got work with UNICEF in Guyana I substituted "Guyana" for "Mexico" *passim* in my research proposal and happily set out to carry on much as before. However, as we were stationed in Georgetown, many miles from any indigenous communities, I spent several frustrating months after our arrival wondering how I was going to get started. Eventually I made contact with Janette Forte, a sociologist specialising in Amerindian matters (see Forte 1994, 1996a, 1996b; Forte and Melville 1989). Janette was working with Iwokrama at the time, and through her my first trip to the Rupununi was organised. By this time I had decided that CDA was the discipline for me and, fired with enthusiasm, it was on this trip that I made my confident promise to help the local communities even up the discursive playing field in their dealings with Iwokrama—one of a range of ambitious research topics I had put on the table to Iwokrama, including such grandiose schemes as a comparison of English and Makushi from a Whorfian perspective, despite the fact I spoke no Makushi and was yet to visit a Makushi community. It should therefore be clear that I was not fully integrated into the ethnographic paradigm as I started my fieldwork. I was, however, beginning to appreciate the need to provide a contextual background to any linguistic analysis I would undertake, though I imagined this as being more or less within the limited tradition of the CDA with which I was familiar. And this lack of preparation affected my data collection once my fieldwork began. While I made recordings of over 40 hours of discourse, this was not backed up with the bagfuls of assorted data that Blommaert and Dong (2010:59) describe arriving home with, though I had several notebooks and copious envelopes on the back of which I had scribbled and doodled. So, while there was an emergent ethnographic sensibility developing within me at this time, I cannot claim to have collected my data either as thoroughly or as systematically as I now would have liked. However, I had become aware during my fieldwork, as I transcribed my data and began to analyse it, that something interesting was happening within NRDDB meetings: that skilled orators were in some way

228 *Hybrid Voices and Collaborative Change*

appropriating the conventions of such meetings towards their own ends. This now became the principal angle of my research, and I began to collect data and to carry out interviews in a more focused manner. While this was still not of a standard that merits the name *ethnography*, it did enable me to start building the framework that I have outlined in this book, a framework that has been developed in the years since I left Guyana. It is for this reason that I have presented this book as a theoretical discussion of the limitations of CDA and PDA—that, after all, was my personal trajectory—as much as an ethnographic account of discourse on the North Rupununi. Similarly, not wanting to fall foul of Hymes's (1996:19; see also Blommaert and Dong 2010:50) injunction against confusing fieldwork with ethnography, I have been cautious in using the term "ethnography" when referring to my own work, with Chapter 2 simply entitled "Background". In the following sections I will outline some of the more specific limitations that my personal trajectory has entailed and hint at how I might have undertaken things differently.

Angle of Analysis

As a result of the limitations on my data collection in the field the particular angle of analysis I have adopted is potentially too text-oriented. While this is not an entirely bad thing—a positive interpretation would be to see my work as a development of SFL and CDA rather than as a diminished ethnography—it does mean that my work is centred on the relationship between voice and the linguistic concept of register and that my background description has been specifically tailored so as to mesh with the contextual categories of field, tenor and mode. While such a language-led approach is adopted in much work within linguistic anthropology (e.g. Duranti 1994), there is a clear danger here of working back in linear fashion from *a priori* categories to discover these in operation, an approach criticised by Foucault (1984:76), who advocates a wider examination of the conditions of possibility within a particular social context through a *genealogical* approach which:

> must record the singularity of events outside of any monotonous finality; it must seek them in the most unpromising places, in what we tend to feel is without history—in sentiments, love, conscience, instincts; it must be sensitive to their recurrence, not in order to trace the gradual curve of their evolution, but to isolate the different scenes where they engaged in different roles.

In similar vein, Scollon and Scollon (2007:621) talk of the need "to document or record everything that might be relevant to understanding the historical antecedents of a social action as well as the unfolding outcomes of that action". Clearly, my focus on field, tenor and mode has delimited rather than opened up my description of "the singularity of events" and, while I believe that my descriptions added insights to my analysis, rather than appearing *ex machina* to back up already-reached conclusions, a more far-reaching and open-ended ethnography might well have led to more unexpected questions and findings. This leads to the following point.

Methods of Analysis

Related to my angle of analysis is the question of the specific methods I have used to analyse the various texts. While I have explained my reasons for focusing on the SFL concept of register in analysing for the presence of distinct voices, and have supplemented my analysis of the realisation and contestation of different voices with methods from Conversation Analysis and Interactional Sociolinguistics, I do not doubt that a more far-reaching use of these and other methods would have revealed much of interest. In particular, in taking a different analytical approach from those used by Hymes and others under the label of *ethnopoetics* I will have missed some of the key ways in which distinct voices can be identified and the ways in which these are significant. Uncle Henry's contribution discussed in Chapter 6 is a particular stretch of discourse that I never tire of looking at, and each time it reveals something new to me; adopting an ethnopoetic analysis would no doubt add to my appreciation of Uncle Henry's oratory skills and this is something that must be considered as part of any future work that brings together the insights from ethnopoetics and the approach to analysing voice that I have adopted here.

Analyses of Failed and Non-Existent Discourse

In similar vein, my analyses might be limited inasmuch as I focused on examples where local community representatives were successful in appropriating dominant institutional formats, subsuming Iwokrama and government voices to their own ends and taking control over participation and content in discourse, with Text 3.1 provided as the sole counter-example. An examination of more examples of discourse where the community failed to attain such control, as well as a consideration of the types of discourse that did not appear (Blommaert 2005:34–35), might well have provided further insights into the dynamics of community–Iwokrama discourse that both strengthened and challenged my analytical framework and conclusions.

Understanding, Empathy and Uptake

Kramsch and Boner (2010) talk of the problem of mutual understanding in intercultural discourse and point to the possibility of different communities working with different conceptions of key points while appearing on the surface to be using the same terms to refer to these. While in the present study I have divided the term *understanding* into the complementary components

230 Hybrid Voices and Collaborative Change

of *comprehension* and *empathy* and suggested that Uncle Henry was able to enhance community understanding of the SUAs through the empathy he engendered, the question remains as to whether Uncle Henry's *reformulation* of this concept might have led to different understandings at a deeper level and that this might have significant effects on the decision-making process. Further work, therefore, remains to be done in order to ascertain in what ways understanding of key concepts differs between the local communities and professional development workers.

Relatedly, while I stated in Chapter 4 that the success of Uncle Henry's account of the SUAs was a result of his ability to reformulate Sara's more abstract account in locally relevant terms in combination with his symbolic capital as local elder and expert in outside knowledge, this reasoning was to some extent based on my own theoretical assumptions. Although the claim was backed up through relating Uncle Henry's authority to the sociocultural background provided in Chapter 2, more work remains to be done to test in practice the level of *uptake* of different speakers' discourse within different *marketplaces* over both the short and long term. Such work, which would have far-reaching applications, might be based on an analysis of features including, but not limited to, the field, tenor and mode of different speakers' discourse; relating these to the patterns of *socialisation* of different audiences; and evaluating the ways in which features of these discourses are reproduced and reformulated by different members of the audience at later dates. My initial feeling, based on the analyses and theoretical framework of this book, is that fostering empathy with an audience is the essential intermediary stage between comprehension and uptake, and this is a hypothesis that requires further testing in more ethnographically grounded studies.

Co-optation

Related to the question of mutual understanding beyond a superficial level, raised above, is the question of whether the seemingly collaborative approach taken by Iwokrama representatives in their dealings with local communities is not ultimately *co-optive* (either unintentionally or by design).[3] While this is not my understanding of the events described in this book, it could be argued that the very existence of the NRDDB is an elaborate means of getting the local communities 'on board' with regards to predetermined plans, as with Henríquez Arellano's (2002) discussion of the Mexican government's concessions to 'indigenous practice' in order to extend their control over Amerindian communities. As a counter-argument, it could be argued that the discourses of the NRDDB make community input into higher-level decision-making possible. In Chapter 3 I contrasted the government's disdain for local knowledge with both their over-acceptance of 'scientific' discourse and Iwokrama's appreciation of the value of local knowledge. Combining these two factors, it could be claimed

Positive Discourse Analysis 231

that Iwokrama's acceptance of local input will be *formalised* (Iedema 1999) within their dealings with the government and so lead indirectly to the government's acceptance of local knowledge. Work therefore needs to be done in analysing the degree to which community-based practice and ideas are reformulated in official policies at a higher level and how they ultimately affect practice, an area of research that would take on board Blommaert's (2005:35) questions of where texts go and what "happens to language users long after they have shut their mouths".

Acceptance of Community-Based Knowledge outwith the NRDDB

Related to the last point is the question of whether community-based practices and knowledge will be accepted by organisations less committed to sustainable social development than Iwokrama. At the Iwokrama Workshop on Critical Issues in the Guiana Shield (Pegasus Hotel, Georgetown, 6/12/00), involving government officials and scientists working on sustainable development from within the natural sciences, Sam presented a community perspective of the issues, a presentation which appeared to me to be met with indifference by many of the assembled experts (see Bartlett 2006 for an analysis of Sam's presentation). While this impression is, of course, anecdotal, it suggests that while Iwokrama workers, with their experience and understanding (including empathy) of local community practices, are keen to adopt community perspectives within their work, many other organisations are less positively inclined. In line with the framework developed in this book, it would seem that the voice adopted by Sam at the Guiana Shield Workshop was not appropriate to the specifics of that marketplace while adoption of another voice might not have been deemed appropriate, and that one possible approach to improve this situation would be to consider how Iwokrama scientists could recontextualise the contributions of community members in such external fora in terms that are more understandable to the scientific community—an exercise that would represent the converse of Uncle Henry's recontextualisation of Sara's abstract explanation of the SUAs into terms that made sense to the local community.

Entextualisation and Personal Investment

I have been working on this book since the time of my fieldwork in Guyana (1999 to 2002), during which time my understanding of the NRDDB and the discourses that surround it has altered considerably, as has the framework for analysis that I have developed. This carries with it the very real danger that, removed from the everyday reality of life on the North Rupununi, I will have adopted the same textualist orientation for which Escobar (see Chapter 3) criticises international development agencies; that in presenting and writing about my work over the years I will have *entextualised* the discourse that I recorded (Baumann and Briggs 1990:78, 80)

232　*Hybrid Voices and Collaborative Change*

so that my presentation no longer represents, for example, Uncle Henry's original *performance* before the NRDDB, but is *recontextualised* as part of my own academic performance. Such a process is, I am sure, inevitable as discourse becomes text and the dynamics which originally propelled it fade ever further from our awareness. One way to mitigate against this loss might be to return to the Rupununi, to reacclimatise myself, to hear local *voices* again and to discuss the issues behind this book. But that would be to assume that the voices I heard would be the same as those from a decade ago and that the process of development described in this book had come to an end.

CODA

The preceding sections point to the conclusion that there is still much work to be done. I am thus minded of a proverb from another minority culture in danger of being colonised, the Gaelic speakers of northwest Scotland, and a rejoinder from the Gaelic lexicographer Edward Dwelly (1988:1034). The proverb captures a feeling that will be familiar to many academics as they sit down to translate their thoughts to the printed page: *Is obair-là tòiseachadh*—It's a day's work starting. To which Dwelly added his rejoinder: *Ach is obair beatha crìochnachadh*—But it's a life's work finishing. My thanks to the communities of the North Rupununi Savannahs for their hospitality and insights and to Iwokrama for theirs and for making it possible for me to begin. I hope that my representation of life on the Savannahs and the understanding I have developed, though far from finished, have done you some justice.

Appendix 1

Cloran's (2000) Classification of Rhetorical Units

EVENT ORIENTATION CENTRAL ENTITY	HABITUAL	REALIS		IRREALIS		
		CONCURRENT	PRIOR	GOODS/SERVICES EXCHANGE	INFORMATION EXCHANGE	
Within material situational setting (MSS)			Recount	Action	FORECAST	HYPOTHETICAL
Interactant	Reflection	Commentary			Plan/Prediction	Conjecture
other: -person/object	Observation				Prediction	
Not within MSS						
person/object	Account	Report			Prediction	
Class	Generalisation					

Continuum of role of language in social process:

ancillary [e.g. contextualised]———————————————————— constitutive [e.g. decontextualised]
Action-Commentary Observation-Reflection Report Account Plan-Prediction Conjecture Recount Generalisation

Appendix 2
Textual Examples of End-Terms in Figure 4.2

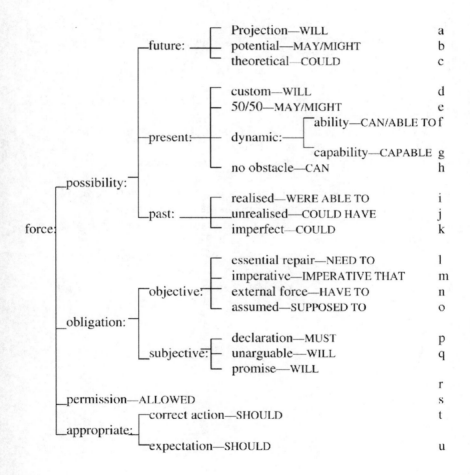

Examples. Letters refer to place in network.
SA = Steve Andries; UF = Uncle Fred; GW = Graham Watkins.

a. SA: We tried last year, we'll come up a little bit.
b. SA: It might be a little food basket, or whatever,

236 *Appendix 2*

c. SA: We could produce our own feed here. We will then be able to supply.

d. SA: They give us notice . . . and we'll have a final discussion on this, right?

e. GW: This is not consultation in terms of what the government might think of [as] consultation.

f. SA: By mixing with other people . . . you're able to gather something.

g. GW: The Zacks and Williams and Freds and Sydneys of the world are perfectly comfortable with communicating at that level and are capable of going back to the communities and communicating at the other level as well.

h. UF: If they can be blended together I think we can get something.

i. SA: And in that meeting we were able to come up with all of this review of the poultry.

j. UF: They could have been gone there to ask their questions and get their answers.

k. GW: We sat down at a meeting . . . but we couldn't get NRDDB together.

l. GW: There needs to be a set of processes for communicating.

m. UF: It's imperative that we find a site.

n. SA: They teach you . . . when you have to mulch.

o. GW: We're supposed to write a river management plan.

p. UF: These buildings must be at least two feet from the ground.

q. SA: You will be responsible, in charge of this community.

r. GW: A lot of the management planning will be based on that.

s. GW: They're allowed to sit there for a week.

t. GW: There is the question of whether . . . you should be managing from Annai.

u. GW: In the end what you should end up with is action which pleases Fishereies.

Notes

NOTES TO CHAPTER 1

1. The names of all the participants in the events I describe in the book have been changed.
2. The Guyana Amerindian Act was revised in 2005, after the period of my fieldwork. For an overview of the changes, see http://www.amerindian.gov.gy/legislation.html (last viewed 14 October 2011).
3. 'Iwokrama' is used to refer to this organisation, though it is properly the name of the rainforest in which they work and in and around which the 13 local communities live and work.
4. Humphrey (2006) is a notable exception.
5. The Conservative prime minister of the United Kingdom at the time Toolan was writing.
6. This is not to say that I accept uncritically my respondents' views on why specific contributions were effective or not as such factors can be assumed to generally operate below the level of consciousness. However, where respondents identify a contribution as having been good or effective this is in itself a reason to believe that it was so, at least to some extent.
7. Formalising the relationship between grammar, meaning and context is a central concern within SFL. However, the concept of context in SFL relates to how language *construes* a context within a given situation rather than to a consideration of the non-linguistic features that make such construals both possible and meaningful, which is my focus here. The SFL notion of context, and its relation to the current work, is discussed in more detail in Chapter 6, and for a fuller discussion of this issue, see Bartlett (forthcoming).
8. I say "markedly" for, as Blommaert (2005:75) points out, all contexts are polycentric to a greater or lesser degree.
9. Ninety percent of the Guyanese population lives along a ten-mile strip of the coast. These who live in 'the Interior' often view Coastlanders as overbearing in dealings with them.
10. The United Nations Development Programme, one of several UN organisations operating in Guyana, with a history of work in the North Rupununi.
11. 'Na' is a general negative marker in Guyanese English.
12. The Amerindian Act establishes the legal balance between Amerindian autonomy and government sovereignty. It is discussed in depth in Chapter 2.
13. Guyanese dollars. G$1000 was roughly £3.75 at the time of writing.
14. Standard English subject pronouns are used as possessives in Guyanese English.
15. The phoneme /t/ is used in Guyanese English where /θ/ is used in Standard English.
16. That is, roughly, two clauses that share a common starting point but which contrast in ending.
17. It is worth stressing in passing, however, that while Iwokrama may often be seen to be dominating the talk, it is only through their comparatively egalitarian approach to discourse and development, and the strong contrast

240 *Notes*

between this and other approaches, that these tensions appear at all, opening up 'wiggle room' that can be positively exploited through further discourse.
18. As opposed to grammatical roles, as will be described in Chapter 2.

NOTES TO CHAPTER 2

1. Since the period of my fieldwork the road has been further improved.
2. However, Guyana's only local radio station, Radio Paiwomak, named after the three mountain ranges of the Rupununi, was being run by a number of volunteers at the time.
3. Funding for Iwokrama from these international sources has been inconsistent since the time of my fieldwork and at times the programme's survival has been in serious doubt.
4. In the election of 2011 the PNC were the central party in a coalition called "A Partnership for National Unity".
5. I appreciate that these categorisations are based on the distinct criteria of colour and geographic origin. However, they are the terms used within Guyana and underlie perceptions of group identity and history and I will therefore use them throughout the book.
6. "Uncle" is a general term of respect for elders and distinguished figures in Guyanese communities.
7. In Guyanese English the possessive is characteristically unmarked.
8. The Amerindian Act was revised in 2005 and several key changes were agreed after consultation with the communities. See http://www.amerindian.gov. gy/legislation.html.
9. The rebellion was an attempt at secession after Guyana's independence and the increased marginalisation of the interior as Georgetown-based politics became ever more embroiled in the interracial disputes that characterise it today.
10. That is a person who can take on the shape of other beings, usually for evil purposes.
11. Non-marking of past tense and past participles is another characteristic of Guyanese English.
12. A popular programme on national radio at the time of writing was *Caught in the Slips*, a title that plays on Guyana's love of cricket but which is dedicated to promoting "good English".
13. The Act was revised again in 2005, but the 1976 Act was in force at the time of my fieldwork. See note 8 above.
14. These roles are based upon and often equate to Participant Roles identified within the lexicogrammatical system of English within systemic linguistics, but they do not correspond directly with these and for that reason are not written with an initial capital.
15. This single example is Article 7.2 , which begins "Contributions to the Fund may be solicited from funding agencies". This is analysed in part as Process:contribute; Performer:GOG/NGO; Beneficiary:NRDDB. However, as the article finishes with "agreed to and sanctioned by the membership of the Board", NRDDB also fills the overseer role and so the idea of paternalism is tempered.
16. The sole example here is Article 42(2), which states that exemption certificates "may, with the consent of the Amerindian, be revoked by the Chief Officer". This is analysed as Process:revoke; performer:GOG; overseer:Amerindian.
17. A position reflected in other South American states with large Amerindian populations such as Guatemala, where efforts have occasionally gone as far

as claiming that the present indigenous population are not the true descendents of the pre-colonial Maya who built the pyramids and crafted the artefacts assiduously promoted as representing the true soul of the country.

NOTES TO CHAPTER 3

1. 'Matty' is a local variant of 'mate' and appears to be used ironically here to question the possibility of the Guyanese water board being willing to help the local community.
2. 'Gaan' = 'going'.
3. This has been the case with several such projects in Guyana, particularly where the wells are in the interior but both the coordinating group and the construction company are based on the coast.
4. The Positioning Triangle can be used to analyse any act. I have modified it here to refer specifically to discourse. My apologies to Sigrid Norris, who has often been at pains to point out to me that language is not the only semiotic act!
5. N.B. this triangle is not meant to represent the local perception of events, but a possible *local perception of Sara's perception of events* and therefore how they interpret her motives and how they respond to this.

NOTES TO CHAPTER 4

1. Though as Blommaert and Dong (2010:52–56) point out, this is always a dangerous assumption.
2. More accurately, the contextual variable of tenor is construed through the semantics of Andrew's discourse which is then construed through the lexicogrammar.
3. Line 19 is less clear-cut. While the use of CAN here refers to what the community will be able to produce, it is possibly just a formulaic collocation with EXPECT.
4. The usage of NEED in line 13 is in fact as a main verb, though the effect is the same.
5. One instance of permission not included as this fits with none of the categories as set up and contrasted here.
6. The subjective/objective split is not beyond question an analytical distinction, especially in a context such as the Rupununi where English is not the first language. However, the main contrasts analysed here do not rely heavily on this distinction but on those between HAVE TO, NEED TO.
7. In contrast to Halliday (1994), who distinguishes between a future and a modal use of WILL, I consider all uses of WILL as modal.
8. Examples of knowledge as process such as NOTICE are not considered appropriate here as they are as much processes of observation as knowledge.

NOTES TO CHAPTER 5

1. NONE OTHER THAN was commonly used as marker of importance rather than with the standard English meaning of surprise.
2. In Guyana WALK WITH is used to mean BRING WITH YOU.
3. I am using context in its everyday use here rather than in the specialist SFL use.
4. A failure to recognise the distinction made in SFL between the semiotic context and what I have labelled the environment has led many critics to dismiss

242 *Notes*

the SFL notion of context, by which is meant the semiotic context only, as too restrictive.

NOTES TO CHAPTER 6

1. In Bartlett (2003) I also analysed the texts in terms of the structural complexity of clauses across a number of parameters. This analysis showed that Sara consistently used more complex structures and I suggested there that this might be a reflection of a tendency in Iwokrama to "get through" information in a prescribed time rather than taking time to ensure comprehension. As this analysis would deflect too much from current purposes, however, I have decided not to include it here.
2. This is not as objective as it sounds, as the sense relations developed in real-time texts are emergent constructs of the speaker and hearer, rather than externally defined aspects of the language system (Brazil 1995:34–36).
3. Even though this does not represent Uncle Henry's complete contribution, as he goes on to expand on these main themes, comparisons between the two texts are justified in that this extract essentially represents an account of the SUAs leading to a check on comprehension and 'call to action' in the same way as Sara's contribution.
4. This is an approach similar to that of Hasan (1996), which deals with a fuller "Generic Structure Potential".
5. In the texts subordinate RUs are marked as embedded, which implies that they are contained within a matrix RU as a contributing factor to a greater purpose. Looking at the discourse function of these lines, however, it would be more accurate to see lines 11–13 as prefacing or *projecting* the long Account that follows.
6. Bernstein refers to *instructional contexts*, but as this term is, to me at least, ambiguous between providing information and regulation, I shall use the term *informative context*.
7. In Bartlett (2003) I also analysed field in terms of the technical level of the lexis and grammar. While this provided the interesting finding that Uncle Henry used considerably more technical language than Sara, I have omitted this analysis here as it deflects from the immediate purpose of these analyses.
8. It should be emphasised here that these are not the same thing. Familiar concepts can be referred to in terms of abstract Generalisations or Predictions, for example, while unfamiliar concepts can be referred to through the highly contextualised language of Commentaries and Reflections.
9. What counts as a significant measure of consistency and what counts as a significant shift in register is a matter of the analyst's judgment and hence any representation of a text as a progression of phases is to some extent a subjective rather than a definitive schematisation.

NOTES TO CHAPTER 7

1. Nicholas's use of "even" here betrays something of the complex social stratification in Guyana.
2. Canadian International Development Agency.
3. My thanks to my colleague Gerard O'Grady for bringing this seemingly obvious point to my attention.

References

Allan, Christie. 2002. *Amerindian Ethnoecology, Resource Use and Forest Management in Southwest Guyana*. Roehampton University: Unpublished PhD Thesis.

Amerindian Peoples' Association. 1998. *A Plain English Guide to the Amerindian Act*. Georgetown, Guyana: APA.

Bakhtin, M. M. 1981. *The Dialogic Imagination: Four Essays*. Ed. Michael Holquist; tr. Caryl Emerson. Austin: University of Texas Press.

———. 1984. *Problems of Dostoevsky's Poetics*. Ed. and tr. Caryl Emerson. Minneapolis: University of Minnesota Press.

Bartlett, Tom. 2000. Dictionary, Systemicity, Motivation. *Edinburgh Working Papers in Applied Linguistics* 10: 1–14.

———. 2001. Use the Road: The Appropriacy of Appropriation. *Journal of Language and Intercultural Communication* 1, no 1: 21–39.

———. 2002. Unpublished presentation to Iwokrama on discourse within NRDDB meetings. Iwokrama Offices, Georgetown, Guyana, 24/4/2002.

———. 2003. *The Transgressions of Wise Men: Structure, Tension and Agency inIntercultural Development Discourse*. Edinburgh University: Unpublished PhD Thesis.

———. 2004. Mapping Distinction. In Lynne Young and Claire Harrison (Eds.), *Systemic Functional Linguistics and Critical Discourse Analysis: Studies in Social Change*, pp.68–84. London and New York: Continuum.

———. 2005. Amerindian Development in Guyana: Legal Documents as Background to Discourse Practice. *Discourse and Society* 16, no 3: 341–364.

———. 2006. Genre as Ideological Mediation. In *Linguistics and the Human Sciences* 2, no. 2. Special Issue on Genre: 257–274.

———. 2008. Wheels within Wheels or Triangles within Triangles: Time and Context in Positioning Theory. In Fathali M. Moghaddam, Rom Harré and Naomi Lee (Eds.), *Global Conflict Resolution through Positioning Analysis*. New York: Springer: 169–187.

———. 2009. Legitimacy, Comprehension and Empathy: The Importance of Recontextualisation in Intercultural Negotiations. *European Journal of English Studies* 13, no. 2. Special Edition on Intercultural Negotiation: 179–192.

———. Forthcoming. *"I'll Manage the Context"*: Context, Environment and the Potential for Institutional Change. In Lise Fontaine, Tom Bartlett, and Gerard O'Grady (Eds.), *Systemic Functional Linguistics: Issue of Choice*. Cambridge: Cambridge University Press.

Baumann, Richard, and Charles L. Briggs. 1990. Poetics and Performance as Critical Perspectives on Language and Social Life. *Annual Review of Anthropology* 19:59–88.

244   References

Berger, Peter, and Thomas Luckmann. 1966. *The Social Construction of Reality: A Treatise in the Sociology of Knowledge*. Harmondsworth: Penguin.

Bernstein, Basil. 1971. *Class, Codes and Control, Volume 1: Theoretical Studies towards a Sociology of Language Learning*. London and Boston: Routledge and Kegan Paul.

———, ed. 1973. *Class, Codes and Control, Volume 2: Applied Studies towards a Sociology of Language Learning*. London and Boston: Routledge and Kegan Paul.

———. 1975. *Class, Codes and Control, Volume 3: Towards a Theory of Educational Transmission*. London: Routledge.

———. 1990. *Class, Codes and Control, Volume 4: The Structuring of Pedagogic Discourse*. London: Routledge.

———. 2000. *Pedagogy, Symbolic Control and Identity: Theory, Research, Critique*. Lanham, MD: Rowman and Littlefield Publishers.

Bhabha, Homi. 1994. *The Location of Culture*. London and New York: Routledge.

Bhatt, Rakesh M. 2010. Unraveling Post-Colonial Identity through Language. In Coupland (Ed.).

Billig, Michael. 1999a. Conversation Analysis and the Claims of Naivety. *Discourse and Society* 10, no. 4: 572–576.

———. 1999b. Whose Terms? Whose Ordinariness? Rhetoric and Ideology in Conversation Analysis. *Discourse and Society* 10, no. 4: 543–558.

Blair, H. 2003. Civil Society and Local Governance. Report prepared for DFID Bangladesh, Dhaka.

Blommaert, Jan. 2005. *Discourse: A Critical Introduction*. Cambridge: Cambridge University Press.

———.2008. Bernstein and Poetics Revisited: Voice, Globalisation and Education. *Discourse and Society* 19, no. 4: 425–452.

Blommaert, Jan, and Dong Jie. 2010. *Ethnographic Fieldwork: A Beginner's Guide*. Bristol: Multilingual Matters.

Bourdieu, Pierre. 1977. The Economics of Linguistic Exchanges. *Social Science Information* 16, no. 6: 645–668.

———. 1990a. *In Other Words: Essays towards a Reflexive Sociology*. Cambridge: Polity Press.

———. 1990b. *The Logic of Practice*. Cambridge: Polity Press.

———. 1991. *Language and Symbolic Power*. Cambridge: Polity Press.

Bourdieu, Pierre, and Loïc Wacquant. 1992. *An Invitation to Reflexive Sociology*. Chicago: University of Chicago Press.

Brazil, David. 1995. *A Grammar of Speech*. Oxford: Oxford University Press.

Bremer, Katharina, Celia Roberts, Marie-Thérèse Vasseur, Margaret Simonot and Peter Broeder. 1996. *Achieving Understanding: Discourse in Intercultural Encounters*. Harlow: Longman.

Briggs, Charles, and Clara Mantini Briggs. 2003. *Stories in the Time of Cholera: Racial Profiling during a Medical Nightmare*. Berkeley: University of California Press.

Brown, Penelope, and Stephen C. Levinson. 1987. *Politeness*. Cambridge: Cambridge University Press.

Cameron, Deborah, Elizabeth Frazer, Penelope Harvey, M.B.H. Rampton and Kay Richardson. 1992. Introduction. In Deborah Cameron, Elizabeth Frazer, Penelope Harvey, M.B.H. Rampton and Kay Richardson. . *Researching Language: Issues of Power and Method*. London: Routledge.

Canagarajah, A. Suresh. 1993. Critical Ethnography of a Sri Lankan Classroom: Ambiguities in Student Opposition to Reproduction through ESOL. *TESOL Quarterly* 27:601–626.

References 245

Celce-Murcia, Marianne, and Elite Olshtain. 2000. *Discourse and Context in Language Teaching: A Guide for Language Teachers.* Cambridge: Cambridge University Press.

Chambers, Robert. 1997. *Whose Reality Counts? Putting the First Last.* Southampton: ITDG Publishing.

Chouliaraki, Lilie, and Norman Fairclough. 1999. *Discourse in Late Modernity: Rethinking Critical Discourse Analysis.* Edinburgh: Edinburgh University Press.

Cloran, Carmel. 1999. Contexts for Learning. In Frances Christie (Ed.), *Pedagogy and the Shaping of Consciousness: Linguistic and Social Processes.* London: Cassell: 31–65

———. 2000. Socio-Semantic Variation: Different Wordings, Different Meanings. In Len Unsworth (Ed.), *Researching Language in Schools and Communities: Functional Linguistic Perspectives.* London: Cassell: 152–183.

———. 2010. Rhetorical Unit Analysis and Bakhtin's Chronotope. *Functions of Language* 17, no. 1: 29–70.

Colchester, Marcus. 1997. *Guyana, Fragile Frontier: Loggers, Miners and Forest Peoples.* London: Latin America Bureau.

Cooke, Maeve. 1994. *Language and Reason: A Study of Habermas's Pragmatics.* Cambridge, MA: MIT Press.

Cornwall, Andrea. 2002. *Making Spaces, Changing Places: Situating Participation in Development.* IDS Working Paper 170. Brighton: Institute of Development Studies.

Cornwall, Andrea, and John Gaventa. 2001. *From Users and Choosers to Makers and Shapers: Repositioning Participation in Social Policy.* IDS Working Paper 127. Brighton: Institute of Development Studies.

Coupland, Nikolas, ed. 2010. *The Handbook of Globalization.* Chichester: Wiley Blackwell.

Cummins, Jim. 1996. *Negotiating Identities: Education for Empowerment in a Diverse Society.* Ontario: California Association for Bilingual Education.

———. 2000. *Language, Power and Pedagogy: Bilingual Children in the Crossfire.* Clevedon: Multilingual Matters.

Despres, Leo A. 1975. Ethnicity and Resource Competition in Guyanese Society. In Leo Despres (Ed.), *Ethnicity and Resource Competition in Plural Societies.* The Hague: Mouton: 87–117.

Duranti, Alessandro. 1994. *From Grammar to Politics: Linguistic Anthropology in a Western Samoan Village.* Berkeley: University of California Press.

Dwelly, Edward. 1988. *Faclair Gàidhlig gu Beurla le Dealbhan.* Glasgow: Gairm Publications.

Erjavec, Karmen. 2001. Media Representation of the Discrimination against the Roma in Eastern Europe: The Case of Slovenia. *Discourse and Society* 12, no. 6: 699–728.

Escobar, A. 1992. Planning. In W. Sachs (Ed.), *The Development Dictionary.* London: Zed Books: 132–145.

———. 1995. *Encountering Development: The Making and Unmaking of the Third World.* Princeton, NJ: Princeton University Press.

Fairclough, Norman, ed. 1992 *Critical Language Awareness.* Harlow: Longman.

———. *Discourse and Social Change.* Cambridge: Polity Press.

———. 1995. *Critical Discourse Analysis.* Harlow: Longman.

———. 2001. *Language and Power.* Harlow: Longman.

———. 2003. *Analysing Discourse: Textual Analysis for Social Research.* London and New York: Routledge.

Fishman, Joshua. 1989. *Language and Ethnicity in Minority Sociolinguistic Perspective.* Clevedon: Multilingual Matters.

246   References

Forte, Janette, ed. 1994 *Proceedings of Amirang: National Conference of Amerindian Representatives. April 11th–14th 1994.* Georgetown, Guyana: Amerindian Research Unit.

———. 1996a. *About Guyanese Amerindians.* Georgetown, Guyana: Janette Forte.

———. 1996b. *Thinking about Amerindians.* Georgetown, Guyana: Janette Forte.

Forte, Janette, and Ian Melville, eds. 1989. *Amerindian Testimonies.* Georgetown, Guyana: Janette Forte.

Foucault, Michel. 1972. *The Archaeology of Knowledge.* London: Routledge.

———. 1984. *The Foucault Reader.* Ed. Paul Rabinow. Harmondsworth: Penguin.

———. 1991. *Discipline and Punish: The Birth of the Prison.* Tr. Alan Sheridan. Harmondsworth: Penguin.

Giddens, A. 1993. *New Rules of Sociological Method.* Cambridge: Polity Press.

Goetz, A. M., and J. Gaventa. 2001. *From Consultation to Influence: Bringing Citizen Voice and Client Focus to Service Delivery.* Report prepared for DFID. Brighton: Institute of Development Studies.

Goffman, E. 1974. *Frame Analysis.* New York: Harper and Row.

———. 1981. *Forms of Talk.* Philadelphia: University of Pennsylvania Press.

Gotsbachner, Emo. 2001. Xenophobic Normality: The Discriminatory Impact of Habitualised Discourse Dynamics. *Discourse and Society* 12, no. 6: 729–759.

Gregory, Michael. 1988. Generic Situation and Register: A Functional View of Communication. In J. D. Benson, M. Cummings and W. Greaves (Eds.), *Linguistics in a Systemic Perspective.* Amsterdam: John Benjamins: 301–329.

Gumperz, John J. 1982. *Discourse Strategies.* Cambridge: Cambridge University Press.

Habermas, Jürgen. 1984. *The Theory of Communicative Action, Volume 1.* Tr. T. McCarthy. Boston, MA: Beacon Press.

Hagerman, Ellen. 1997. *Tales from Guyana: An Examination of Some Communicative Practices between Members of an Amerindian Village and Outsiders.* Université du Québec à Montréal: Unpublished MSc Thesis.

Halliday, M.A.K. 1978. *Language as Social Semiotic.* London: Arnold.

———.1994. *An Introduction to Functional Grammar.* London: Arnold.

Halliday, M.A.K., and Ruqaiya Hasan. 1976. *Cohesion in English.* London: Longman.

———. 1985. *Language, Context and Text: Language in a Social-Semiotic Perspective.* Victoria: Deakin University Press.

Hasan, Ruqaiya. 1995. The Conception of Context in Text. In P. Fries and M. Gregory (Eds.), *Meaning and Choice in Language.* Westport and London: Ablex: 183–283.

———. 1996.The Nursery Tale as Genre. In Carmel Cloran, David Butt and Geoff Williams (Eds.), *Ways of Saying: Ways of Meaning: Selected Papers of Ruqaiya Hasan.* London: Cassell: 51–72.

———. 2009. A Sociolinguistic Interpretation of Everyday Talk between Mothers and Children. In Jonathan J. Webster (Ed.), *The Collected Works of Ruqaiya Hasan Volume 2. Semantic Variation: Meaning in Society and in Sociolinguistics.* London and Oakville: Equinox: 75–118.

Heath, Shirley Brice. 1983. *Ways with Words: Language, Life and Work in Communities and Classrooms.* Cambridge: Cambridge University Press.

Henríquez Arellano, Edmundo. 2000. Usos, costumbres y pluralismo en Los Altos de Chiapas. In Juan Pedro Viqueira and Willibald Sonnleitner (Eds.), *Democracia en Tierras Indígenas: Las Elecciones en Los Altos de Chiapas (1991–1998).* Mexico City: CIESAS, El Colegio de México and IFE: 29–60.

References 247

Hobley, Mary. 2003. *Power, Voice and Creating Space: Analysis of Local-Level Power Relations*. Paper prepared for DFID Bangladesh, Dhaka.

Holmes, Janet, and Maria Stubbe. 2003. *Power and Politeness in the Workplace*. Harlow: Longman.

Hornberger, Nancy, and Luis Enrique López. 1998. Policy, Possibility and Paradox: Indigenous Multilingualism and Education in Peru and Bolivia. In Jasone Cenoz and Fred Genesee (Eds.), *Beyond Bilingualism: Multilingualism and Multilingual Education*. Clevedon: Multilingual Matters: 206–242.

Humphrey, S. 2006. 'Getting the Reader On Side': Exploring Adolescent Online Political Discourse. *E-Learning* 3, no. 2: 143–157.

Hutchby, Ian, and Robin Wooffitt. 1998. *Conversation Analysis*. Cambridge: Polity Press.

Hymes, Dell. 1996. *Ethnography, Linguistics, Narrative Inequality: Towards an Understanding of Voice*. London: Taylor and Francis.

Iedema, Rick. 1999. Formalizing Organisational Meaning. *Discourse and Society* 10, no. 1: 49–65.

Kabeer, N. 2002. *We Don't Do Credit: Nijera kori Social Mobilisation and the Collective Capabilities of the Poor in Rural Bangladesh*. BRAC Printers: Nijera Kori, Dhaka.

Kohonen, Viljo. 1992. Experiential Language Learning: Second Language Learning as Cooperative Learner Education. In David Nunan (Ed.) *Collaborative Language Learning and Teaching*. Cambridge: Cambridge University Press: 37–56.

Kramsch, Claire, and Elizabeth Boner. 2010. Shadows of Discourse: Intercultural Communication in Global Contexts. In Coupland (Ed.).

Kress, Gunther. 2000. Design and Transformation: New Theories of Meaning. In W. Cope and M. Kalantzis (Eds.), *Multiliteracies: Literacy Learning and the Design of Social Futures*, pp. 153–161. London: Routledge.

Kymlicka, W. 1995. *Multicultural Citizenship: A Liberal Theory of Minority Rights*. Oxford: Clarendon Press.

Makushi Research Unit. 1996. *Makusipe Komantu Iseru: Sustaining Makushi Way of Life*. Ed. Janette Forte. Annai, Guyana: North Rupununi District Development Board.

Martin, J. R. 1992. *English Text: System and Structure*. Philadelphia and Amsterdam: John Benjamins.

———. 2004. Positive Discourse Analysis: Power, *Solidarity and Change*. *Revista Canaria de Estudios Ingleses* 49: 179–202.

May, Stephen. 1999. Critical Multiculturalism and Cultural Difference: Avoiding Essentialism. In Stephen May (Ed.), *Rethinking Multicultural and Antiracist Education*. London and Philadelphia: Falmer: 12–41.

———. 2001. *Language and Minority Rights: Ethnicity, Nationalism and the Politics of Language*. Harlow: Longman.

Narayan, Deepa, with Raj Patel, Kai Schafft, Anne Rademacher and Sarah Koch-Schulte. 2000. *Voices of the Poor: Can Anyone Hear Us?* New York: Oxford University Press.

National Development Strategy. 2000. *National Development Strategy (2001–2010), A Policy Framework: Eradicating Poverty and Unifying Guyana*. Georgetown: Civil Society Document.

Norton, Andrew, with Bella Bird, Karen Brock, Margaret Kakande and Carrie Turk. 2001. *A Rough Guide to PPAs. Participatory Poverty Assessment: An Introduction to Theory and Practice*. Overseas Development Institute: London.

Norton, Bonny. 2000. *Identity and Language Learning: Gender, Ethnicity and Educational Change*. Harlow: Longman.

248 References

NRDDB and Iwokrama. 1999. *Community-Based Wildlife Management in the North Rupununi*. Annai and Georgetown: NRDDB and Iwokrama.

O'Halloran, Kieran. 2003. *Critical Discourse Analysis and Language Cognition*. Edinburgh: Edinburgh University Press.

Parekh, B. 1995. The Concept of National Identity. *New Community* 21:255–268.

Rattansi, Ali. 1999. Racism, 'Postmodernism' and Reflexive Multiculturalism. In May (Ed.).

Redford, Kent H., and Steven E. Sanderson. 2000. Extracting Humans from Nature. *Conservation Biology* 14, no. 5: 1362–1364.

Regional Democratic Council for Region 9, Guyana. 2001. *Report on Region 9's Poverty Reduction Strategy Consultations*. Lethem, Guyana.

Richardson, Kay. 1987. Critical Linguistics and Textual Diagnosis. *Text* 7, no. 2: 145–163.

Roberts, Celia, and Sarangi Srikant. 1999. Hybridity in Gatekeeping Discourse: Issues of Practical Relevance for the Researcher. In S. Sarangi and C. Roberts (Eds.), *Talk, Work and Institutional Order: Discourse in Medical, Mediation and Management Settings*, pp. 363–390. Berlin: Mouton de Gruyter.

Said, Edward. 1995. *Orientalism: Western Conceptions of the Orient*. Harmondsworth: Penguin.

Sánchez Gómez, Francisco Javier. 1998. *Sociedad y educación tseltal en Oxchujk'*. San Cristóbal de las Casas: Consejo Estatal para la Cultura y las Artes del Estado de Chiapas y CELALI.

Sanders, Robert. 1976. American Indian or West Indian: The Case of the Coastal Amerindians of Guyana. *Caribbean Studies* 16, no. 2: 117–144.

Schegloff, Emanuel A. 1999a. Naiveté vs. Sophistication or Discipline vs. Self-Indulgence: A Rejoinder to Billig. *Discourse and Society* 10, no. 4: 577–582.

———. 1999b. 'Schegloff's Texts' as 'Billig's Data': A Critical Reply. *Discourse and Society* 10, no. 4: 558–572.

Scollon, Ron. 2005. The Rhythmic Integration of Action and Discourse. In Sigrid Norris and Rodney H. Jones (Eds.), *Discourse In Action: Introducing Mediated Discourse Analysis*. London and New York: Routledge: 20–31.

Scollon, Ron, and Wong Suzie Scollon. 2007. Nexus Analysis: Refocusing Ethnography on Action. *Journal of Sociolinguistics* 11, no. 5: 608–625.

Sealey, Alison, and Bob Carter. 2004. *Applied Linguistics as Social Science*. London: Continuum.

Silverstein, M. 2003. Indexical Order and the Dialectics of Sociolinguistic Life. *Language and Communication* 23:193–229.

Spiegel, A., V. Watson and P. Wilkinson. 1999. Speaking Truth to Power? Some Problems Using Ethnographic Methods to Influence the Formulation of Housing Policy in South Africa. In Angela Cheater (Ed.), *The Anthropology of Power*. London: Routledge: 175–190.

Spivak, G. C. 1990. *The Post-Colonial Critic: Interviews, Strategies, Dialogues*. Ed. S. Harasym. New York: Routledge.

Stubbs, Michael. 1997. Whorf's Children: Critical Comments on Critical Discourse Analysis (CDA). In A. Ryan and A.Wray (Eds) *British Studies in Applied Linguistics 12: Evolving Models of Language*, pp. 100–116. Clevedon: Multilingual Matters.

Talbot, Mary, Karen Atkinson and David Atkinson. 2003. *Language and Power in the Modern World*. Edinburgh: Edinburgh University Press.

Thibault, Paul J. 1995. Mood and the Ecosocial Dynamics of Semiotic Exchange. In Ruqaiya Hasan and Peter Fries (Eds), *On Subject and Theme*. Amsterdam and Philadelphia: John Benjamins: 51–90.

References 249

Toolan, M. 1997. What Is Critical Discourse Analysis and Why Are People Saying Such Terrible Things about It? *Language and Lit* 6, no. 2: 83–103.

Upper Mazaruni Amerindian District Council, Amerindian People's Association of Guyana, Forest People's Programme and Global Law Association. 2000. *Indigenous Peoples, Land Rights and Mining in the Upper Mazaruni*. Georgetown, Guyana: APA.

van Dijk, Teun A. 1997. Discourse as Interaction in Society. In Teun A. van Dijk (Ed.), *Discourse as Social Interaction*. London: Sage.

———. 2001. Critical Discourse Analysis. In D. Tannen, D. Schiffrin and H. Hamilton (Eds.), *The Handbook of Discourse Analysis*. Oxford: Blackwell: 352–371.

———. 2008. *Discourse and Context: A Sociocognitive Approach*. Cambridge: Cambridge University Press.

Van Langenhove, Luk, and Rom Harré. 1999. Positioning as the Production and Use of Stereotypes. In Rom Harré and Luk van Langenhove, eds *Positioning Theory*. Oxford: Blackwell.

Voloshinov, V. N. 1973. *Marxism and the Philosophy of Language*. Tr. Ladislav Matejka and I. R. Titunik. Cambridge, MA: Harvard University Press.

Wetherell, Margaret. 2007. A Step too Far: Discursive Psychology, Linguistic Ethnography and Questions of Identity. *Journal of Sociolinguistics* 11, no. 5: 661–681.

Widdowson, H. G. 2000. Critical Practices: On Representation and the Interpretation of Text. In Srikant Sarangi and Malcolm Coulthard (Eds.), *Discourse and Social Life*. Harlow: Longman: 155–169.

———. 2004. *Text, Context, Pretext: Critical Issues in Discourse Analysis*. Malden,   MA: Blackwell.

Williams, Patrick E. 1997. Ecotourism and Environmental Education in the Amazon Region: A Case Study of Guyana. In Patrick E. Williams and James G. Rose (Eds.), *Environment and Sustainable Human Development in the Amazon*. Georgetown: Free Press and University of Guyana: 50–100.

Wood, G., and P. Davies. 1998. *Engaging with Deep Structures: Linking Good Governance to Poverty Elimination in Rural Bangladesh*. Paper prepared for DFID.

Index

A

accommodation, 77, 87
activation (by context), 23, 30
advocacy: in Amerindian Act/NRDDB Constitution, 71; and Amerindian groups 86; by Iwokrama 95–96, 101; as means of empowerment, 65, 85, 220
Alicia, 82, 96
Amerindian Act: analysis of, 35, 64–77; attitudes to Amerindians, 81, 174, 203, 220; and local autonomy, 25; revision of, 239n2
analytical methods, 20–22, 35–38, 219–226, 228–229
Andrew: analysis of symbolic capital, 13–137, 140–141, 144–156, 177; on collaboration, 90–91, 93,122; on "mixing it up", 214
appropriation, 4, 195, 214, 225
assimilation, 9, 16, 63–64, 77, 87, 207, 221
audience, 9, 130, 152–153, 178, 181, 199–203. See also linguistic marketplace, uptake
authorised language, 122–124, 153
authority, 199–203; institutional, 161, 164, 168–169, 171, 173, 178, 200, 223; local, 184, 220; moral, 164, 187, 200, 202, 207, 222–223, 225

B

Bakhtin, M., 13–24
behavioural potential, 15
Bernstein, B., 15
Bhabha, H., 211–213, 219
Bilingualism, 57–58
Bina Hill Institute, 161, 174, 178

Blommaert, J.: on CDA, 5, 35–38; on globalisation, 11, 16; on voice, 16

C

Canadian International Development Agency (CIDA), 90–91, 214
capital, symbolic and cultural: analyses, 130–153, 160–161,164–165,175–180,202; and collaboration, 153–156, 216; disruption, 132, 222; strategic manipulation, 132, 222; subsumption of, 207; theory, 11–12, 33–34, 94–95, 122–130, 181, 220–222
Chambers, R., 82–85
cherry-picking, 4
Chiapas, 85–86
Choice,88,208
Chouliaraki, L., 6, 216, 218
Cloran, C.,28
code,15,130,222
collaboration: analysis, 175–180; and external control, 77 ,90; and hybridity, 19; NRRDB and Iwokrama, 149, 203, 221; potential for, 17, 34, 153–156; relation to CDA and PDA, 4,215–219; Uncle Henry on, 198
collaborative interdiscursivity, 184
colonialism, 1–2, 3. See also postcolonialism
colonisation (of lifeworld), 214, 225
communicative action, 52, 214, 225
communicative disadvantage, 27,77,90
communicative rationality, 52, 53, 214, 225

252 Index

Community Environment Workers (CEWs): role, 46, 47; Nicholas on failings, 78, 97; Walter on failings 99; Walter on reporting, 164, 172–174, 177

comprehension. *See* understanding

conditions of possibility, 30, 32, 40

construal (of context), 23, 30

consultation, 82

context, 23, 175–176, 182–184, 224, 239n7

contextualisation, cline of 28, 185–186

contextualisation cue, 171, 177, 223

cooptation: as means of empowerment, 65, 95, 220; by Iwokrama, 101, 203, 230–231; in Amerindian Act and NRDDB Constitution, 71; of government and UNDP by NRDDB speakers, 161; of indigenous groups, 85–86

Creolese, 207–208

Critical Discourse Analysis (CDA), goals, 3, 10; critique,4–9, 35–38, 215–219; and voice,16, 141

cultural capital. *See* capital

cultural maintenance. See Makushi, Nicholas, Sam, Uncle Henry, Walter

cultural nationalism. *See* local autonomy

D

Department for International Development (DFID), 46

development, 1–2, 220; critique of 78–89, 220; local discussion of 22–30; in Amerindian Act and NRDDB Constitution, 66–77; Model-T approaches, 83; on North Rupununi, 48–50, 61

discourse: across difference, 54, 215, 220, 225; contextualisation of, 4, 7–9, 9–12, 13, 17, 20, 21; of Development,33, 76, 78–89, 96, 101, 209, 213; emergent, 7; indigenisation of, 208, 210–215, 225; local vs dominant, 3–4, 33, 87, 89–101, 120, 125; perturbation, 132; recalibration, 30, 131–132, 173, 175, 222; recontextualisation, 87, 207, 213, 225, 232; reformulation, 173, 181, 230; tensions within,

7, 10, 30, 33, 118, 128, 153, 165, 211–218, 225; and text, 9–12, 20

E

ecotourism,,51

emergent conditions, 129

empathy. *See* understanding

empowerment, approaches to, 65–77. *See also* advocacy, cooptation, local autonomy, paternalism

entextualisation, 231

environment, 176, 183, 224

Escobar, A., 78–80

ethnography, 40–41, 218, 226–228

ethnopoetics, 21,229

F

Fairclough, N., 6, 216, 218

Fair Deal, 79–81

familiarity, 28, 173

field, 186–187; analysis of Sara and Uncle Henry, 197–199. *See also* register

footing, 117

formalisation, 231. *See also* reformulation

formality, 171–172

Forte, J., 227

Foucault, M., 10. *See also* genealogy

frames, 118

G

genealogy, 78, 80, 228

genre, 13, 19, 72

globalisation, 11, 16, 32

Gordon: discussing local autonomy , 22–30; on government views of local knowledge, 95–96; informal meetings in Rupununi, 96; on Iwokrama management, 93; on local decision-making, 213–214; on local and Iwokrama concerns, 92; modality and projection analysis, 138–141, 144–156; at NRDDB meetings, 172–174

Government of Guyana, 32, 46–47; and Amerindians, 57, 59–60, 95–96, 231; and Amerindian Act, 66–77; and Iwokrama, 45; and NRDDB, 2, 10

Guiana Shield Conference, 90, 212, 231

Index   253

Guyana: demographics, 41–42; history, 1. *See also* Government of Guyana

H

Habermas, J., 52, 214–215
Habitus, 63–64
Halliday, M.A.K., 15
Heath, S.B., 166–167
hegemony, 7, 10, 15
heteroglossia, 13
Hilda, 170–171, 172–174
hybridity: analysis, 173, 181,184; theory, 19, 77, 87, 211–213, 219
Hymes, D., 15, 20–21

I

imported knowledge, 164, 184, 200, 207, 222
indexicality, 17, 127. See also orders of indexicality
insulation, 216
intercultural communication, 15, 19
intercultural competence, 180, 224
interdiscursivity, 182–208, 224
international development. *See* development
interpersonal awe, 200
intertextuality, 184,224
Iwokrama, 32, 45–46; and NRDDB 2, 3, 10, 47–48, 180,203,220; early communications, 81–82, 89–101
Iwokrama Act, 45, 46, 72

K

knowledge. *See* imported knowledge, local knowledge

L

land rights, 50–51
legitimation, 9, 23, 216, 219; and capital, 140–141, 178, 208; and orders of indexicality, 17, 123, 126; of speakers, 200; and voice, 18–19, 32, 64
lifeworld ,214, 225
linguistic bias, 5. *See also* textualism/ textual attitude
linguistic marketplace, 124–126, 153, 222, 230; analysis, 161; in interviews 133; and Positioning Theory, 130. *See also* audience, uptake

local autonomy: in Amerindian Act/ NRDDB Constitution 68, 71; Andrew on, 214; in development 86–87; in interviews 149; local discussion of, 22–30; as means of empowerment 65, 77, 90, 155, 220; Nicholas on, 61; and perturbation, 174
local knowledge: and book knowledge, 99–100; as capital, 200, 202, 221, 222; and development practice, 2; and interdiscursivity, 184, 198, 207; and Iwokrama, 45–46, 101; local discussion of, 22–30; loss of, 59–64; official attitudes towards, 95; specialisation of, 54; Uncle Henry on, 57; Walter on, 55

M

macrocontext, 176, 183, 224
Makushi, 1, 41–45, 220–221; and development, 32; attitudes to development and cultural maintenance 44–45; demographics, xvii,41–43; language, 42–43, 57–58; social organisation, 43,51–59. *See also* North Rupununi
marketplace. *See* linguistic marketplace
Martin, J.R., 6–7, 216–217
Material Situational Setting, 175
Minister of Amerindian Affairs,46, 47, 50, 73; in NRDDB meetings, 158–161, 177
Misrecognition, 62, 95, 98–99, 123, 221
mode, 185–186;analysis of Sara and Uncle Henry 195–197; and symbolic capital 166–167. *See also* register
modality, 34, 133, 134, 138, 140, 141–144, 241nn6–7; analysis, 144–150, 160, 199–203, 235–236

N

naming procedures. *See* titles
National Development Strategy, 41, 55–56
Nicholas: discussing local autonomy, 22–30; on CEW programme 78, 97; on cultural maintenance,

254 *Index*

39, 61–64, 89–90, 209–219;
on Iwokrama, 82, 91, 94, 97;
on local management, 49,
53–54, 78, 93, 97; in workshop,
101–122
nihil obstat, 147, 155, 174, 180, 203,
213, 222–225
North Rupununi: communication
strategies and formal education, 54–59; infrastructure, 43;
interpersonal relations, 51–54;
material conditions, 48–51;
post-colonial context, 1, 30,
220. *See also* Makushi
North Rupununi District Development
Board (NRDDB), 32, 47–48;
analysis of meetings, 157–180,
181–208; Constitution, 35,
69–77, 174, 220; as hybrid
space, 77, 175, 210–215; and
Iwokrama, 2; meetings 3, 158,
170

O

orders of indexicality, 17; in intercultural contexts, 19; and perturbation, 131, 134, 173; and
Positioning Theory 128; side
effects, 101; and symbolic capital,33, 123, 125, 129, 153–154,
164, 222; and voice, 220

P

participatory research,83–85
paternalism: in Amerindian Act/
NDDB Constitution, 69, 71,
203; of Government of Guyana,
60, 100–101;
in international development 85; as
means of empowerment, 65,
86, 95, 214, 220; Uncle Henry
on, 89
People's National Congress (PNC), 46
People's Progressive Party (PPP), 46
personal pronouns, 199–203
perturbation potential, 18–20,
174–180, 224
phase,183, 187: analysis of Sara and
Uncle Henry 203–207
piai man, 52–53
polyphony, 14, 19, 64, 215–216
positioning, 160
Positioning Theory, 12, 33, 119–121,
128, 140, 221–222; analysis

175–180; Positioning Star of
David, 130–132,222,224
Positive Discourse Analysis (PDA): critique, 6–9, 12, 215–219; goals
4, 10, 20; and voice, 16
postcolonialism, 30–31, 75–77, 212,
219. *See also* colonialism
post-conventional identities, 215
power: and capital, 130; in CDA, 216;
and control 124–125; as shifting
resource, 127; and voice,19; in
workshops, 117–118; of written
discourse, 166,
presupposition, 159–160
projection, 34, 133, 136, 138, 140;
analysis, 150–156, 160,
237–238

R

rearticulations, 10
recalibration. *See* discourse,
recalibration
recontextualisation. *See* discourse,
recontextualisation
reformulation.*See* discourse,
recontextualisation
register, and context, 182–184; and
indexical order, 127; limitations of analysis, 228–229; and
phase, 203; recalibration/recon-
textualisation, 26–30, 111, 113,
173, 175, 177–180, 213; and
symbolic capital, 129, 132, 134,
138, 153; and voice, 21, 34, 40,
125, 220
relativity of function, 11–12
repertoire, 18–19
respect, 178
revoicing, 19
rhetorical function, 186
rhetorical structure, 203, 224
Rhetorical Units (RUs), 28,185–186,
234

S

Sam: on collaboration, 90; on cultural
maintenance,39; at Guiana
Shield Conference, 90, 231; in
NRDDB meetings, 158–167,
170–171, 177;
Sara: discussing local autonomy,
22–30; informal meetings in
Rupununi, 96; at NRDDB
meetings, 161, 164–167, 181,

Index 255

184–185, 187–207; in workshop, 33, 101–122, 128–129, 131–132
semantic mappings, 197–199
shama man, shaman. *See* piai man
socialisation, 123
socialisation contexts, 196–197
solidarity, 28, 165, 171, 173, 177, 178, 199–203
space, 88–89, 161, 169–170, 178, 208, 223; of contradiction or resistance, 210–215, 217, 225
structural/objective conditions,7–8, 40, 88, 101, 118; as constraints on positioning 130; and emergent relations, 129. *See also* North Rupununi
strategic essentialism, 41
subsumption (of authority), 168–170, 180,181, 207, 223, 225
Sustainable Utilisation Areas (SUAs), 34,98,161; Sara and Uncle Henry's explanations, 195–207
symbolic capital. *See* capital
syncretism. *See* hybridity
system. *See* lifeworld
Systemic Functional Linguistics (SFL),5, 21, 36–37, 141, 175–176

T

taxonomic chains, 187
tenor, 187; analysis of Sara and Uncle Henry, 199–203. *See also* register
text. *See* discourse
textualism/textual attitude, 81, 226. *See also* linguistic bias
third space, 211–213, 217, 219,225
titles, 170–171, 172, 178, 179, 199–203
Traditional Ecological Knowledge (TEK). *See* local knowledge
Trudy, 167–170
Truman, Harry S., 79–81

U

Uncle Henry: on cultural maintenance, 52–53; on development, 48–49; on education, 57; on Iwokrama, 91–92, 94; on local management, 61–62, 74; modality and projection analysis, 137–138,140–141,144–156;

and NRDDB, 47; at NRDDB meetings 34, 181, 184–185, 187–207; on participation at NRDDB meetings, 97; on training, 99–100
understanding, 18–19, 32, 98, 181, 183–184, 208, 216, 225, 229–230
UNICEF, 44
United Nations Department of Social and Economic Affairs, 79
United Nations Development Programme (UNDP), 24, 91; in NRDDB meetings, 158–161, 164
Uptake, 8–9, 181, 183–184, 229–230. *See also* audience, linguistic market place

V

Ventriloquism, 164–165, 173,177
Voice: amplification of, 82, 89; analysis of, 20–21; community, 18, 181, 208, 220; and competence, 14; development perspective, 82–89; individual, 18, 153; and interdiscursivity, 182–184, 216–218, 219; mediation of, 85, 87; negotiation of, 22–30, 125; in NRDDB 34, 77; and perturbation, 18–20, 64, 176–180; and Positioning Theory, 128; theoretical background, 12–18, 31–32
Voloshinov, V., 14

W

Walter, 1–2; on cultural maintenance, 1; discussing local autonomy, 22–30; on CEWs, 157; on education, 55, 58, 100; on Iwokrama, 81–82, 99; on local management, 61, 93; on local participation in NRDDB, 98; at NRDDB meetings, 158–174, 177, 181; in workshop, 101–122, 128–129, 132
Widdowson, H.G., 4–5, 35–36
workshops: analysis, 101–121; different attitudes to function, 113, 116, 118; Sara on, 27; Uncle Henry on, 47
World Bank, 84